LECTIONARY SCRIPTURE NOTES

FOR SERIES C

Norman A. Beck

CSS Publishing Company, Inc.
Lima, Ohio

LECTIONARY SCRIPTURE NOTES FOR SERIES C

FIRST EDITION
Copyright @ 2012 by
Norman A. Beck

All rights reserved. No portion of this book may be reproduced or utilized in any form or by any means, electronic or mechanical including photocopying, without permission in writing from the author. Inquiries should be addressed to: Dr. Norman Beck, Texas Lutheran University, Seguin, Texas 78155.

ISBN-13: 978-0-7880-2672-0
ISBN-10: 0-7880-2672-0   PRINTED IN USA

EDITOR'S NOTE

Prior to 1969, most of the congregations in the denominations of Christians that use pre-selected texts from Scripture as readings during their worship services utilized a one year cycle of texts. In response to a directive from Vatican II that a more comprehensive lectionary be made available, a three year series (cycle) of texts, *Lectionary for Mass*, was developed and was published in 1969, so that approximately 12-15% of the Bible over a three-year period rather than perhaps 4-5% of the Bible repeated each year would be read and heard within the worshiping congregations for those who attended at least once each week. Most Lutheran groups soon approved use of the Roman Catholic three-year lectionary, which they adapted slightly so as not to use readings from the so-called Old Testament Apocrypha. Other Christian groups, initially Episcopal, United Church of Christ, Presbyterian, Disciples of Christ, United Methodist, and United Church of Canada, developed a lectionary based on the Roman Catholic three-year cycle and differing somewhat from the Lutheran selections by selecting consecutive readings in certain instances, especially in their use of texts from the Older Testament.

During the years between 1983 and 1992 a larger group of Christian denominations, attempting to achieve greater uniformity in their selections, produced first The Common Lectionary, and then the Revised Common Lectionary. The work of lectionary revision continues. Particular attention and sensitivity is needed during this task of revision to avoid use of texts that present all Pharisees and in some instances all Jews negatively. For easy access to a discussion of this, please see my article "Removing Anti-Jewish Polemic from our Christian Lectionaries: A Proposal," http://jcrelations.net/en/?item=737 (also in a Spanish translation).

This resource provides guidelines and resources for homilies and sermons, worship planning, and Scripture study based on the texts in Year C (Cycle C) in *The Revised Common Lectionary: Consultation on Common Texts* (Nashville: Abington, 1992). Leaders in worship and worship planning and other members of Christian congregations and communities will find this book to be helpful for use as individuals and in study groups as they prepare for more meaningful worship experiences each weekend.

BACKGROUND INFORMATION

This resource provides guidelines for preaching, worship planning, and Scripture study based on the texts in Year C in *The Revised Common Lectionary: Consultation on Common Texts* (Nashville: Abingdon, 1992). It is a revised and updated replacement for Norman A. Beck, *Scripture Notes C* (Lima, Ohio: CSS Publishing, 1985).

Unique to this resource is its sensitivity to the lectionary selections that include negative statements about Jews in general and about Pharisees in particular. For additional information regarding these negative statements, please see my article, "Removing Anti-Jewish Polemic from our Christian Lectionaries: A Proposal," http://jcrelations.net/en/?item=737. For a more comprehensive study of the negative statements about Jews in our texts, see my *Mature Christianity in the 21st Century: The Recognition and Repudiation of the Anti-Jewish Polemic of the New Testament* (New York: Crossroad, 1994). For translations of the Greek New Testament into modern English that are sensitive to the negative statements about Jews, see the Contemporary English Version of the Holy Bible published by the American Bible Society in 1995 and my *The New Testament: A New Translation and Redaction* (Lima, Ohio: Fairway Press, 2001). The latter work includes as an Appendix, A New Four Year Lectionary, in which, instead of the texts within the Revised Common Lectionary that are negative about Jews, much more edifying texts are provided. Gospel selections for Year 1 are from the Gospel According to Mark, and Gospel selections for Year 4 are from the Fourth Gospel.

Gospel Selections in Year C

Among the writers of the Four Gospels, only the person who provided the Gospel According to Luke provided a rationale and an explicit reason for writing the document that we have, the Gospel from which most of the Gospel selections for Year C are taken. Although this very important preface, Luke 1:1-4, is not used anywhere within The Revised Common Lectionary, in one extensive sentence written in excellent Greek style, it provides for us much material that helps us understand the Lukan Gospel. In this preface, in my own translation, we read that

> In view of the fact that within the past few years many people have endeavored to compile a narrative account with regard to these most important events that have occurred among us, adhering as closely as possible to what those who from the beginning have been eyewitnesses of the events and have assisted in transmitting the oral tradition have handed down to us, it seemed appropriate to me, since I have followed all of this very carefully for a long time, to write to you, most noble Theophilus, a more coherent and meaningful account, so that you may have a more adequate understanding of these traditions that have become of such great interest also to you.

Intense study of this preface and of the entire Four Gospels helps us to see with considerable clarity the materials, both written and oral, that were used, and the process followed by the Lukan writer. We identify four of these materials that this writer-redactor utilized and are able, so to speak, to look over the shoulders of this person as this person compiled this Gospel, a document that is in many ways, as its writer intended, a more adequate and more excellent account than had previously been available.

The first of these four materials was almost certainly a form of what we call the Gospel According to Mark, in the form in which it was accessible to the person who compiled what we call the Gospel According to Luke. Where the writer-redactors who produced what we call the Gospel According to Matthew used approximately 90% of Mark, the writer-redactor of the Gospel According to Luke used only 60-65% of Mark, and used it much more freely, with no sentence incorporated unchanged and much of the material re-arranged and modified in order to provide what the writer described as a "more excellent account than had previously been available."

The second of these materials was the major translation into the Greek language of the Hebrew Scriptures with supplements and additions in Greek that we call the Septuagint, the Bible of most of the followers of Jesus at the time the Four Gospels were written.

The Lukan writer used the Septuagint for ideas and for literary style. Among the ideas used was the motif of an old woman who with her husband has been unable to have a child until God intervenes with a miraculous blessing (Sarah the wife of Abraham who finally has Isaac and Hannah the wife of Elkanah who finally has Samuel) as a prototype of Elizabeth the wife of Zechariah who finally has John the Baptist (Luke 1:5-25). Just as interspersed into the narrative accounts in Genesis, and in portions of Exodus, Judges, 1 Samuel, there are poetic songs, so also was done repeatedly in Luke, especially in Luke, chapters 1-2, most notably the Song of Hannah in 1 Samuel 2:1-10 serving as the model for the Song of Mary (the Magnificat) in Luke 1:47-55. Just as the man Jacob, the father of Joseph, is said in Genesis 37:11 to have pondered the dreams and actions of his son Joseph, so also Mary the mother of Jesus is said in Luke 2:51 to have pondered the life and the actions of her son Jesus. The Lukan writer, who easily could have continued the excellent Greek literary style demonstrated in the Luke 1:1-4 preface, chose instead to follow the literary style of narratives in the Septuagint, in which most sentences as translations of biblical Hebrew narrative begin with the words "And," "And it came to pass," "And it happened that," and so forth. Thus the Lukan writer-redactor sacrificed good Greek literary style to produce the Gospel that sounds the most "biblical."

The third of these materials was either an early draft of what later was to be called the Gospel According to Matthew or of what we call "Q" materials (from the German noun *Quelle*, meaning "source"). The use by the Lukan writer-redactor of an early draft of Matthew or "Q" materials, or both, is our best explanation for the reason that significant portions of Matthew and of Luke are similar, but are not in Mark.

The fourth of these materials and most interesting of all was the Lukan writer's own "inspired creativity." This accounts for the excellent narratives that we have only in Luke, such as the accounts of the conceptions of John the Baptist and of Jesus, the Christmas story, the boy Jesus in the Temple in Jerusalem, the story parables of the "Prodigal Son" and of the "Good Samaritan," the "Road to Emmaus" account, and that we have in Acts, such as the story of the Ascension of Jesus, the gruesome account of the death of Judas Iscariot, the choosing of a replacement for Judas Iscariot, the vivid Pentecost account, the conversations between Philip and the Ethiopian eunuch, the messages of Peter, of Stephen, and of Paul expressed in excellent Greek rhetoric, and so on. In ways that have similarities to the Lukan writer's use of biblical and contemporary sources and developing accounts with "inspired creativity," in our sermons and teachings we too use biblical and contemporary sources with "inspired creativity."

Finally, because the Third Gospel and Acts of Apostles were written much more than the other canonical Gospels from a woman's perspective (the perspective of Mary the mother of Jesus, and with Mary and Elizabeth depicted as bonding together and talking about their pregnancies), and because women are much more prominent in Luke and Acts than in the First, Second, and Fourth Gospels, there is the possibility that Luke and Acts were written by a woman or by a man who was very sensitive to a woman's perspective. The names of the writers of the Four Gospels and of Acts are not given anywhere in those documents. The "According to Mark, Matthew, Luke, and John" designations were developed during the second century in order to distinguish one Gospel from another. Since the second century developing Christian tradition was a very male-dominated tradition, it would not have been acceptable for the men who controlled the tradition during the second century to credit the Third Gospel to a woman writer. Therefore, Luke, the physician mentioned in some of the Pauline tradition documents, was chosen and the Third Gospel was designated as the Gospel According to Luke.

SELECTIONS IN SERIES C
The Revised Common Lectionary

Since Series C of this lectionary is based primarily on the Gospel According to Luke, let us take a few moments to look again at what the writer of this "Third Gospel" wrote as a preface to it. I am providing it in my own translation from *The New Testament: A New Translation and Redaction* (Lima, OH: Fairway, 2001).

In view of the fact that within the past few years many people have endeavored to compile a narrative account with regard to these most important events that have occurred among us, adhering as closely as possible to what those who from the beginning have been eyewitnesses of the events and have assisted in transmitting the oral tradition have handed down to us, it seemed appropriate to me, since I have followed all of this very carefully for a long time, to write for you, most noble Theophilus, a more coherent and meaningful account, so that you may have a more adequate understanding of these traditions that have become of such great interest also to you.

From this Preface to the document and from the content of this Third Gospel when compared to "The Gospel of Jesus Christ" (Mark) and "The Book of the Genesis of Jesus Christ" (Matthew), it is obvious that the writer of this Third Gospel extensively researched (primarily in the written sources of Mark, possibly in "Q" materials and most likely in an early form of what would later be labeled Matthew, and in the Septuagint Greek translation of the Hebrew Scriptures) the subject of the significance of the events associated with belief in Jesus as *the* Messiah (Christ) and with inspired creativity wrote freely about these events so that Theophilus and/or anyone who "loves God" would be able to respond with personal perceptions.

Are we not called in our time to research as extensively and to write and to speak as freely and with as much inspired creativity as did this writer so that those who "love God" today and hear us will be enabled to form their own perceptions just as Theophilus was encouraged to do in this document? May God guide and inspire us, just as we believe God guided and inspired the Lukan writer!

Among many books written in response to the Third Gospel, the following are among the ones that are especially noteworthy and valuable for our task:

Bovon, François. *Luke the Theologian: Fifty Years of Research (1950-2005)*. Waco, TX: Baylor University Press, 2006

Brown, Raymond E. *The Birth of the Messiah*. Garden City, NY: Doubleday, 1979.

Cassidy, Richard J. *Jesus, Politics, and Society: A Study of Luke's Gospel*. Maryknoll, NY: Orbis, 1978.

Conzelmann, Hans. *The Theology of St. Luke*. New York, NY: Harper and Row, 1961.

Danker, Frederick W. *Jesus and the New Age According to St. Luke*. St. Louis: Clayton, 1972.

_____. *Luke*. (Proclamation Commentaries) Philadelphia: Fortress, 1976.

Drury, John. *Tradition and Design in Luke's Gospel*. Atlanta: John Knox, 1977.

Ellis, E. Earle. *The Gospel of Luke*. Greenwood, SC: Attic Press, 1974.

Fitzmyer, Joseph A., *The Gospel According to Luke (I-IX)*. (Anchor Bible 28a) Garden City, NY: Doubleday, 1981.

Franklin, Eric. *Christ the Lord: A Study of the Purpose and Theology of Luke-Acts.* Philadelphia: Westminster, 1975.
Green, Joel B. *The Gospel of Luke.* Grand Rapids: Eerdmans, 1997.
Jervell, Jacob. *Luke and the People of God.* Minneapolis: Augsburg, 1972.
Karris, Robert J. *Invitation to Luke.* Garden City, NY: Doubleday, 1977.
Koester, Helmut, François Bovon, and Christine M. Thomas. *Luke I, A Commentary on the Gospel of Luke 1:1—9:50* (Hermeneia: a Critical and Historical Commentary on the Bible). Minneapolis: Fortress, 2002.
Maddox, Robert. *The Purpose of Luke-Acts.* Edinburgh: T. and T. Clark, 1982.
Marshall, I. Howard. *The Gospel of Luke.* Grand Rapids: Eerdmans, 1978.
Phillips, John. *Exploring the Gospel of Luke: An Expository Commentary.* Grand Rapids: Kregel, 2005.
Pilgrim, Walter. *Good News to the Poor.* Minneapolis: Augsburg, 1981.
Talbert, Charles H. *Literary Patterns, Theological Themes, and the Genre of Luke-Acts.* Missoula: Scholars Press, 1974.
_____ ed. *Luke-Acts: New Perspectives from the Society of Biblical Literature Seminar.* New York: Crossroad, 1984.
_____ ed. *Perspectives on Luke-Acts.* Danville, VA: Association of Baptist Professors of Religion, 1978.
Tiede, David. *Prophecy and History in Luke-Acts.* Philadelphia: Fortress, 1980.
Tyson, Joseph B. *Marcion and Luke-Acts: A Defining Struggle.* Columbia: University of South Carolina Press, 2006.

SEASON OF ADVENT
FIRST SUNDAY OF ADVENT

Advent, as the season of anticipation for the coming of the Lord, is unique within our Church Year in that during Advent each year we are encouraged to look forward to new and future acts of God, not only with all other Christian people, but with all who are theists throughout the world. Approximately 67% of all people alive at this time, i.e., virtually all Christians, Jews, Muslims, and Hindus, as well as most people whose religions are spin-offs of Judaism, Christianity, Islam, and Hindu Religions, look forward in some way to new actions of God within their future. All of the other seasons of the Church Year are more specifically Christian, limited for the most part to God's actions as perceived to have occurred in Jesus of Nazareth, whom we believe is raised from the dead by the power of God and is one with God within what we call the Trinity perception of God.

It would be appropriate for us, as least on this First Sunday in Advent, to recognize this broad perspective that the season of Advent provides as we study the texts appointed for this day and as we proclaim God's Word for our time and place this coming weekend. It is within this broader perspective that the season of Advent provides that our Advent hope for peace and justice for all of the people of the world emerges.

Finally, it should be noted that the "Lord" in the texts appointed for this day does not refer solely to Jesus or to Jesus Christ. It refers to Adonai as Lord, as well as to Jesus as Lord. Therefore, if we have Jewish, Islamic, and Hindu friends whom we wish to invite to join with us in a Christian worship service, the service on Advent 1 will be the best time during the year to do this.

Psalm 25:1-10

This psalm is primarily an individual lament. It is an acrostic psalm, with each successive verse in Hebrew beginning with the next letter of the Hebrew alphabet. Because of this rather artificial form, the sequence of thought is somewhat irregular, as it would be if we attempted to write sentences beginning sequentially with each letter of the English alphabet.

Many of us may remember the use of this psalm in opening Sunday school worship services during our childhood. We may still cringe somewhat over its "Remember not the sins of my youth," wondering whether for the sake of our young people should we not translate it more adequately as "Remember not my past sins," at least when it is to be used by young people who can easily see that generally speaking young people are no more sinful than are the older people around them.

The psalm is a prayer to the Lord that with loving kindness the Lord would remember the psalmist. As such, it is a prayer for the present *and for the future*, that a person's present and the person's future may be lived according to the way of the Lord.

The portions of the psalm that are included in this lectionary selection can be used by any theists, especially when the Hebrew divine *tetragrammaton* is translated as "Lord." It is the context and the community within which the psalm is used that make it specifically Jewish, Christian, Islamic, or Hindu.

Jeremiah 33:14-16

The selection is a promise of fulfillment for Israel and for Judah, one of many Israelite expressions of hope for a political ruler in David's line, one who will rule in a way that will give to Jerusalem a good name.

The larger section, Jeremiah 33:1-26, appears to be a redactional addition to the chapter 30-31 "Book of Consolation," following in the Hebrew text the story about Jeremiah's purchase of a field in Anathoth, his hometown. The section Jeremiah 33:14-26 repeats, redacts, and comments upon Jeremiah 23:5-6. The absence of Jeremiah 33:14-26 from the Septuagint text suggests that Jeremiah 33:14-26 may have been a relatively late addition to the Hebrew text of Jeremiah.

As Christians, we can use upper case letters for the branch, for the political messiah, if we wish, and we can see in Jesus the fulfillment of this expression of prophetic hope. There are some insurmountable problems with this interpretation, however, since we can hardly say with Jeremiah 33:16 that "in those days Judah will be saved and Jerusalem will dwell securely." The birth, life, and death of the Jesus of history and his resurrection as the Christ of faith have not made Jerusalem and Judah safe and secure. At no time since the time of Jeremiah has Judah been "saved" and at no time has Jerusalem "dwelled securely." Certainly this is *still a future hope*, not one that has been realized, in spite of important new efforts to make this possible.

1 Thessalonians 3:9-13

The key portions of this text for use on Advent 1 appear to be 3:11-13 (a doxology that concludes with a reference to the "Advent" or "Parousia" of Jesus as Lord). In this portion the *future* emphasis predominates. The extension of the reading into 4:1-2 adds a segment of parenesis, sound advice in view of the coming Advent of the Lord.

Luke 21:25-36

As we read and ponder over the significance of these words for our own time and place, with the apocalyptic expectations in this text regarding the coming of the Son of

Man, cosmic distress, the end of heaven and earth, and the continuance of the words of Jesus into the future, our emphasis in the use of this text should be on *futuristic* eschatology rather than on realized eschatology. Particularly this should be the case on Advent 1 when we stand with the Israelite people, with the writers of the Newer Testament epistles and gospels, with Jews, Muslims, Hindus, and other theists and look ahead with joyful anticipation toward God's new acts in the time that is still to come. We are now in a new Church Year, looking forward to Christmas once again, to new acts of God in the future in which we may participate, not looking backward to the past.

SECOND SUNDAY OF ADVENT

In each of the texts selected for this day, those who are addressed are urged to look forward in anticipation of good things that will occur when God will act decisively in behalf of people who are in need. Each of the situations differs from each other, and our situation differs from each of these. Nevertheless, in each situation someone speaks as a representative of God. In our own situations, each of us is being called to be that representative of God next Sunday. What are we being called to proclaim as God's representative where we are next Sunday? What message of judgment and of hope shall be spoken through us? Let us look more closely at the situations depicted in each of these texts. Then let us look more closely at our own situations.

Baruch 5:1-9

In this final portion of the beautiful call for courage and hope in view of the imminent saving intervention of God that extends from Baruch 4:5—5:9, Jerusalem is commanded to dress appropriately for this great occasion of salvation. She is told to remove her tattered garments of mourning and affliction and to put on the everlasting robe of righteousness that is a gift from God and the diadem of the glory of the Holy One, so that her beauty will be seen everywhere on the earth.

It is also said that Jerusalem will soon see her children gathered together from the east and the west to return to her. All of nature will cooperate in this glorious restoration.

This final portion of Baruch could easily be a segment of the Isaiah tradition from the late exilic and early restoration periods upon which it is heavily dependent. For us as Christians on Advent 2, this reading can become an expression of our solidarity with the Jewish people as together with them we look forward to saving acts of God.

Malachi 3:1-4

According to this text, good and needed actions will occur at any moment, for "Behold, I am sending Malachi ('my messenger') to prepare the way in front of me" (v. 1a). Many in the early Church disregarded the original context of this prophetic word of assurance and identified John the Baptist as "my messenger" and Jesus as the Lord. Leaders in the early Church had every right to do so, even though in its context and "life situation" Malachi 3:1-4 refers to a series of conditions that prevailed in restoration Jerusalem somewhere between 515 and 445 BCE, not to the first century CE. When Malachi 3:1-4 is read next Sunday, it would be appropriate to provide a brief explanation of the Malachi tradition's concern for sincere, carefully guided cultic actions. Within our proclamation of the message for our time we would help the people in our situation if we would point out that early Christian leaders saw in this Malachi text a reference to John the Baptist as the Lord's messenger and to Jesus as the Lord, even though that was not the intention of this text in its original setting. The Malachi 3:1-4 text, therefore, comes to us in the Jewish tradition in which it continues to be a call for sincere, carefully guided cultic actions and in the Christian tradition in which it continues to function as a prediction of the work of John the Baptist as the Lord's messenger and of Jesus as the Lord. Within our sincere, carefully guided cultic actions we now function as John the Baptist to prepare our people for the Lord.

Philippians 1:3-11

The "day of Jesus Christ" about which the Apostle Paul wrote to the Philippians is obviously the point of contact with the other texts chosen for use on Advent 2. That "day of Jesus Christ" was an important day for the Apostle Paul, and it is an important day for us. It is a day for which we also should be filled with the "fruits of righteousness," to the "glory and praise of God." That day, for us as for Paul, is a day when God will act decisively. That day is not merely the Christmas Day of incarnation of God in the past. It is also a day in our future and in the future of the world.

Luke 1:68-79

Liturgically, this "Benedictus" of Zechariah provided by the inspired Lukan writer, following in the Older Testament tradition of songs and canticles, has a prominent place in the Morning Prayer (Matins) Service for many of us. In it there is a confident expectation that the Lord God of Israel will soon deliver us from the heavy hand of our oppressors to serve God without fear, guiding our feet on the path of peace. In what ways do we suffer under the heavy hand of *our* oppressors? How do we expect that the Lord God will deliver us from our oppression? How do we proclaim and expect the Lord God to act in *our future*? How must we change so that we do not oppress others, so that we will turn back to God instead of turning our backs to God?

Luke 3:1-6

Since this is the major text for Advent 2, let us take the time for a somewhat extended exegetical study of it before we consider its application in *our* own situations.

Exegetical study:

1. An analysis of the literary genre of the text
It is an introduction of a religious precursor. (Compare this pericope with Luke 3:21—4:30, in which Jesus is introduced.)

2. Themes in the text

a. The word of God comes upon a person selected by God (v. 2b).

b. That word of God results in the proclamation of a baptism of repentance for the forgiveness of sins and the preparation of the way of the Lord to bring God's saving action to all people (vv. 3-6).

3. Structure of the text

a. External structure

1) Parentage, conception, pre-natal development, birth, circumcision, growth and development of Jesus accounts precede this pericope.

2) The message of John and an introduction of Jesus as the beloved Son of God follow this text.

b. Internal structure

1) The time and place setting that "Luke" supplies for the beginning of the public appearance of John (3:1-2a)

2) The call of John (3:2b)

3) The work of John as a "voice of one crying in the wilderness" (3:3-6)

4. Matrices (Life-situations) in which the text probably developed

All four Gospels and Acts associate the work of John the Baptizer with the beginning of Jesus' public actions. In Mark this is done almost immediately. In Luke, as Mark's gospel genre is recast more along the lines of a "drama" genre, the Lukan playwright provides a time and place setting for the beginning of the public appearance of John. Only Luke provides this time and place setting, because only Luke uses a modified "drama" genre. Neither Matthew nor Luke adopts Mark's identification of both Malachi 3:1 and Isaiah 40:3 as "written in Isaiah the prophet" without modification. Matthew utilizes the Malachi concept in Matthew 11:10 as words of Jesus, and Luke uses it in Luke 1:76 in Zechariah's "Benedictus" considered above. Only Luke includes Isaiah 40:4-5, apparently in order to include a reference to a universal witness that Luke has changed from the "glory" of the Lord to the "salvation" of God. All four Gospel accounts omit the parallelism "our God" in their quotation of Isaiah 40:3, thereby making John the messenger of Jesus as Lord rather than the messenger of God. The extensive Lukan account concerning John the Baptist combines Markan material, possible "Q" materials, and Lukan composition. Because of the apparent tendency within the Gospels and Acts to subject the John the Baptist traditions to the Jesus traditions, it is not possible for us to uncover with certainty what the historical Jesus said and did. Therefore, we shall concentrate on the Lukan level here and not attempt to reconstruct the Jesus of history level.

5. Purposes and meanings of the text

a. to show that God was speaking and acting in a powerful manner through John the Baptist to open the way for the Lord (Jesus) to come to offer the salvation of God to all people who wish to receive it.

b. to indicate that the Isaiah 40:3-5 portion of the Isaiah tradition had its most significant application in the person and work of John the Baptist, the most important precursor of Jesus as Lord.

6. Usage of this text from the first century CE until the present time

Most Christian commentators, teachers, and preachers have followed "Luke" quite closely in seeing the person and work of John the Baptist as *the* fulfillment of the Isaiah 40:3-5 text. They have considered Isaiah 40:3-5 to have been a long-range prediction and have read Luke 3:1-6 as its historical fulfillment. More objective biblical studies during the past bicentennial put more emphasis upon the original matrix and purposes of the Isaiah 40:3-5 tradition during the latter years of the Babylonian exile period and upon the tendency within the Gospels and Acts to subject the John the Baptist traditions to the Jesus traditions.

Applications now

We are now in the precursor role, the role of John the Baptist, the role of the messenger of the Lord, today! It is for us next Sunday to proclaim that God will act decisively in behalf of the people of the world in *our present and in our future*. We may be inspired to proclaim that action of God in continuity with our present, or in discontinuity with our present, or partially in both. Since our situations differ and are always dynamic, the specific content of that inspired, revealed, and authoritative word that we proclaim cannot be depicted here, except in general terms. Since we believe in God and believe that God does act decisively in Jesus the Christ, we shall certainly proclaim decisive acts of God on behalf of people who desire such action. We will look forward in joyful anticipation to the good things that will occur when God acts and when we by faith see those actions as God's actions for the people of the world. In each specific situation, that is, in each congregation at a specific time and place, our proclamation as inspired, revealed, and authoritative word of God should address the needs of people for economic opportunity, political freedom, education, and civil rights. Nothing less than that will be adequate. Anything less than that is likely to be merely repetition of messages that the people have heard many times before on Advent 2. Then most of them will lose interest in the message.

THE THIRD SUNDAY OF ADVENT

The dominating theme of these texts and of Advent 3 is *eager expectation*. The message for Advent 3 in Series C, therefore, differs from the message for Advent 2 not in substance but in intensity. Not only is the Lord going to do something good for people; the Lord is coming now! The proclamation is now more insistent; the *parenesis* is now more urgent. Promises and assurances of the coming *parousia* of the Lord are punctuated again and again in these texts by *parenetic* directions of how to live in view of the arrival of the Lord. We see this in all of these texts, even though their situations differ from each other and from ours.

Isaiah 12:2-6

In the first of the two brief psalms (12:1b-3 and 4b-6) that conclude Isaiah 1-12, the person who sings in the psalm is directed to say, "I will trust in the Lord and not be afraid!" On that day, which is coming soon, the psalmist will sing, "The Lord has become my salvation!"

In the second psalm the psalmist will draw water from wells of salvation. The Holy One of Israel is in the middle of Jerusalem. What the Lord has done shall be proclaimed throughout all of the earth. Our Advent hymn, "Joy To The World! The Lord Is Come!" expresses the same thought as we sing it during this season. Like Isaiah 12:2-6, this hymn is a mixture of realized and futuristic hope.

Zephaniah 3:14-20

This concluding portion of the Zephaniah traditions portrays the Lord as a great military leader whose presence assures Jerusalem and its people that the Lord will bring peace and safety to them. The eager expectation with which the tradition is expressed indicates that at the time this tradition was formed there was good reason to hope that the Lord would soon restore Jerusalem. On Advent 3 we too are filled with eager expectation. As the Spirit of God engenders our words, the mood and message of eager expectation must be communicated next Sunday also where we are.

Philippians 4:4-7

Appropriate and acceptable lifestyle for Christians during this twenty-first century continues to concern us. At the time when Paul was writing his letters and while the Four Gospels were being formed, new religious communities of followers of Jesus self-consciously identifying themselves as separate from other religious communities had the responsibility of determining what lifestyle was appropriate and acceptable for themselves. From the evidence that we have in the documents within the Newer Testament, it is likely that more than any other individual within these communities Paul was instrumental in shaping the lifestyle of the people within these new communities of faith. Paul was instrumental in this regard during his lifetime and again late in the first century when many of his letters that he had sent to five specific house church communities and to one individual, Philemon, were gathered together, edited by several persons within the Pauline communities, and circulated more widely. We are beginning to realize that Paul was probably more instrumental in shaping the lifestyle of early followers of Jesus than he was in establishing their theology. Because Paul's letters, as collected, edited, and distributed within the developing followers of Jesus, have continued in use as sacred Scriptures, they, more than any other parenetic material, have continued to determine what shall be appropriate and acceptable behavior for Christians. The Epistle to the Philippians and the segments of Philippians to be read within our congregations at worship next Sunday are important evidence of lifestyle considerations in Paul's letters as they have been brought to us within our Christian tradition.

Within Philippians 4:4-7, 8-9, and 10-13 Paul alternates repeatedly between telling his hearers *how* they should live and *why* they should live that way. In eager expectation they should "Rejoice in the Lord!" and their gentle graciousness should be apparent to all people. This is necessary because "The Lord is at hand!" They should not be anxious about anything, even though Paul himself is now a prisoner of the Roman state, and it is likely that the Roman state will execute him for proclaiming that Jesus raised from the dead rather than Caesar is Lord and ruler "above the earth, on the earth, and under the earth." It was the conviction and proclamation of Paul that Jesus as the Christ rather than Caesar is Lord and ruler *on the earth* that was so objectionable to the zealous advocates of Roman Civil Religion. These were the men who had made Paul their prisoner and would soon be bringing him into a Roman court and charging him with proclaiming someone other than Caesar as Lord and ruler within the Roman state. If Paul had proclaimed Jesus rather than Caesar as Lord only in the heavens and only in the graves under the surface of the earth, the zealous advocates of Roman Civil Religion who had power and wealth because of their loyalty to the Roman state would not have been concerned. It was Paul's proclamation that Jesus the Risen Christ is Lord and ruler *on the earth* and the fact that significant and increasing numbers of Greeks were acclaiming this also that was alarming to the zealous Greeks who had responsibilities to maintain Roman sovereignty in their areas.

    Nearly 2,000 years after Paul had been killed by the Romans, it was the Lutheran pastors in the so-called Confessing Church in Germany who proclaimed that Jesus as the Risen Christ rather than Adolf Hitler was Lord and ruler *on the earth* in Germany who were oppressed by the Nazis. The much larger number of Lutheran pastors who proclaimed that Jesus as the Risen Christ was Lord and ruler in the heavens above the earth and in the graves under the earth, but accepted Adolf Hitler as the Lord and ruler *on the earth* were praised by the Nazis, but discredited after Germany was defeated at the end of World War II.

Regardless of what may happen to him and to them, Paul wrote that the peace of God will keep their hearts and minds in Christ Jesus. Paul in Philippians 4 gently guided the Philippians to follow the model of his own lifestyle as they waited with eager expectation for the coming of the Lord. It was clear to Paul that the Lord will surely come, whether he and they live or die. So also it is for us.

Luke 3:7-18

As we compare this text with its parallels in Mark and in Matthew, and as we attempt to reconstruct the history of the development of the text, we see that by the time it reached the level of development that we have in Luke 3 it had become in terms of genre a prophetic word, specifically a prophetic word of judgment of the "old" People of God.

Verse by verse analysis of Luke 3:7-18 indicates that we have in 7-9 name calling and judgments directed against the Jews (material in common with Matthew 3:7-10 and possibly "Q" source in origin). Verses 10-14, in Luke only, are parenesis for the multitudes, for tax collectors, and for soldiers (probably not Roman soldiers but poor Jews who were paid to protect the persons and the wealth of the Jewish tax collectors). Verse 15 provides expectations about the possibility that John the Baptist might be the Messiah (Luke only). In verse 16 it is said that John baptizes with water, but that the mightier one who is to come will baptize with the Holy Spirit (Markan material used also by Matthew and by Luke). Verse 17 asserts that the mightier one will judge everyone, gathering the "wheat" and burning the "chaff" (material in common with Matthew 3:12). Verse 18 is a summary statement that with many different types of exhortation John the

Baptist proclaimed "good news" to the people, good news obviously for those who are "wheat" (Luke only).

Four levels of development of this tradition can be seen with considerable clarity as we study the Luke 3:7-18 text and its parallels. These are the John the Baptist of history level, the Markan level, the Matthean level, and the Lukan level. Life situation and purpose at each level can also be recovered with some certainty as we examine these texts within the context of other texts.

At the John the Baptist of history level, the life situation is Jewish, specifically Jewish prophetic self-criticism coupled with eager expectation of the coming of the transcendent though human Son of Man. The visible expression of a water baptism of preparation was used. The purpose at this Jewish level of prophetic self-criticism was to gather a people prepared for the Lord, after the analogy of the Isaiah traditions during the last years of the exilic period. Similarities to the Qumran literature are numerous. The polemic at this level is not anti-Jewish. It is intra-Jewish. It is designed for the improvement of one's self, not for the improvement of other people.

At Markan level (Mark 1:5-8) John the prophet has now become the messenger "foretold" by Isaiah. John the Baptist has now become securely subordinate to Jesus. Nevertheless, he is portrayed as the most important precursor of Jesus, the mightier one who is to come. The purpose at the Markan level is to show that the person and work of John the Baptist was clearly foretold by Isaiah and that Jesus is the Lord (the imminent Adonai by implication) who came and will come again to baptize his followers, the new People of God, with the Holy Spirit.

At the Matthean level (Matthew 3:5-12) the intra-Jewish internal self-criticism has become external anti-Jewish polemic directed viciously against the Pharisees and the Sadducees. The Pharisees and the Sadducees are judged and condemned to destruction by fire. The purpose at the Matthean level is to show that the Jewish groups are going to be cut down and thrown like tree brush and chaff into the fire (with the recent destruction of Jerusalem in 70 CE undoubtedly in mind) in accordance with the prophetic word. In place of these discredited Pharisees and Sadducees the tradition represented here asserts that God can certainly raise up new children for Abraham, i.e., the followers of Jesus, and definitely will do so.

At the Lukan level (our Luke 3:7-18 text) the Jewish multitudes are condemned as in Matthew. However, for the new People of God there is good news. It is essential that these new People of God, the followers of Jesus and those who will join themselves to them, be honest, considerate, and content. By this time the invitation is extended even to Roman military personnel, in the hopes that they too would join in the new community of faith and accept Jesus rather than Caesar as their Lord. The purpose of the text at the Lukan level is to provide guidelines of ethical behavior for followers of Jesus baptized by the Holy Spirit and by fire on the Lukan Pentecost and later.

Perhaps a few suggestions for liturgical and homiletical use of these Synoptic traditions next Sunday may be in order. If we wish to go back through these texts to the ground floor of the John the Baptist of history level, we can emphasize the Advent message of sincere self-criticism in anticipation of the Lord who comes (came, comes, and will come) to us and to all people. This level is most appropriate for us for use on Advent 3.

If we wish to go no deeper than the Lukan level, we should deemphasize the Lukan judgment of the "old" People of God (the Jews), since especially within our post-Auschwitz era such condemnation is certainly neither appropriate nor is it necessary. Instead, we should concentrate on the words of assurance and of parenesis for the People of God today, ecumenically gathered wherever God gathers them in many traditions throughout the world. It is our privilege to proclaim the good news that there is salvation in Christ to everyone, without standing in judgment of them or claiming an exclusive monopoly over the sharing of God's grace.

Finally, we should be reminded that the great Advent hymn "Joy To The World" belongs with these texts for use on Advent 3 next Sunday.

THE FOURTH SUNDAY OF ADVENT

The Collect (Prayer of the Day) for Advent 4 is truly a classic. It is not a weak "Help us to do so and so." Instead, it is a bold call in the best Older Testament style with its "Stir up your power, O Lord, and come! Take away our sins and make us ready for the celebration…" The words "celebration *of your birth*" clearly indicate the double meaning of the word "Lord" here, as well as in many other places within our Christian prayers, since "the Lord" (Adonai) is not perceived as having a birth, but "the Lord" Jesus is. With its Trinitarian conclusion the prayer takes us to the farthest reaches of the Newer Testament and beyond it into the early Church.

Just as the Gospel account for Advent 3 directed our attention fully to John the Baptist, the Gospel account for Advent 4 focuses on Mary, the mother of Jesus.

Psalm 80:1-7

The geographical areas mentioned in this community lament imply that this psalm may have had its origin in the Northern Kingdom. Its words "Listen, O Shepherd of Israel! Get yourself going! Come and save us! Restore us, O God! You have the power to do it. Let your face shine upon us, in order that we may be saved! Give us life! Then we shall call upon your name!" and others like them in similar psalms provide the basis for the Collect cited above. In our liturgical use as Christians, this psalm is a final call for help before we celebrate the coming of God to us in Christ Jesus our Lord on Christmas.

Micah 5:2-5a

This well-known text may be said to exist in two separate but related genres, one in terms of its Jewish Older Testament context and the other in the Christian Newer Testament setting. It is first of all an Israelite-Jewish text, one of many within what may be called the "Messianic Problem" grouping. These texts are concerned with the problem of "Whom will God raise up from among the descendants of David to become our new king who shall under God lead us to political independence and freedom? Which of the descendants of the great king David shall give us the security that our ancestors enjoyed?" Just as David had been born in Bethlehem, so also it was expected by many that a son of David destined to become a political messiah would someday be born in that little village. In a most interesting way, the Jewish Messianic Problem of who would be this great new king became the basis for what would later be seen as many Christian Messianic Prophecies pointing specifically to Jesus. It is important that intelligent, educated Christians in our time become aware of this basis for the so-called Christian Messianic Prophecies of this type. The Matthean and the Lukan traditions "solved" the Jewish Messianic Problem to the satisfaction of the early Church by placing the birth of Jesus in Bethlehem and turning the Micah 5:1-5a Jewish Messianic Problem text into a Christian Messianic Prophecy that has remained basically unquestioned in popular Christianity. Christian Christmas carols such as "O Little Town Of Bethlehem" have brought Micah 5:2-5a fully into our Christian Christmas setting. Nevertheless, the little town (now city) of Bethlehem remains a holy place for both Jews and Christians for separate but related reasons. With greater understanding of the varied use of Micah 5:2-5a by both Jews and Christians, the text and the town can and should become focal points for fellowship and shared community between Jews and Christians, and for Muslims as well.

Hebrews 10:5-10

This text is a small segment of the extended persuasive presentation of the writer of this document in which its writer was attempting to convince Jewish background followers of Jesus within an evolving Christian community, perhaps in Alexandria, Egypt, to remain followers of Jesus and not return to their Jewish practices and lifestyle. We read in Hebrews 10:5 (my translation), "Therefore, coming into the world, Christ said, 'The sacrifice of animals and the offering of material gifts are not what you (God) wish most. But a body for me you have prepared for your purpose.' " Through our Christian use of this text on the Sunday immediately prior to Christmas Eve, we are in effect having the about-to-be-born baby Jesus addressing God by quoting from the Septuagint text of Psalm 40 (39):6-8 regarding the much greater importance of doing the will of God than of offering animal sacrifices and making material gifts!

The last instance in which Jews offered animal sacrifices as a religious action was just prior to the destruction of Jerusalem and its Temple by the Romans in 70 CE, and even for many centuries prior to that date animal sacrifice was little more than a symbolic action by Israelite-Jewish priests. Jews and Christians agree with this writer of Hebrews 10:5-10, and certainly all Muslims as well, that doing the will of God is far more important than butchering animals so that their meat can be eaten. As for the giving of material gifts to be used in helping people who are in need, Jews, Christians, and Muslims find this to be important and in accordance with the will of God. As Christians, we certainly bestow material gifts on family members and friends on Christmas Day, actions that are of great significance to merchants and a necessary stimulus to the global economy!

Luke 1:39-45 (46-55)

In verses 39-45 we have a fascinating drama scene involving two pregnant women. With inspired creativity, the Lukan writer brought the mother of John the Baptist and the mother of Jesus into a close kinship relationship in which the themes of prenatal signs and the superiority of Jesus as

Savior over John the Baptist could be utilized fully. In verses 46-55 (the Magnificat) the Lukan writer, again with much inspired creativity, produced a hymn of glorification, based this time on the song of Hannah in 1 Samuel 2:1-10, with a focus on the Lukan theme of the exaltation of the lowly.

New Testament scholars such as Richard A. Horsley, Warren Carter, William R. Herzog II, and others currently identify and explain within texts such as Luke's Magnificat "hidden transcripts" of resistance by oppressed persons against their powerful oppressors. My own *Anti-Roman Cryptograms in the New Testament: Hidden Transcripts of Hope and Liberation* (New York: Peter Lang, 2010) is an analysis of such texts throughout the Newer Testament. These "hidden transcripts" characteristically include political connotations as well as theological content. Our sermons and homilies, if they are grounded in biblical texts, will inevitably also have political and economic implications as well as primarily theological content, especially during the Advent-Christmas-Epiphany and during the Lenten and Easter Seasons, as well as throughout the Church Year.

SEASON OF CHRISTMAS
NATIVITY OF THE LORD
CHRISTMAS, PROPER I (A, B, C)

Isaiah 9:2-7

The usage of religious traditions affects the form and even the content of those traditions. For example, usage of evergreen trees that are brought into our homes, stores, and churches during the season of Christmas over periods of time has affected the trees themselves. The use of such trees, especially when they are placed into stores and even into homes and churches many weeks prior to Christmas, has mandated that unless the trees are constructed out of materials that are made to look as if they were live trees cut from a forest or tree farm, even though they were not, they will deteriorate to the point that they are no longer useful objects of beauty. When automobiles began to be used not only to transport people slowly from one place to another on gravel roads, but to become portable sound systems transported at high speeds on superhighways, the form and the content of the vehicles have been changed radically. The automobiles themselves have become, in a sense, religious traditions. The time when teenagers are able to drive and to own their own cars or trucks becomes a "religious rite of passage" for them and for their families. Usage affects form and content.

Usage has affected the form and the content of Isaiah 9:2-7 dramatically, and, of course, of other religious texts as well. While the precise details of the environment in which Isaiah 9:2-7 had its origins are unknown to us, it is likely that life conditions had been difficult for the Israelite people and for their nation. Now, however, there was reason to be hopeful. A young man, a descendant of King David, was being acclaimed as the new king. There was an expectation that, unlike their recent kings, this one would be wise, compassionate, strengthened by God, as concerned for them as a loving father would be, a king whose reign would be a reign of justice and of peace. Unfortunately, the hopes and the dreams of the people were never realized. Once the king had power and authority, his power and his authority were misused and lost and the people again suffered, sometimes even more than they had earlier.

As the ancient Israelites and the Jews who came after them experienced repeated injustices and hardships, their hopes for an ideal king repeatedly rose and fell. Especially when for long periods of time they had no autonomy as a nation, their hopes and expectations for their own fair and just "king" and "messiah" were embellished by their poets and heroes. The Isaiah 9:2-7 text, along with Isaiah 11:1-9 and others, are evidence of their efforts, and remain useful as expressions of Messianic expectations for Jews today. For many Orthodox Jews, expectations of the coming of a truly worthy earthly ruler sent by God continue, even after countless disappointments. For most non-Orthodox Jews, these texts are treasured as expressions of the coming Messianic Age of justice and of peace, for which they should strive.

For followers of Jesus whose efforts eventually resulted in the Christian tradition, these same texts initially provided expressions of hope that were similar to those of Jews who did not become Christians. Many of these followers of Jesus developed a belief that Jesus was the ideal Messianic King, not merely human, but also divine. Their usage of Isaiah 9:2-7, and of other Israelite-Jewish texts, affected the form and the content of the texts. Long before Handel composed his magnificent "Messiah," and certainly ever since that time, translations of Isaiah 9:2-7, and most of all of the titles given to the ideal king in the latter portion of Isaiah 9:6 were affected for Christians in ways that departed significantly from the texts and translations used by Jews. As is well known, in most of our Christian translations into the English language we see the adjectives beginning in upper case form as "Wonderful!" "Counselor!" or "Wonderful Counselor," as "Mighty God," "Everlasting Father," "Prince of Peace." The usage has almost indelibly affected the form and the content of Isaiah 9:2-7, for Christians differently than for Jews.

Does this mean that we should not use Isaiah 9:2-7 as it has evolved for us? Should we use instead the text in its most primitive possible form? Not at all. We should no more do that than we should use only Christmas trees cut live from the forest or make and utilize only automobiles that are like the first horseless carriages. We should use and enjoy fully the text of Isaiah 9:2-7 as we have it, while at the same time fully appreciating and respecting Jews who use it as it has been affected by their experiences.

Psalm 96

This is one of a series of psalms in which the Israelites were and Jews and Christians are called upon to worship the Lord God, the Creator and Righteous Ruler of the earth. In this beautiful psalm even the elements of nature are urged to sing praises to the Lord God. Since we as Christians perceive the Christmas season as the primary time when we give thanks to the Lord God as the Father of the one who is for us God's Son, Jesus the Christ, God in another form, it is in every way fitting that we, together with all Jews, praise the Lord God on Christmas Eve. Jews praise God in a universal sense at all times; we as Christians, especially during the Christmas season, praise God in a particular, as well as in a more general, universal sense at this time. It is essential that we emphasize that the Christmas season is first and foremost a celebration of God's unique gift to us all.

Titus 2:11-14

Although this text was written from a post Good Friday and Easter Christian perspective rather than from a festival of Christmas Christian perspective, it is also adaptable to our use here on this occasion. Its emphasis is on the grace of God and on our lives that are to be appropriate responses to God's grace. This text also from its perspective provides for us an early link to Good Friday and to Easter, which for us are only a few short months away.

Luke 2:1-14 (15-20)

Within popular Christianity, this vivid Christmas drama written by the inspired author of the "Gospel According to Luke" dominates all other texts. We as leaders in public worship services should, therefore, center our proclamation upon it every Christmas Eve. If we were to do otherwise, it would hardly be Christmas Eve for us and for the people worshiping God as Christians among us, so powerful has this Lukan drama become! Here and in the other instances in which the writer of Luke-Acts was not dependent upon written sources known to us, it is likely that the writer researched the subject thoroughly and then composed freely and with inspired creativity, much as we do when we prepare sermons and homilies.

We must read this text with every oral interpretation skill given to us, or perhaps, after memorizing a particular translation of the text, proclaim it with the techniques employed in dramatic biblical storytelling. We can also portray it in vivid chancel drama with parts for children and adults and with the "holy family" of the parents of the youngest child in the congregation and their infant "baby Jesus" seated in the chancel. (We did this in a young mission congregation in which I served many decades ago. During the worship service, the infant cried and the mother discreetly nursed him.) Infants and children should certainly be highlighted during the worship service on Christmas Eve.

But what in addition can we do to make this worship experience as meaningful and as memorable as possible? We all want to sing our favorite Christmas carols, hear well-rehearsed anthems from the choirs, and gaze at the Christmas trees in the chancel. How can we best explicate and apply the message of the Lukan Christmas story? What will God do within us that will be a continuation of what God has done within the Lukan writer? How shall we paraphrase the text with a bit of additional historicizing?

If then, now, and always *the Lord comes within the activities of the People of God*, as we see in all of the texts selected here, should we not proclaim some specifics about how God comes as Savior, Christ, and Lord (the three designations used in the message of the angel in Luke 2:11) within the parishes in which we serve? We can, also with well-researched and inspired creativity like that of the Lukan writer, proclaim something such as "During the early decades of the twenty-first century, while _____ was the President of the United States and _____ was the governor of _____, within a local congregation in (your location), the Lord God came to a woman stricken by cancer and sustained her and her family and friends in their grief. The Lord came to a young businessman who would not sacrifice his moral principles to gain an advantage over his competitor. The Lord came to an old rancher and his wife who shared some of their land with people who were unemployed, and *the Lord was born here*, and the angels in the church choir sang, 'Glory to God in the highest, and on the earth peace and good will!' and the shepherds in the congregation told this story, and Jesus was Savior, Christ, and Lord among all of them."

Are we not the "shepherds" where we are? Can we not repeat what the "angels" have sung about what happens when the Lord comes *within the activities of the People of God where we are*? This can then be our most meaningful Christmas Eve message, a proclamation and application of the texts selected for this night. Perhaps it would also be a proclamation and application that Jews and Muslims, Hindus and Buddhists, and our other non-Christian guests could receive in a Christmas Eve worship service to which they were invited. They may want to be invited to this Christian mountaintop experience, if they know that *their* religious traditions and practices are respected by us.

I cannot leave this text, most of all Luke 2:7 with its depiction of the mother of the baby Jesus wrapping him in soft material and tenderly placing him into a "manger" so that he and she could sleep, until I share with you an experience that I had during the years in which I was growing up on our small farm in Northwest Ohio. While my friends in town were playing sandlot baseball after school and later going to football, basketball, and track practices and games, I, five miles from town, was doing what my parents wanted and expected me to do, the daily chores of feeding our chickens, hogs, and calves, and helping to cut and husk corn with hand tools. I drove our Farmall H tractor so that my mother could come back to our house to begin to prepare our supper and bring in our 4-5 cows to be milked by hand as well, which she often did so that my father and I could keep the tractor and team of horses going until dark during planting and harvesting times.

We had a calf shed, which unlike our other farm buildings we never painted, in which at any given time, we had one or two calves. There was a narrow walkway along the north side of the shed we used so that we could bring straw to soak up the manure that the calves produced, hay and corn fodder for roughage, water for the calves to drink, and a small scoop of oats, which the calves relished eagerly. Apart from the larger area where we placed the hay and the corn fodder, there were two feedboxes into which I would pour the oats. (There had to be two feedboxes for two calves. If you know anything about animals eating oats, you know why there had to be two feedboxes.)

The relation of all of this to Luke 2:7 is that these feedboxes, built into the feeding area by my grandfather, were raised from the floor perhaps 24 inches, were approximately ten inches wide and eighteen to twenty inches long, with sides perhaps six inches high so that the calves as they licked up the grains of oats would not spill them out of the manger. Many generations of calves, over a period of more than four decades had with their raspy tongues licked the boards smooth, even wearing away with their tongues over the years grooves in the soft wood between the darker bands of hard wood. These feed mangers were just the right size into which a mother could place her newborn child! We did not use these mangers for that, but in the Lukan Christmas story the Virgin Mary did. In Luke's Christmas story the mother of Jesus placed him into a feedbox like the ones into which I had poured scoops of oats for our calves. The mangers in the feedlots in Bethlehem were intended for use by the sheep and goats, but in Luke's Christmas story Mary placed the baby Jesus into one of them, while Caesar and Herod languished in their richly adorned palaces.

CHRISTMAS, PROPER II (A, B, C)

Isaiah 62:6-12

After many years during which the grain and the wine from the vineyards of Jerusalem had been given by the Lord God to the enemies of its people, the people of Israel are depicted here as streaming back to the city from the broad highway cleared of all stones and obstructions over which they were returning from their exile in Babylonia. The people who return to the city are called "holy," because they are the people of the Lord; they are called "redeemed" because the Lord has purchased them from their captors. The people of the Lord will again eat their bread and drink their wine in the holy city.

Psalm 97

The land and its people will rejoice, because the Lord God is now the King. The throne of the Lord God is built upon the foundations of righteousness and of justice. All adversaries of the Lord God are consumed by his fire. The earth trembles under his feet. Those who are righteous will welcome the coming of the Lord and give thanks to their God.

Titus 3:4-7

While in the Isaiah 62:6-12 and Psalm 97 texts God is depicted as the Savior, active in the lives of the righteous, the people here in Titus 3:4-7 have been washed and reborn. What is new and different in this text from the Newer Testament is that God as the Holy Spirit is said to have been poured out upon the people through the activity of Jesus Christ our Savior. The Lord God is coming in new forms. As arranged in Proper II of our texts for Christmas, Titus 3:4-7 provides a transition from the idea that the Lord God comes in power and might to the belief that the Lord God comes in the birth of the baby Jesus in the Lukan Christmas story.

Luke 2:(1-7) 8-20

For this, see the notes under Luke 2:1-14 (15-20) above for Christmas, Proper I.

CHRISTMAS, PROPER III (A, B, C)

All four of the texts chosen for our use on Christmas Day refer to the coming of the Lord God. That coming is perceived in a way that is unique to each text. The most noticeable differences are that in the two texts from the Older Testament the coming of the Lord is expressed by use of a series of *anthropomorphisms* (depictions of God using various features and characteristics of humans), while in the two texts from the Newer Testament the Lord is depicted as coming *incarnate* (in the actual form of a human person). Let us look more closely at each of these texts. Perhaps the differences between these two depictions are not as large as they may at first appear to be.

Isaiah 52:7-10

This delightful portrayal of watchmen on the walls of Jerusalem singing joyously when they see the first indications of the return of the Lord God to Jerusalem is an entirely appropriate text from the Older Testament to serve as the First Lesson in Christian worship services on Christmas Day. The feet of the messenger who will be able to announce the return of the Lord God as they skip at a rapid pace over the hills approaching the city are described as beautiful, for their arrival means that the Lord God has come to the city to make it holy once more. The Lord God comes in the form of the feet of the messenger and of the voices of the watchmen. May our longing on this Christmas Day for the peace and salvation that only God can give to us be as great as that of the inspired poet of the Isaiah tradition during the period of the restoration of Jerusalem. May we, like the ancient Israelites, see the coming of the Lord in the feet of the messenger and in the voices of the watchmen among us.

Psalm 98

The primary anthropomorphism that is used in this psalm is that of a victorious military hero who becomes a king. The most notable human model for this achievement in ancient Israel was David and in our own history in the USA is George Washington. Most nations have military heroes who become political figures highly honored within the national-civil expressions of religion. Within the Older Testament use of anthropomorphisms, even when there are many references to physical characteristics such as the "right hand" and the "holy arm" of the Lord, it is not likely that a physical coming, an incarnation, a presence of God in human form is intended. Anthropomorphisms such as these are used with great frequency in the Older Testament and continue to be used widely among Jews and Christians, as well as among many Muslims, Hindus, and others, simply because such anthropomorphisms are the most vivid way in which people can attempt to describe God and depict actions of God. The use of anthropomorphisms in the language with which we and other people express faith in God does not imply incarnation. There is no doubt, however, that the heavy use of anthropomorphisms in Israelite-Jewish sacred scriptures and in Jewish theology contributed very significantly to the development of incarnation theology in the Christian Church and to our understanding of the meaning of Christmas.

In the final verse of Psalm 98 the entire world is called upon to sing praises to the Lord, who is depicted as the righteous, equitable judge of the entire world. For us as Christians during this Christmas season and throughout the year, it is easy to see Jesus as Lord with powers and responsibilities that are similar to those ascribed by the Israelites and Jews to Adonai as Lord.

Hebrews 1:1-4 (5-12)

The primary contrast in the initial portion of this treatise in which the writer argues that Jewish background followers of Jesus should not return to their Jewish lifestyle is between what is written here about Jesus as the Incarnate Son of God and the important but inferior prophets through whom God spoke and the angels who merely delivered messages from God. Jesus as the Son of God is said to be the heir of God, the one who will receive all that belongs to God. As in the Gospel According to John, the Prologue of which follows here as the Gospel selection for Christmas Day, Jesus is said to have been the one through whom God created the world. To Jesus is ascribed the reflection of the glory of God, the imprint of God's nature. It is claimed in this document that after Jesus had himself gone into the "Holy of Holies" and offered not the blood of sheep and of goats but his own blood upon the altar in order to purify us from our sins, Jesus took his position at the right hand of God on high. Within these few verses we have a brief abstract or synopsis of the entire Christian understanding of salvation. It is a huge, adult-size gift package under our Christmas tree! It is far more than a series of anthropomorphisms; it is fully an incarnation theology. Its high Christology is matched only in the Fourth Gospel within our New Testament and surpassed only by the Gnostic Christians for whom Jesus was perceived to have been only divine and never incarnate.

John 1:1-14

How different this hymn of acclamation of Jesus the Christ as the *Logos* face-to-face with God and *as* God is from the Lukan writer's literary drama scenes! Who would ever attempt to portray this hymn to Christ in a Sunday school or chancel Christmas drama? How many Christmas greeting cards have you seen that are based on John 1:1-14? The reading from the Epistle to the Hebrews, however, has prepared us for this.

The most perceptive among the members of the congregations in which we serve will be aware from their study of our biblical traditions and from their participation in Christian worship that there is not one theology but many "theologies" and not one Christology but many "Christologies" within our Newer Testament collection of documents. It would be appropriate within the message on Christmas Day to show that we are aware of the richness of our biblical tradition in these various Christologies, as a "preview of coming attractions" during the subsequent Sundays of this year. It would be helpful to share that for the Apostle Paul, divine powers were bestowed upon Jesus by God the Father through Jesus' death and resurrection. For the Markan writer, God "adopted" Jesus and gave to Jesus powers as God's Son at the time of the Baptism of Jesus by John the Baptist. For the Matthean and Lukan redactors, God made Jesus the Son of God by means of Jesus being conceived within the reproductive system of a virgin woman by the power of the Spirit of God. Here in the Gospel According to John, as well as in the Epistle to the Hebrews, God had apparently made Jesus divine "before the foundations of the earth were laid," and Jesus had participated fully or perhaps even with no involvement by God as God the Father in the creative process. We see, therefore, as we proclaim the Christmas message on Christmas Day using Hebrews 1:1-4 (5-12) and John 1:1-14 that we are at the extreme outer edge of the Christologies presented within our Newer Testament documents, Christologies in which there is no "baby Jesus" and, therefore, actually no "Christmas" as such at all!

JANUARY 1 — HOLY NAME OF JESUS (A, B, C) (MARY, MOTHER OF GOD)

The name by which a person is addressed is important. The name of a person, even the name of a thing, such as the name given to a file in a computer, provides a means of access to the person and to the thing. The name may also identify a particular characteristic of a person. Parents in Native American tribes, for example, usually waited to give a name to a baby until a particular characteristic of the baby could be identified. Infants are taught to respond when the name given to them by their parents is spoken.

The names by which God is identified and addressed are obviously especially important. God is depicted in many languages by words that suggest transcendence. Political and religious groups often develop personal names for God to designate God specifically for their group, that is, for God as their Lord or "Boss," their on-the-job supervisor who teaches them their tasks, guides and disciplines them, and requires respect and loyalty from them.

The personal name for God that was developed in Ancient Israel and is used by Jews is said in the Exodus 3 "burning bush" account to be the designation for "being" or "essence." Written using four Hebrew consonants, the so-called divine *tetragrammaton*, it is read but not spoken, lest it might be made common or profaned. Because it is considered to be so holy, a substitute (Adonai), which in the Aramaic language means "Lord," is used by many Jews. Orthodox Jews generally do not even use the substitute word Adonai, but instead the Hebrew word *HaShem*, *Ha* being Hebrew for "the" and *Shem* being Hebrew for "Name." They say, *HaShem* says, meaning "The Name" says. Most Orthodox Jews, when writing the general word for Deity in English, "God," write it with consonants only and not the vowel, as "G-d." They do this not only out of profound respect, but also so that any material on which the complete word "God" is written will not be erased or trashed.

Most of the texts selected for our worship services on January 1 when this day is observed as "The Holy Name of Jesus" day include emphasis on the Name. The Name of God is highlighted at the conclusion of the Aaronic Benediction in Numbers 6:22-27 and in Psalm 8, verses 1 and 9. The Name of Jesus is of utmost importance in Philippians 2:9-10 and in Luke 2:21. Galatians 4:4-7 has no mention of the Name, but when the Apostle Paul wrote in 4:4 that "when the fullness of time had come, God sent God's Son, born from a woman, born under the Torah" (my translation in *The New Testament: A New Translation and Redaction* [Lima, Ohio: Fairway Press, 2001]), indirectly Paul mentioned the mother of Jesus. Mary is prominent, of course, in the Luke 2:15-21 Gospel account selected for this day.

Before we look briefly at each of the four texts selected for use on this day, it may be helpful to sketch a variety of emphases on Mary within the Christian Church today.

For some Christians, Mary as the mother of Jesus is mentioned when the Lukan Christmas story is read, but she is mostly only a silent figure in the manger scene. She appears again at the cross of Jesus, but again is basically a silent figure. She is respected but not highlighted. For these Christians, especially within groups in which the Apostles' Creed and the Nicene Creed are not used, there is little emphasis on her as "the Virgin Mary."

For other Christians, those who use the Apostles' Creed and the Nicene Creed in most of their major corporate worship services, references to Jesus' mother as "the Virgin Mary" are frequent, but these Christians do not consider it to be necessary nor appropriate to address her in prayer. She is called "the Virgin Mary" because that is designated as her name in the Luke 1-2 accounts. She is honored throughout the Church Year, but is basically also a silent figure.

For large numbers of Christians, she is not only "the Virgin Mary"; she is referred to and prayers are addressed to her as "Mother of God." This was a result of theological development after the Newer Testament documents had been formed, but relatively early within the history of Christianity. The line of reasoning was that "Jesus is God." Mary is "the mother of Jesus." Therefore, Mary is the "Mother of God." Women especially, but men also, among these Christians find it helpful and easier in many respects to pray to her with certain requests than to Jesus as the Christ. She is perceived as having a mother's understanding of Jesus and of them. She *is* their mother. For these Christians, it is a natural and somewhat necessary theological development to believe that Mary had not and does not sin, since Jesus would not have been born sinless to a sinful mother. Therefore, she also must have originated, theologically, from an immaculate conception. Additionally, it came to be believed that she had never died, that she had been taken into heaven to be with God and with her Son Jesus without experiencing death. We experience death because we sin. If Mary has never sinned, death is not needed for her. Also, there was no interruption, therefore, in her hearing and responding to the prayers of the faithful.

Finally, there are millions of Christians, going beyond the third group in their Mariology, who now perceive Mary as not only the mother of Jesus, the Virgin Mary, and Mary as Mother of God, but also Co-Redemptrix with Jesus, with power along with Jesus to grant forgiveness of sins. These Christians reason that Mary suffered horribly along with her Son Jesus as he was nailed to the cross, as he died on the cross, and as she held his lifeless body after his death. She shares, therefore, with him as a dispenser of his redeeming grace. For Christians in the third and fourth of these groups, theological development continues; it did not cease after the Newer Testament documents were accepted as canonical.

All of our Scripture is Tradition, but not all of our Tradition is Scripture. The Word of God is dynamic, not static. God continues to inspire us, to reveal God's Self to us.

Numbers 6:22-27

It is entirely appropriate that we read this text with its familiar Aaronic Benediction on this day. This helps us to realize that this is actually an Israelite benediction that we happen to use in the Church along with many other "gems" from the Older Testament that we claim as our own. For us, of course, as we use this benediction in our Christian worship setting, the "Lord" is not primarily the Lord God of the Ancient Israelites. For us, the "Lord" is our Lord Jesus Christ, the Son of God, our Savior and Redeemer. Many among us are able to believe that there is one Lord and God, Savior and Redeemer, of us all, certainly of all Jews and Christians, as well as of all Muslims, Hindus, and so forth, and that we merely experience God in different ways.

Psalm 8

O Lord, our Lord, how awesome is your Name throughout the earth! Just as this psalm begins and ends with this acclamation; so also we should acclaim God at the beginning and at the ending of each day. We cannot overuse this acclamation and this psalm. No matter how heavily we use this acclamation and this psalm, when we focus on the Name, the words will always be dynamic for us.

Galatians 4:4-7

In this text Paul expressed no rejection of the Jews who remain Jews. Instead, he wrote that followers of Jesus are adopted into the family of God, to live together with the Jews, those who are not merely adopted but are biological members of God's family. Paul wrote that followers of Jesus are redeemed just as Israelites-Jews are redeemed and are now heirs together with them. God's inheritance is not limited. Our shares in it are not decreased, no matter how many people share in it.

Philippians 2:5-11

In this beautiful "hymn," whether quoted from another source by Paul or composed by him, what is written in Isaiah 45:23 about the Lord God as the one to whom every knee will bend and every tongue will profess is applied to Jesus as the Risen Christ. Here Jesus as the Risen Christ is Lord, to "the glory of God the Father." With this text, we as Christians are distinguished from Jews, but we are also united with Jews. In the end, there will be one Lord and God for us all. In the end, all will be one.

Luke 2:15-21

In this text we have a presentation of the "holy family." We see Mary and Joseph and we see the baby Jesus lying asleep in the feedbox where Mary has placed him. Later, theologically, Joseph as the father has to fade away and the "Holy Family" becomes God the Father, the Virgin Mary the Mother, and the Risen Christ the Son. In this text Mary ponders in her heart what the shepherds reported that the angels had said, and we ponder with Mary the Holy Name of Jesus and the significance of all of this for us today.

JANUARY 1 —
WHEN OBSERVED AS NEW YEAR'S DAY (A, B, C)

Even though from the perspective of the Christian Church Year we have already observed "New Year's Day" approximately one month ago on the First Sunday of Advent, we can be grateful if people will come together to worship God on the first day of our secular calendar year. It is good to see that for some people worship of God in Christian community on the first day of the secular year is more meaningful than "celebrating" with alcoholic drinks and watching football games.

It is interesting to see the texts selected for us as we prepare this worship service, since the American secular year is obviously not noted in our biblical tradition. They provide for us a challenging set of choices rather than a unified theme.

Ecclesiastes 3:1-13

This popular selection from the *Qoheleth* supplies for us on this day a collection of philosophical reflections over contrasting activities in our lives. It concludes with the observation that it is a gift from God that our eating, our drinking, and our occupations, even if tedious, should be enjoyable to us.

The wisdom tradition here has some similarities to Eastern philosophy, to Oriental wisdom, especially to the Taoist concept of yin/yang, the combination of opposites to attain completeness. As we have completed one secular year and as we begin another, it can be comforting to realize that although much of what occurred for us during the previous year was beyond our control, we can believe that, in spite of it all, God wants us to enjoy life and wants us to believe in God and to believe that, ultimately, God is in control of our lives and of our destiny.

Psalm 8

Psalm 8 in this context is a reminder to us that God, awesome as God is for us, has given tremendous responsibilities to us to care for the creatures of this world. As we ponder this, perhaps it would be appropriate for us to make some serious New Year's resolutions with regard to our God-given responsibilities to care for this world and its creatures and for our own bodies, as individuals and as groups of Christians in communities of faith. If we make resolutions, we should keep them.

Revelation 21:1-6a

Although we are not on this day in a new heaven nor on a new earth, we are beginning a new secular year and the old year has passed away. The sea, however, is still with us and is rising! On this New Year's Day and every day God is the Alpha and the Omega for us, present from the beginning to the ending of our lives.

There is an expression of faith in this text that God will be with us at every moment in our new year to "wipe away every tear" that may come into our eyes. We should be ready and prepared to see the hand of God in whatever form that hand may be expressed for us during the coming year.

Matthew 25:31-46

The clear emphasis in this text upon judgment of people by the Risen Christ based on works of mercy and acts of kindness that they may or may not have done may appear to be in stark contrast to the insistence by the Apostle Paul that we are being judged by God and saved from eternal suffering and death by the undeserved grace of God, not based on our own good works. Certainly different and even contrasting emphases can be and are present in our biblical collection of documents. Also, it is helpful to see contrasting teaching as present in creative tension within our Scriptures.

A key factor in this Matthew 25:31-46 text, however, is that it is "all the nations" that are said to be judged by the Risen Christ as the "Son of Man" here in 25:32, not the People of God, not those who believe and trust in God. Perhaps the people who do not believe in God and who do not trust in God are considered here in this text to be judged by criteria that are different from the criteria under which we are to be judged. In any event, during the coming year as in the past, eternal judgment is the work of the eternal God, not of mortal humankind.

SECOND SUNDAY AFTER CHRISTMAS DAY
(A, B, C)

Jeremiah 31:7-14

This thoroughly optimistic text is a reminder to us that the concept "salvation" in much of the Older Testament is primarily corporate and this-worldly and in most of the Newer Testament is primarily individualistic and is often other-worldly. By accepting both the Older and the Newer Testaments as its biblical canon, the early Church assured itself of well-balanced and well-rounded salvation concepts. Our teaching and our proclamation should reflect this balance, not overemphasizing the individualistic and other-worldly. When the corporate and this-worldly aspects of salvation are underemphasized and neglected, as they have been for so many centuries in most of the Church and still are in significant segments of it, oppression inevitably results and social justice is neither valued nor considered to be important for the Church. Instead, the Church offers only "pie in the sky by and by" and persons and groups of people who understand the necessity for social justice look with contempt upon the Church or at least consider it to be irrelevant.

Corporate and this-worldly and individualistic and other-worldly salvation is a gift from God for us. Life is itself a gift from God. Although we are individuals, we are members of the Church, the corporate body of Christ.

Sirach 24:1-12

This extensive personification and praise of *Wisdom* introduces the second half of the document known and used in major portions of the Christian Church as "The Wisdom of Jesus the Son of Sirach," "Ecclesiasticus" (the Church's book), or simply as "Sirach." After emanating from the "mouth of the Most High," *Wisdom* is said in this text to have permeated the world before being commanded by the Creator to dwell in Israel.

Psalm 147:12-20

As in so many of the songs in the Psalter, praise of the Lord (Adonai) is the dominant theme here. It is possible that there are three extended "verses" (vv. 1-6, 7-11, 12-20) in this psalm as we have it today, much as we may have hymns with three verses in our hymnals. The third verse selected here (vv. 12-20) was probably at one time separate from verses 1-6 and 7-11, as it is the Septuagint (Greek) and in the Vulgate (Latin) major translations of the Hebrew Bible. The emphasis in verses 12-20 on the Lord sending out the *Word* of the Lord (v. 18), declaring the *Word* of the Lord to Jacob (v. 19), and the statement that the *Word* of the Lord runs swiftly (v. 15) explains the reason for the selection of this portion to be placed between the personification of *Wisdom* in Sirach 24:1-12 and the personification of the *Word* of the Lord in Jesus perceived as the Christ in John 1:1-18, the pre-existent *Logos (Word)* who became flesh and "camped" among us, full of grace and truth.

Wisdom of Solomon 10:15-21

In this other major wisdom document within the so-called Older Testament Apocrypha that is sacred Scripture for most Christians, *Wisdom* is personified and acclaimed throughout the first ten chapters of the Wisdom of Solomon. In this segment, as in the portion from Sirach 24:1-12, *Wisdom* is said to have provided guidance for and become a blessing for Israel. It is written that *Wisdom* entered into Moses and led the former slaves through the Red Sea to freedom. We can believe that just as God via *Wisdom* provided salvation for Israel, God via the *Word* (the *Logos*) Jesus the Christ, provided salvation for the members of the Johannine community and offers salvation to the world.

Ephesians 1:3-14

The key words that connect this text selected from the "blessing" portion of this epistle to the Johannine Prologue (vv. 1:1-18) are *Grace* in verse 6 and the *Word of Truth* in verse 13. It should be noted that in Greek the entire "blessing" section of this epistle (vv. 3-14) is one extended sentence. When we translate this sentence into the English language for readers of modern English, we have to divide it into at least six sentences. Greek readers from the period of classical Greek and from what is for us the "biblical" period enjoyed well-constructed, "edifice" sentences; most modern readers of English want their sentences in simple, small bites.

John 1:(1-9) 10-18

Since the references to the witness of John the Baptist interrupt the flow of thought of this Prologue in the Fourth Gospel, even though they link the Prologue to the materials in the Gospel proper that begin with 1:19, on this particular occasion on the Second Sunday after Christmas Day when the *Word*, the *Logos* is emphasized, it would be appropriate to focus our attention on the portions of the Prologue (vv. 1-5, 9-14, 16-18) apart from the references to John the Baptist that we see in 1:6-8 and 15. The main and perhaps original portions of the Prologue (vv. 1-5, 9-14, 16-18) express one of the highest Christologies that were included within the Newer Testament canon.

Here in Jesus, the pre-existent *Logos*, divine grace is said to be so abundant that it is literally "grace piled on top of grace." Here the only begotten God the Son, who is in the close presence of God the Father, has "exegeted" (from the final verb in v. 18) God, has brought God out so that those who follow God will be able to see the meaning of God, God whom no human has ever seen at any time.

Particularly if we have used John 1:1-14 as the Gospel text on Christmas Day, we should put our emphasis on 1:16-18 on this present occasion. A biblically based message from this text on the Second Sunday after Christmas Day will demonstrate from Jesus as Jesus is revealed to us in the Newer Testament and from our experiences within the Church as it should be as the "Body of Christ" what it means to us to receive God's "grace piled on top of God's grace." Our message will also show how the Jesus of history in his life brought out for others to see the meaning of God whom no human being has ever seen at any time. It will be God who graciously forgives and Jesus who goes to the cross for us whom we, therefore, will proclaim and will depict with our lives. This will mean offering ourselves for others. It will mean giving up our life by trusting and believing in God who is the one who gives "grace piled on top of grace." Our words will be effective if our lives demonstrate these things.

SEASON OF EPIPHANY (ORDINARY TIME)
EPIPHANY OF THE LORD (A, B, C)

We have a responsibility in our ministry to observe and to preserve the festival of the Epiphany in some way each year, not only on the years in which January 6 happens to be a Sunday. The Sundays *after* the Epiphany will not have much special meaning unless we observe Epiphany itself in some way that will bring it to the attention of the members of the congregation. If we do not have a worship service within our usual setting, perhaps we could gather a group of young people — or people of all ages — and go Epiphany caroling to members of the congregation and community who are older, are shut-in, or otherwise are special in some way. This activity would also be a reminder to us that a substantial portion of the Church, i.e., the Eastern Orthodox tradition, observes January 6 as the Festival of the birth of the Christ. A carol singing would also highlight the beautiful Epiphany hymns on the Day of Epiphany.

If an Epiphany carol singing event is not chosen, some other unusual worship setting produced by the Worship Committee of the congregation could be most meaningful for those who plan it and participate in it. For example, worship could be in a public place to illustrate that this is the festival of revealing Christ to the "nations." It could be held in a circle on the floor or within a circle of chairs. The setting should be appropriate for a relatively small number of participants, and the setting as well as the message should be memorable. With a little imagination and some preparation, a group of youth or adults could act out each of the four texts in simple drama form, not necessarily with a narrator and following the dialogue verbatim, but with a measure of creative inspired imagination not unlike that displayed by the writer of the Matthean tradition that became Matthew 2:1-

12. The accounts could also be memorized by four different persons and presented in the form of biblical storytelling.

Isaiah 60:1-6

This is a truly beautiful text, especially when we consider its original "life situation." Certainly the people who first shared this message had vivid memories of the darkness that they and their parents and grandparents had experienced through defeat, the destruction of Jerusalem, and decades of exile in Babylon. Now they dared to hope and to dream of a glorious future when the glory of the Lord God would shine again on them and when people from all nations would come to that light. In their minds they pictured the return of parents with young children coming to Jerusalem from every direction. They visualized also pilgrims and foreigners bearing gifts that — in contrast with the total losses suffered during deportation and the flight of refugees — would restore the economy of their city. They expressed this in terms of camels laden with precious metals and perfumes, a picture of the greatest imaginable value brought on the largest "trucks, trains, cargo planes, and ships" known to them at that time. We can be joyful with them within our imaginations without at this point trying to make any Newer Testament application of this text. The Newer Testament application can come in our use of the Matthew 2:1-12 account.

Psalm 72:1-7, 10-14

This is obviously a Royal Psalm intended for use at the coronation of a new king or at some commemoration in honor of a king. We notice the high expectations of the song writer and of the people with respect to their king. They were especially concerned about justice for all and about righteousness in all relationships within the realm. Most of all, they were concerned about justice for the poor.

Within our own experience the theme of justice for the poor becomes extremely significant when national, state, and local governments directly or indirectly withdraw sustenance from those who have the greatest need among us. As members of communities of faith, we have the responsibility to hold our government units accountable through our direct actions and participation in government, advocacy, voting, and so on. In addition, we can and should do everything that we can to employ those who are poor, provide skills training opportunities, and to provide immediate assistance in terms of food, medical care, rent, mortgage payments, and utility payments. The Day of Epiphany can become a time when we recover some of this kind of service, a service that the Judaisms of the time of Jesus' public ministry, the early Church, and traditionally people within the Islamic tradition have provided. Our efforts locally and through regional and national church bodies have sometimes been very significant. Certainly much more can and should be done.

The mention in Psalm 72:10 of kings from Sheba and Seba in Arabia bearing gifts of great value and falling down in front of the Israelite king — something that was very rare within Israel's history — is apparently the reason for the selection of this psalm in connection with Matthew 2:1-12 on this occasion within our lectionary. The writers of the Matthean tradition probably used both Isaiah 60:1-6 and Psalm 72 when, inspired by the Spirit of God, they prepared the Matthew 2:1-12 account.

Ephesians 3:1-12

This text was most likely chosen for use on the Day of Epiphany because of the mention in Ephesians 3:6 and 8 of participation by Gentiles, along with those who were of Jewish background, in the one Church with its one faith and one Lord. These are very important Epiphany themes.

Matthew 2:1-12

This story is so well known that we may hardly notice how it was constructed. The inspired writers made good use of their Older Testament resources and in the process produced some quite remarkable subtle polemic against the Persian Zoroastrian magi religion that was still a significant factor in the East at the time of the development of this text. According to the subtle polemic in this text, Zoroastrians who are truly wise will bring their most precious gifts and fall down to worship the baby Jesus. The story is told so simply and beautifully that, accustomed to it as we have been from our childhood, we hardly stop to think about it. With some mature reflection we might ask whether the Herod of history would be so careless that he would not send spies to follow the magi to the home of any newly born "king of the Jews" who would be a threat to his own plans to be followed in power by one or more of his favorite sons. Also, with mature reflection we might be interested in how differently the Matthean and Lukan redactors developed their infancy narratives. The Matthean writers moved the action from Bethlehem to Egypt, back to Bethlehem, and then north to Nazareth. Luke started in Nazareth, moved the action to Bethlehem, and then returned to Nazareth. If we try to understand the story genre used in both of these infancy accounts, we shall not be unduly troubled by these very different geographical scenarios. Each writer used research, inspiration, and creativity. The purpose of each writer was primarily theological and only secondarily historical. Should our purpose not be the same today, since we believe that we are inspired and led by the same God who inspired and led them?

BAPTISM OF THE LORD
(FIRST SUNDAY AFTER THE EPIPHANY)

There are no texts within the Older Testament that point specifically to the "Baptism of the Lord." It is difficult, therefore, for those who construct lectionaries to identify Older Testament texts that can be related to the baptism of Jesus. It is also difficult for us who prepare and present homilies and sermons based on the lectionaries to ground our presentations on the Older Testament texts selected to be read on this day in which we focus attention on the baptism of Jesus.

Psalm 29

The specific life setting of Psalm 29 is obviously a thunderstorm hitting the entire west coast of Canaan and moving inland along a broad front that extends from Lebanon in the north to the wilderness of Kadesh in the south. The awesome sounds of the storm are attributed anthropomorphically to Adonai, whose voice is acclaimed as full of power and majesty. It is only in regard to this voice of Adonai that there is any notable connection with the specifics of the Luke 3:15-17, 21-22 account of Jesus' baptism.

Isaiah 43:1-7

This text is a poetic celebration of the redemption of the people of Israel announced by the Lord God who has created, formed, and bought back from slavery God's people Israel. God is said to love the people of Israel, who are honored and precious in the eyes of God. God is presented as promising to be with the people to lead and guide them safely through every danger that they might encounter, as well as to give the people of Egypt and the lands to the south of Egypt as a ransom price to buy back the people of Israel.

We can best connect this account to the baptism of Jesus texts by noting how God is said to love God's people Israel in this Isaiah 43:1-7 text and to be pleased with Jesus, adopted through his baptism to become God's chosen Son in the Luke 3:15-17, 21-22 text. By our baptism in the name of the Father, and of the Son, and of the Holy Spirit, we too are adopted into God's chosen family of people. Through the use of this Isaiah 43:1-7 text as we celebrate the baptism of Jesus and our own baptism, we are symbolically united with the Israelites and Jews, not separated from them, but joined together with them. The Older Covenant and the Newer Covenant become one Covenant with one God.

Acts 8:14-17

Acts 8:14-17 is a small segment of the Lukan writer's story about a man named Simon who wishes to purchase the power to bestow the Holy Spirit of God by placing his hands on people. In this text baptism in the name of Jesus was followed sometime later by the gift of the Holy Spirit. For the Lukan writer there apparently was some sort of progression from the baptism of Jesus to baptism in the name of Jesus to the gift of the Holy Spirit before, during, or after baptism in Jesus' name. Possibly it was to illustrate a growing perception of the Trinity concept of God, i.e., God the Father bestows the gift of baptism on Jesus the Son of God and together they provide the gift of the Holy Spirit of God. We can compare this to the Trinitarian formula for Baptism in Matthew 28:19, "Go, therefore, and make disciples of all kinds of people, baptizing them in the name of the Father and of the Son and of the Holy Spirit" (my translation). Various Christians since the first century have interpreted the gift of the Holy Spirit in many different ways. The concept should be a unifying factor within Christianity, not a cause for boasting or division. Each of us has a share in the responsibility of making it and keeping it a unifying factor.

Luke 3:15-17, 21-22

The Lukan writer linked the baptism of Jesus more closely to the baptism of "the people who had come to John" than did the Markan and Matthean writers. Also, the Lukan writer depicts the Holy Spirit of God as coming down in "bodily form," as a dove coming down and landing upon his head.

For the writers and people of the Synoptic traditions, the baptism of the Jesus of history, his life, teachings, and everything that he did were pleasing to God and to them. Just as they perceived Jesus as in many ways recapitulating the life and experiences of all of the chosen ones of God who had preceded him (the Israelites and the Jews), so also should we. We should live so that everything that we do will recapitulate the life and teachings of the Jesus of history in his Jewish context, the Jesus of history who, after God raised him from the dead, is perceived by us to be the Christ of faith. Therefore, we shall want to learn as much as we possibly can about the specifics of the life of the Jesus of history. Then we shall live with him, die with him, and we believe that we shall also be raised from the dead with him, to the glory of God! This is essentially the message that we are called to share during the Epiphany season, the bridge between Christmas and Lent and Easter.

SECOND SUNDAY AFTER THE EPIPHANY

The Greek word *epiphaneia*, transliterated into English as "Epiphany," is widely used in biblical and in non-biblical literature in the technical religious sense of "the visible appearance or manifestation of deity." In this literature the presence of deity is manifested in a great variety of ways. Anthropomorphisms are commonly employed. Past events are interpreted as evidence that deity has entered into the human sphere. Extraordinary phenomena in nature are said to be revelations of divine power. These visible manifestations of deity are said to have occurred during the past, in some instances they are claimed for the present, and frequently they are anticipated for the future.

The texts selected for Epiphany 2, Series C, in our lectionary are excellent choices for our celebration of God's self-manifestation in our lives. They depict divine-human encounters. They tell us in many ways that God cares about us and that God comes to us. We have the call and privilege of sharing this good news next Sunday.

Psalm 36:5-10

This portion of Psalm 36 focuses on characteristics and manifestations of Adonai Elohim (the Lord God) as perceived by many Israelites. The illustrations and analogies are beautiful, vivid, and descriptive. The human response to the manifestation of the divine is a mixture of praise and supplication. The best of human poetic expressions are offered in service to God. The Lord (Adonai) is said to save not only people, but animals as well. The steadfast love of God is depicted as the most precious gift that we can ever receive.

"Salvation" is the overall theme of the text. For our message this coming weekend, we are called to provide explicit examples of how God has provided salvation among us. We are also expected to permit and to encourage the people of the congregation to define "salvation" as each person perceives it.

Isaiah 62:1-5

At the time of the writing of this text, Jerusalem was still a "desolate widow." The time was near, however, when the desolate widow Jerusalem will be given a new name within a new marriage, with the Lord rejoicing over "her" just as a bridegroom rejoices over his bride. Then Jerusalem and Zion will be a crown of beauty in the hand of Adonai. Her salvation will go forth as does a burning torch carried by the lead runner in a group bearing good news that cannot wait until the morning.

Each of us is that torch-bearing runner rushing out into the night where we are during this Epiphany season. We add our message of salvation to the messages of these texts. We proclaim what God (in every way that we perceive God) has done and is doing for us. As Christians, what God has done and is doing through Jesus our Lord will be central in our proclamation next Sunday. The 1 Corinthians 12 and John 2 texts will provide our basic themes.

1 Corinthians 12:1-11

One God, one Lord, one Spirit provides for us a great variety of *charismata* (spiritual gifts). In God there is unity in the midst of all of this God-given diversity. Paul calls for mutual recognition and fellowship within the diversity of spiritual gifts with which the Spirit of God has endowed us. Why, we must ask, have so many people of the Church consistently ignored this call of Paul and this Word of God and refused mutual recognition and fellowship? Can our divided state of the Church, our exclusive enclaves, our superior attitudes and claims, be in any way pleasing to God? Why do we not use this 1 Corinthians text written by Paul to call the hand of the sectarians, those who will withhold their presence, refuse to share their offerings, threaten to separate themselves and their congregations from us if they cannot force their opinions on everyone else with regard to interpretation of the Word of God, participation by persons who have minority sexual orientations who are called to serve in the Church, or any other issue that they may choose? In their arrogance, they blunt the Epiphany message. They dim the Epiphany torch.

John 2:1-11

The "good wine" in this smallest of the miracles among the Fourth Gospel stories, this first "sign" by which the Johannine Jesus manifested his glory, is often considered to have Eucharistic significance. Perhaps it would be more precise to say that the "good wine" here is Johannine rather than to say that it is Eucharistic. It is an indication of something that was important to the people of the Johannine community. Within the context of the Fourth Gospel, this account may be saying that Jesus, not merely by a word of command but by his life and death, produced in bountiful quantities the "good wine" that is far better than all other wine, a symbol not of overindulgence or of alcoholism but of never-ending celebration of life. As a result, his disciples believed in him.

Today we are Jesus' disciples. We have this "good wine" from Jesus, given through his life, his death, and his resurrection. What shall we do with it? What did Jesus do with it in this text? Did he keep it? Did he sell it? Or, did he give it away?

Perhaps not merely for this text, but for all of the texts selected for next Sunday we might use a theme such as "The Best Product on the Market!" We might begin by saying that according to these texts we have the best product on the market, and that we agree with these texts that we do have this "best product" as a gift from God. We might involve the members of the congregation by asking, "What shall we do with it, with this best product on the market?"

Shall We Keep It for Ourselves?

Shall We Sell It to Those Who Can Afford to Buy It?

Or Shall We Give It to All Who Need It and Want to Receive It?

THIRD SUNDAY AFTER THE EPIPHANY

The emphasis in Psalm 19 is on the Torah and in Nehemiah 8 on the reading and validation of the Torah. In the Luke 4 text we are taken to a story about Jesus reading from an Israelite/Jewish sacred text, not from the Torah but from the Isaiah traditions.

Psalm 19

Poetically, this psalm emphasizes the value to be gained by living in accordance with the Torah. The value system derived from Torah observance is to be desired far more than precious materials such as gold and the sweetest food such as honey. Those who are wise will understand, respond appropriately, and be blameless. These words and actions have been and continue to be celebrated by Jews throughout the ages. They are vitally important also to us.

Nehemiah 8:1-3, 5-6, 8-10

This text reports a highly significant reading of the Torah by Ezra with commentary upon the text provided by the Levites. The deliberate, public reading of the Torah, the assembly of the religious leadership as witnesses, the explanations provided by the Levites, and the joyous acceptance of the authority of the Torah are indications that this text is meant to describe the process by which the Torah was formally validated as inspired, revealed, and authoritative sacred Scripture, "Word of God" for the Israelites. From this point on, the lives of the Israelites and Jews were to be guided by this written Word.

Ezra's opening the document in the sight of all of the people and reading from it (Nehemiah 8:5) may have been one of the many ideas that the writer of the Gospel According to Luke with inspired creativity used and adapted from the Septuagint. Like Ezra the scribe opening the Torah and reading from it in the Nehemiah 8:5 text, Jesus was depicted by the Lukan writer in Luke 4:14-21 as opening the scroll of the prophet Isaiah and reading from it in the synagogue in Nazareth.

Luke 4:14-21

Comparison of Luke 4:14-30 with its antecedent in Mark 6:1-6a reveals how freely the inspired Lukan writer reshaped the Markan tradition in order to produce, as the Lukan writer in the Luke 1:1-4 preface puts it, "a more excellent account of the things that have happened among us."

The most important written resources used by the Lukan writer here were obviously Mark 6:1-6a, Isaiah 61:1-2, and Isaiah 58:6. The Lukan writer moved Jesus' return to his own region in Mark 6:1-6a to the earliest period of Jesus' public activity, and left the disciples of Jesus out of the picture. The Lukan writer added that it was Jesus' custom to go to the synagogue in his hometown of Nazareth on the Sabbath day. The Lukan writer also provided the text for the Lukan Jesus to read, a combination of two portions of the Isaiah tradition, Isaiah 61:1-2 and 58:6.

The dramatic scene developed by the Lukan writer of pride by the people of Nazareth in this "hometown boy" that turned into vicious hatred and attempted lynching of Jesus supplies "in a nutshell" a look at the entirety of the Luke-Acts composition. Certainly Luke 4:14-30 is more vivid and consequently more memorable than Mark 6:1-6a and has been much more significant within the Church, just as the Gospel According to Luke as a whole has been more significant than the Gospel According to Mark. Unfortunately, however, in this instance the anti-Jewish polemic was also increased greatly in the Lukan writer's reshaping of the Markan tradition, as it was increased elsewhere by the Lukan writer.

As we apply these texts to our own specific life situations, it will be appropriate to concentrate on the Luke 4:14-21 portion that has been selected in our lectionary and on the mission of the Church today. According to these texts, we too should feel that the Spirit of the Lord is upon us, as the Spirit of the Lord was upon the prophet of the Isaiah 61 and 58 traditions and as the Spirit of the Lord was upon Jesus. We too in our times are anointed "to proclaim freedom to the oppressed," "to announce that those who have been in bondage shall be released and those who have been blinded shall see, to send out from captivity those whose spirits have been broken," and "to announce the time of the favorable action of the Lord."

These scriptures are fulfilled in our time when we as People of God in the name of Jesus Christ put these words of Isaiah 61:1-2, Isaiah 58:6, and Luke 4:18-19 into action. This is our responsibility as parts of the Body of Christ in the world. We are called to be players and player-coaches, not spectators and bystanders in this process.

1 Corinthians 12:12-31a

The somewhat continuous reading of 1 Corinthians texts during most of the Epiphany season continues here with little direct connection with the other readings for next Sunday. Through Baptism and the Eucharist it is said that all who are members of the Body of Christ have valid and very important functions. How much more grievous then is our current situation in the Church in which in so many instances sectarian Baptists are hurting other Baptists, sectarian Lutherans are hurting other Lutherans, sectarian Episcopalians are hurting other Episcopalians, and sectarian Roman Catholics are hurting other Roman Catholics! How foreign are the actions of these to the Word of God that the sectarians like to use as a weapon rather than as a means of God's grace.

FOURTH SUNDAY AFTER THE EPIPHANY

The connection is rather tenuous. Nevertheless, there is a point of contact in all four of these texts in the concept of *prophetic powers*. In Psalm 71 an old man in distress relies on the Lord to continue the prophetic powers of inspiration that the Lord has given to him since the time of his birth. In the call story in Jeremiah 1:4-10 prophetic powers are said to have been virtually forced upon the reluctant young man Jeremiah. He is said to have been known, consecrated, and appointed to be a prophet even before he had been born. For the Apostle Paul, prophetic powers, important as they are, are of no avail unless they are accompanied by God's kind of self-giving love. In the Lukan writer's story about Jesus in his hometown, prophetic powers are said to have gone unrecognized not only at the time of Elijah and Elisha, but also in Jesus himself. As we read and use these texts, we are called to consider the concept of prophetic powers in our own lives and in our own ministries.

Psalm 71:1-6

This psalm is the lament of an old man who asks the Lord for deliverance from personal enemies. Although there is no specific reference to the expression of prophetic powers in the old man, his need for deliverance from personal enemies is characteristic of any person who is given and demonstrates prophetic powers. There is an important connection with the Jeremiah 1:4-10 call story in the psalmist's claim to have been taken from his mother's womb by the Lord. The psalm is noteworthy for its vivid images and for its emphasis on proclamation of the mighty deeds of the Lord. These are exactly what is typically associated with the exercise of prophetic powers.

Jeremiah 1:4-10

The two principal purposes of a prophetic call story are to establish the credentials of the prophet and to indicate the major themes of the prophet's life and message. Particularly significant in this Jeremiah call story is its emphasis on the power of the prophetic word over the nations. We should perhaps tie this to the concern for the nations implied in the Luke 4:21-30 account. In Jeremiah 1:17-19 it is said that Jeremiah will be given prophetic powers to stand up against the powers and people of his own land. Jeremiah is given no choice; he is impelled by the Lord into his life situation. Nevertheless, there is a promise that ultimately the Lord will deliver him.

Perhaps as we ponder our own God-given call and responsibilities as we prepare for the worship service next Sunday, we should think more about our own personal call story in relation to the principal motifs of our particular ministry. To what themes are we driven by the Lord? Into what areas of ministry are we impelled? How does the Lord validate our credentials in these areas of ministry? When our credentials are challenged in these areas, what is our defense? What can we say about our call from the Lord? How can our sharing of our call from the Lord help other people to recognize and to accept their call from the Lord?

1 Corinthians 13:1-13

The individual members of the "Body of Christ" have various and diverse *charismata* (spiritual gifts). None of the members are able to perform the functions of *all* of the others. All are urged, however, to desire the higher gifts and to follow the way that Paul will show, the way of agape-type love, God's kind of love, revealed by God through Jesus the Christ and through Paul. While Jesus and Paul are our most important role models for Christian ministry, we also as inspired individuals within the Church are called to be reflective role models to demonstrate and to proclaim the same kind of self-giving love that Jesus and Paul exemplified. This call to reflect God's kind of self-giving love is experienced not merely to those who are clergy. It comes to all of us.

Luke 4:21-30

This is the rejection portion of the acclaim and rejection drama composed by the Lukan writer to present the principal motifs of the Third Gospel and of Acts. The violent reaction of the men of the synagogue in Jesus' hometown is almost certainly somewhat of an exaggeration and of an anachronism. This story about the vicious wrath of all of the men of the synagogue and their abortive attempts to lynch and to kill Jesus (and on the Sabbath!) is much more likely a Lukan composition late in the first century CE than it is the reporting of a historical occurrence from the time of the Jesus of history. After the atrocities committed by Christians against Jews during the Christian Crusades, after the abuse and execution of Jews ordered by the Christian Inquisition courts, after the horrendous pogroms in Eastern Europe during which over a period of several centuries more than six million Jews were killed, and after the death of an additional more than six million Jews in lands dominated by Christians during the Holocaust, as inspired people within the Church today it is unconscionable for us to include Luke 4:28-30 in our lectionaries and to read these three verses during our worship services.

Those who included Luke 4:28-30 in the Roman Catholic three year lectionary commissioned by Vatican II and used within the Lutheran and Common lectionaries derived from the Roman Catholic lectionary, and those who continued to include verses 28-30 in the Revised Common Lectionary were inexcusably insensitive. Those during the first few centuries of the early Church who through usage and decree accepted Luke 4:28-30 and similar materials into the New Testament canon were callous. The Lukan writer who composed Luke 4:28-30 was guided by that writer's own anti-Jewish bias and prejudice and as a result perpetrated much greater violence against the Jesus of history than did the fictitious people of the synagogue in Nazareth created to be characters in this story. As inspired people in the Church today, we must not perpetuate the destructive polemic of texts such as Luke 4:28-30 by continuing to include them in our lectionary. We are well aware that when we speak out against the reading of texts such as Luke 4:28-30 within our congregations we will be attacked and condemned by well-meaning traditionalists within the Church who will say that we must not object to these verses, because what is written in Luke 4:28-30 "is what those Jews did to our Jesus." We are fully aware that we are speaking against material that has been perceived as a part of the "Word of God" within our Christian tradition for many centuries.

Nevertheless, we speak because, like Jeremiah, we are called and compelled by God to do so; we cannot be silent. We speak for the sake of our children and for the sake of the children of others. We cannot continue to be silent bystanders and spectators. We, along with the writer of the Epistle to the Hebrews, consider the Word of God to be living and active, sharper than a two-edged sword, piercing to the essence of our being. The Word of God is an excellent sword, but we are aware that there are serious "nicks" in that sword. We must, therefore, appeal beyond canonical scripture and tradition directly to God. We must appeal because we believe in God, not in the Bible as if it were God, and not in the Church as if it were God, but because we perceive that God is "a consuming fire" to whom we are ultimately accountable.

As inspired people, we have no power of our own. We are captive to the unwanted gift of *prophetic powers*, the "red thread" that runs through the four texts chosen for this day.

May these prophetic powers be accompanied by what the Apostle Paul called "God's kind of self-giving love!" (For a much more extensive rationale for the necessity of our repudiation of the content of Luke 4:28-30 and similar texts, see my *Mature Christianity: The Recognition and Repudiation of the Anti-Jewish Polemic of the New Testament* [Susquehanna University Press, 1985], or my *Mature Christianity in the 21st Century: The Recognition and Repudiation of the Anti-Jewish Polemic of the New Testament* [New York: Crossroad, 1994]). (For an extensive article in which *The Revised Common Lectionary: The Consultation on Common Texts* and other lectionaries are analyzed regarding anti-Jewish polemic in their selections, see my "Removing Anti-Jewish Polemic from our Christian Lectionaries: A Proposal" at http://jcrelations.net. Select "English," "Articles," and "Beck, Norman A.")

FIFTH SUNDAY AFTER THE EPIPHANY

The calling of Isaiah, the calling of Peter, and (by implication) the calling of each of us dominate the series of texts selected for our use next Sunday. Each is called for a purpose, to carry on a mission, to be commissioned.

Isaiah 6:1-8 (9-13)

Prophetic call stories typically reveal much about the life and nature of the person called and about the reception that the message of that prophet received. The call story in Isaiah 6 does this well for the Isaiah 1-39 traditions.

The placing of the call of Isaiah story so far into the Isaiah 1-39 text, as Isaiah 6, is unusual. (Compare the positions of the call of Jeremiah in Jeremiah 1, of Ezekiel in Ezekiel 1-3, and of Moses in Exodus 3:1—4:23.) Perhaps this position was chosen by the editors of the Isaiah traditions so that much of the message of the Isaiah 1-39 traditions could be given prominence before the call of the prophet was described.

This call story emphasizes the overwhelming holiness of the Lord and the glory of the Lord over the entire land. *"Kadosh, kadosh, kadosh, Adonai Sabaoth; melo kal-ha-aretz kevodo!"* Three times both for emphasis and for euphony the Lord is acclaimed as holy. And the cry is passed back and forth between the seraphim. The holiness of the Lord overwhelms Isaiah in the call story. Then the burning coal touches his lips, and his sin and guilt are taken away. He is compliant. He is willing to be sent.

This call story suggests that the message of Isaiah will not be understood; the people will not be healed. This will continue until the land is desolate. Hardly a remnant will remain. Isaiah is expected to be obedient to the Lord even when destruction surrounds him on every side. The same is certainly expected of us.

Psalm 138

Although this psalm is not a call story, there are significant connections between Psalm 138 and Isaiah 6. The glory of the Lord is said to be great in Psalm 138:5 and in Isaiah 6:3. The temple of the Lord is the location of each text, and it is written in each that the Lord will fulfill the purpose of the Lord, for the prophet in one and for the psalmist in the other. There is a difference in that the psalmist is said to have called upon the Lord and the Lord responded, whereas in Isaiah 6:8 the Lord asks a question and the prophet responds.

For us as called People of God today, Psalm 138 is an approximate expression of our situation. We too give thanks to God for God's steadfast love and faithfulness in calling us to fulfill the purposes of the Lord.

1 Corinthians 15:1-11

The call of Paul to be an apostle of Jesus Christ, according to Paul himself in this text, was the result of an appearance of Jesus as the Christ raised from the dead by God. The message received in the call, Paul wrote, was that Christ died for our sins in accordance with the earlier Scriptures, that he was buried, that he was raised from the dead on the third day also in accordance with the earlier Scriptures, and that as the Risen Christ he appeared to various disciples and groups of disciples. Like Isaiah in the Isaiah 6 call story, Paul is overwhelmed by the Lord and is not said to have offered resistance to his call. Paul considered his call to be evidence of the grace of God. His response, through the grace of God, was to labor harder than anyone else to proclaim Christ crucified and raised from the dead, a message of hope for both Jewish background and non-Jewish background followers of Jesus.

It is likely that the Lukan writer had access to 1 Corinthians 15:1-11 and used it, together with Galatians 1:11-24, in the composition of the dramatic call of Paul stories in Acts

9:1-22; 22:4-16; and 26:9-18. The simple testimony of Paul himself here in 1 Corinthians 15:1-11 about his call provides a much better model for us of our own call to Christian ministry than does the vivid literary drama composed by the writer of Acts 9:1-22 and liked so much by that writer that the Lukan writer repeated it with only slight variations again in what is for us Acts 22:4-16 and 26:9-18.

Luke 5:1-11

Here again the Lukan writer "improved" the Markan account by using Mark 1:16-20 as the basis for an extensive "Call of Peter" composition that was then placed after the Like 4 account of solo activity of Jesus in Jesus' hometown. The miraculous great catch of fish in Luke 5:1-11 at the command of the Lukan Jesus symbolizes proleptically the great success of the Spirit-filled apostles of Jesus after the Lukan writer's Pentecost account.

Incidentally, the John 21:1-11 story that is similar in some respects to Luke 5:1-11 depicts "the disciple whom Jesus loved" (the Johannine community) as recognizing Jesus as the Risen Lord before Peter does and then together with Peter hauling in the net filled with 153 huge fish. The Fourth Gospel tradition insists that the one net can hold all of those huge fish without breaking. Therefore, the Petrine communities associated with and using the three Synoptic Gospels and the Johannine community developing its own separate Fourth Gospel can be one, so long as the Johannine community of the Beloved Disciple can be preeminent.

This Luke 5:1-11 call of Peter's account with its success orientation contrasts rather sharply with the Isaiah 6:1-13 call of Isaiah story. When these two texts are used together, as they will be by us next Sunday, the conscientious pastors and worship planning committees are faced with several options. Where shall we place the emphasis for our particular time and for our particular place? Prayerful openness to the

Spirit of God actualized within each congregation and community must determine the emphasis to be chosen.

It may be that the Isaiah 6:1-13 text will present the greater challenge and will offer the greater long-term help to the People of God today. At least we could — and perhaps we should — start at Isaiah 6:1-13 before moving to the success-oriented Lukan call of Peter account. In our Christian use, the Isaiah 6 text must not be used to promote the idea that Judaism and the Jews have failed while the Church and Christians as portrayed in Luke 5:1-11 have succeeded. In our Christian use, both texts should point to the cross of Christ and to a biblical Theology of the Cross rather than to a non-biblical Theology of Glory before our homilies are concluded next Sunday.

SIXTH SUNDAY AFTER THE EPIPHANY

With Psalm 1, Jeremiah 17:5-10, and Luke 6:17-26 selected as three of the four biblical bases for the service and message next Sunday, we also can hardly use any other mode of expression than the beatitude ourselves as we lead in worship. Perhaps we should even express the 1 Corinthians 15:12-20 text in part, at least, in beatitude form for coherence in the service, as will be attempted below.

As would be expected, although many people are said to be blessed in these texts, they are said to be blessed for different reasons within different life situations. It is our task to determine with as much precision as possible the specifics of each life situation in these texts so that we shall be able to apply the texts to specific situations within our own life settings.

Psalm 1

There are two ways contrasted sharply in this lead-off psalm of the Israelite Psalter: the way of the wicked and the way of the righteous. The way of the righteous is the way characterized by delight in the Torah. A person who is walking in this way meditates on the Torah night and day, without ceasing. Such a person is known to the Lord. Such a person shall prosper. Such a person is blessed. The person who is wise will follow the way of the righteous and be blessed by the Lord. A person would be absolutely foolish to do otherwise.

Jeremiah 17:5-10

Because of the similarities between this text and Psalm 1, and because this text uses the more primitive form of curses contrasted with blessings, while Psalm 1 focuses on the Torah, which gained status as an authoritative, canonical body of literature after many centuries of development, it is likely that this Jeremiah 17 text was used as a primary source in the composition of Psalm 1. The contrast here in Jeremiah 17:5-8 is between the person who trusts in people and the person who trusts in the Lord. The person who trusts in the Lord will be fruitful season after season, like a tree that is planted near a stream that never runs dry. Such a person is indeed blessed. It is added in verses 9-10 that the Lord judges every person on the basis of that person's ways and fruitfulness.

1 Corinthians 15:12-20

In beatitude form, this text might include the saying, "Blessed is the person who believes that Jesus has been raised from the dead to be the Christ! Such a person does not live in vain." Paul was writing to people who had various opinions about the resurrection of the dead. Some believed that God actually physically raises people who have died back to a much better form of life, a life that is no longer limited by time and space; some people did not believe this. Paul tried to use logical argumentation to convince those who did not believe that God raises people from the dead, or more specifically that God had raised Jesus from the dead. After using this type of argumentation in verses 13-19, Paul simply states what *he* believes in verse 20, that Christ has been raised by God from the dead, just as Paul had expressed this faith earlier in this chapter. Within verse 20, Paul could well have concluded in the form of a beatitude, "Blessed is the person who believes this!"

For us also, while we may think that we shall be able to persuade someone by argumentation that God has raised Jesus from the dead, it is far more effective when we simply say, *"I believe this. I choose to believe this even though I cannot prove it or any other statement about God. I invite you to believe this also, even though you cannot prove it either. Blessed are you when you believe!"*

Luke 6:17-26

The beatitudes in this portion of what we call the "Sermon on the Plain" in Luke probably stem from several different life situations. It is likely that both what we call the "Sermon on the Mount" in Matthew 5-7 and the "Sermon on the Plain" in Luke 6 are collections by followers of Jesus of beatitudes and other sayings of Jesus remembered and repeated by his followers, supplemented by somewhat similar sayings adapted from things Jesus had said or that were added to what Jesus had said by his followers in new and somewhat different life settings.

As we become increasingly aware of the political situation of the Jews in Galilee and Judea during the time of Jesus' public activity, we realize more fully that Jesus was speaking and working among people who were heavily oppressed economically, politically, and socially by the Roman military forces that eventually crucified Jesus because Jesus was providing hope and encouragement to significant numbers of his fellow oppressed Jews. There were a few, of course, among Jesus' own people who cooperated fully with the Roman occupation forces and contracted to do business with them, managing the Temple, collecting various taxes, doing construction work ordered by the Romans, and providing other personal and private services.

If we wish to express the beatitudes of Luke 6:20-21 in the form in which they may have been verbalized by the Jesus of history, we might express Luke 6:20b in English as "Blessed are you who are oppressed, for yours is the kingdom of God!" The Greek word πτωχοί means "begging, dependent, poor, miserable, impotent, and oppressed politically and economically." Within the context of the overwhelming majority of the Jews in Galilee and Judea with whom Jesus interacted, the Aramaic word *anawim* that Jesus would have used to speak to them and that was expressed in the Gospel accounts by use of the Greek word πτωχοί should be translated as "oppressed" rather than the more general word "poor" that has been used in the KJV, the RSV, the NRSV, and in most other translations of the Newer Testament into English. Jesus and the people with whom he worked were poor because they were severely oppressed economically and politically by the Romans, not because they were lazy.

The kingdom of God for Jesus and for his fellow oppressed Jews in Galilee and Judea was sharply contrasted with the kingdom of this world that was oppressing them, specifically the kingdom of Caesar. We are aware that the writers of the documents that later would be identified as the Newer Testament could not write anything directly against the oppressive Roman Empire, against Caesar, and against the zealous advocates of the Roman Civil Religion who demanded political and increasingly religious allegiance to the Roman State, without great risk of severe retaliation by the same Roman State that had crucified Jesus and had killed Peter, Paul, and other leading followers of Jesus. If Jesus had said, "Blessed are *you* who are *oppressed*, for *yours* is the kingdom of God!" to his fellow oppressed Jews, the Matthean redactors of Mark softened this to "Blessed are *those* who are oppressed *in spirit* (spiritually oppressed), for *theirs* is the kingdom of *heaven*." They did this in order to reduce the political risk of this statement by spiritualizing it and by depersonalizing it.

We in the twenty-first century who are no longer threatened by the oppressive Roman State of the Caesars have no need to soften or to tone down the beatitudes expressed by Jesus. We who are no longer threatened by that particular oppressor should be fully aware of the great courage of Jesus when he spoke out publicly to bless and to encourage his oppressed fellow Jews, even though his doing this resulted in his being seized, tortured, and crucified by the Roman oppressors. We should also realize that the Jesus of history could have stopped speaking publicly his message of hope for the oppressed among his people and returned to a private life in Nazareth when his mother and some of his brothers implored him to do so to save his life, as indicated in Mark 3:20-21, 31-35. It is probable that they wanted him to stop and said that it was "crazy" for him to continue not because they did not agree with what he was saying, but because they feared for his life if he would continue. Jesus, of course, continued and was seized, tortured, and crucified by the Romans when he shared his message in Jerusalem.

The references in Luke 6:17-26 to the Son of Man and to what the fathers of those addressed had done to the prophets and the references to the false prophets of the past most likely reflect the life situations of some of the early followers of Jesus several decades after Jesus had been crucified. In our own ministries we can best proclaim the message and the life of Jesus by focusing on the life setting of the Jesus of history rather than on that of some of his followers decades after Jesus had been crucified.

SEVENTH SUNDAY AFTER THE EPIPHANY

The texts chosen for next Sunday, with the exception of the 1 Corinthians 15:35-38, 42-50 reading that continues the sequential readings in that epistle, emphasize the importance of mercy and forgiveness, even of one's adversaries and enemies. The model to be followed is the Lord God as depicted in Psalm 37:1-11, 39-40, "your Father, the Most High" in Luke 6:27-38, Joseph revealing his identity to his frightened brothers in Genesis 45:3-11, 15, and, of course, Jesus himself. Just as God is merciful and just, so also God's people are to be merciful and just. There is no great difference between the Older and the Newer Testament selections to be used next Sunday. There is proclamation and there is parenesis in all of these texts, summed up for us in the Luke 6:36 reading, "You must always show mercy (parenesis), just as God your Father always shows mercy (proclamation)."

Psalm 37:1-11, 39-40

Those who are wicked and oppressive may gain a temporary economic advantage, but their advantage will soon be lost. In a little while, the wicked will be cut off and destroyed. It would be foolish to be envious of them. The Lord will show mercy to those who are righteous; they will dwell securely in the land long after the wicked are gone. Those who are wise will trust in the Lord and wait patiently.

Genesis 45:3-11, 15

Here in the climax of the Joseph story where Joseph finally reveals his identity to his frightened and vulnerable brothers, Joseph is merciful and forgiving. He exhibits the qualities of the ideal young man. He sees the hand of God in his life and beyond his life in the world. He considers himself sent by God to preserve a remnant of his people on the earth. The qualities of mercy, forgiveness, and salvation are exemplified in him. For Jews he remains an excellent role model; for Christians he is often seen as a type of Christ. The Joseph story is, among other things, wisdom literature; it demonstrates in the character of Joseph the way life should be lived, whether in adversity or success, since Joseph has experienced the extremes of both. It is Torah (instruction: proclamation and parenesis).

Luke 6:27-38

It has often been said that the Matthew 5-7 Sermon on the Mount and its counterpart in the Luke 6:17-49 Sermon on the Plain demand a level of ethical behavior that human beings cannot possibly attain, except possibly for a brief interim period before Jesus would return. Actually, however, as indicated above, there is relatively little difference between the ethical requirements of Luke 6:27-38 and the model for behavior provided in the Joseph story. Each of these texts describes life as it should be lived.

As we continue our study of the life of the Jesus of history, it becomes increasingly apparent that Jesus himself probably did not proclaim the Matthew 5-7 Sermon on the Mount or even the shorter Luke 6:17-49 Sermon on the Plain on one specific occasion. He was not in any way in a situation of power similar to that of a President of the United States delivering a carefully crafted "State of the Union" message. Instead, Jesus lived and died and was remembered to have lived and died in such a self-giving manner that his followers later put his manner of living into a parenetic form as "words of Jesus" based on the life of Jesus. Possibly the Jesus of history had on various occasions verbalized the beatitudes that we now have in Luke 6:20-21 and in Matthew 5:3-10 and perhaps he had said other things also that eventually were incorporated into Matthew 5-7 and into Luke 6:17-49, but it is likely that most of the material in the two great "Sermons" in Matthew and in Luke is based upon what Jesus had done rather than specifically upon what he said at any one specific time. There was apparently a tendency and a desire during the decades after the death of Jesus to present him as the great teacher, the "New Moses," more impressive and exacting than the "old Moses" of the Pharisees.

This brings us to our responsibility of developing and sharing this coming Sunday a message and guidelines for living as a Christian, based largely upon the Luke 6:27-38 portion of the Sermon on the Plain. It will be a cop-out if we say that no one except Jesus can live a life of loving one's enemies, turning the other cheek, and lending money to people who probably will not repay the loan. We are called to do more of what we read in Luke 6:27-38 and to say less about it, i.e., we are called to follow the model of Joseph in the Joseph story and of Jesus in the Synoptic Gospels and to put our trust unconditionally in the mercies of God. This is what it means to be a Christian in the world today.

1 Corinthians 15:35-38, 42-50

In this selection, the Apostle Paul contrasts the physical body that dies with the spiritual body that we believe God will raise up from the dead. Through a long series of comparisons and contrasts between the life we now have and know and the resurrected life that we believe we shall be given, Paul tries to make the resurrection hope more tangible. We can and should use the analogies that Paul used, and we can and should add analogies of our own, but when we have finished, we, like Paul, can only trust in the mercies of God who is merciful. And we believe that this will certainly be sufficient.

EIGHTH SUNDAY AFTER THE EPIPHANY

Identifying a unifying theme within the various texts selected for next Sunday is not an easy task. Something, however, is said about the effectiveness of the word of the Lord in each of the readings. Isaiah 55:10-13 expresses this most clearly, especially in verses 10-11 in the affirmation that the word of the Lord shall not return to the Lord empty. The importance of the People of God doing what they are instructed by God to do is stressed in Sirach 27:6, in 1 Corinthians 15:58, and in Luke 6:40, 43-49. Also in Psalm 92:12-15 the righteous are said to flourish in the house of the Lord where the word of the Lord is spoken.

Psalm 92:1-4, 12-15

As in many other individual hymns of thanksgiving, Psalm 92 depicts the enemies of the psalmist as the enemies of the Lord. Those whom the Lord dooms for destruction are surely vanquished. They shall be scattered and perish.

The righteous, on the other hand, shall flourish in the courts of our God. They will be green and vibrant throughout the year; they still produce fruit even when they are old. The lives of the righteous are proof that the Lord is good.

Isaiah 55:10-13

There is a beautiful comparison in verses 10-13 between the coming of the word of the Lord and the falling of the rain and the snow from the sky. The rain and the snow cover everything. Not a spot is missed. The rain and the snow bring the earth to life. They cause vegetation to flourish. The results are apparent immediately. So also it is said to be with the word of the Lord. It shall do what the Lord wants it to do. It shall bring joy and peace to the people. All of nature shall respond with applause and with singing when the world is refreshed by the Lord's word.

Sirach 27:4-7

In this segment of Sirach's wisdom tradition, the emphasis is on a person's thoughts. A person's activities reveal what is happening within that person's mind. A wise person will remain steadfast and true to the word of the Lord. Therefore, what a wise person says will indicate the fruitfulness of the word of the Lord in that person's mind and life.

1 Corinthians 15:51-58

Because of the victory over death that has been won for us through our Lord Jesus Christ, it is all the more important, Paul concludes, that we be firm in our faith and fruitful in doing what the Lord (Adonai as perceived within the Israelite and Jewish traditions as well as Jesus raised from the dead within the new Christian community of faith tradition) says we should do. What we do in faithful response to the word and will of the Lord will never be done in vain. It will always be productive.

Luke 6:39-49

The highest praise is given here to the individual who comes to the Lord, hears the word of the Lord, and does it. This person will be like the Lord. This person's life will bear good fruit. This person will be productive and will help many others. Such a person's life is built upon a firm foundation; it will not be shaken or destroyed by any storm or flood.

It is our responsibility as stewards of the word of the Lord to live our lives in accordance with it. As we mature in our faith and life, living in accordance with the word of the Lord ceases to be a burden and becomes instead a privilege and a pleasure, far more satisfying than any evil thought or deed.

NINTH SUNDAY AFTER THE EPIPHANY

A consideration of these texts is included in the notes on Proper 4, Ordinary Time 9, Second Sunday after Pentecost for use later this year.

LAST SUNDAY AFTER THE EPIPHANY (TRANSFIGURATION SUNDAY)

Transfiguration accounts, whether in the Hebrew Scriptures (Exodus 34:29-35) or in the Newer Testament (Mark 9:2-8; Matthew 17:1-8; Luke 9:28-36) or in the sacred writings of other religious traditions, are primarily validation texts. They are similar in some respects to call stories. Call stories are used to authenticate the messages and ministries of *persons*, especially of prophetic figures whose authority is being questioned. Transfiguration accounts, on the other hand, are used to validate not persons but *writings*.

Call stories and transfiguration accounts are far more than merely historical records of events that have occurred at a certain time and place. They serve to establish the authority of a person or of a written document within a religious community. The dominant texts selected for this coming Transfiguration Sunday are designed to validate very important documents. The Exodus 34:29-35 text is a validation of the Torah and the Luke 9:28-36 (37-43) Transfiguration account is a validation of the Gospel According to Luke, a continuation of the validation of the Gospel According to Mark in the Transfiguration account in Mark 9:2-8 and of the validation of the Gospel According to Matthew in Matthew 17:1-8.

Psalm 99

For use with the Transfiguration texts, it is obvious that Psalm 99 was chosen by the theologians who selected the texts for our lectionary because of verse 7, in which we read that "From within the cloud formation the Lord spoke to them; they kept the precepts and the statutes that the Lord gave to them." This is the portion of Psalm 99 that provides a link to the Exodus 34:29-35 and the Luke 9:28-36 (37-43) accounts.

Exodus 34:29-35

In the narrow sense, this account validates the Decalogue only, since it was the two tables of the covenant, the ten words (sentences) rather than the entire Torah that Moses is said to have carried with him as he came down from Mount Sinai. Nevertheless, since verse 34 indicates that Moses went in before the Lord many times after that, to speak with the Lord and later to relate to the people of Israel whatever the Lord had commanded Moses to relate, Exodus 34:29-35 serves to validate the entire Torah and not merely the ten words on the two tables of the covenant.

It is of interest to note how the Qur'an speaks about the many times that Muhammad went to the cave near Mecca to receive the words of the Qur'an in small installments so that he could remember them and write them in excellent Arabic even though it is believed that he was not otherwise able to read or to write. Those accounts serve the same function within the Qur'an that Exodus 34:29-35 serves for the Torah and the Transfiguration accounts serve within the Synoptic Gospels, to validate those writings that became canonical and normative for communities of faith and not merely considered to have been the opinions of religious leaders.

2 Corinthians 3:12—4:2

It is unfortunate that this text speaks disparagingly about the Exodus 34:29-35 account and about the "old" covenant in its effort to hold up the "new" covenant as superior. It would have been possible and certainly preferable simply to have added the new revelations to the earlier ones without denigration of the former. We may even wonder whether the interpretation given in this text to the veiling of Moses' face in Exodus 34:29-35 is not in some respects a form of "tampering with God's word" in the very "disgraceful and underhanded ways" that are condemned in the final verse of this 2 Corinthians 3:12—4:2 reading. At any rate, the Exodus 34:29-35 and the Luke 9:28-36 (37-43) texts are so significant that in our proclamation next Sunday we have no need to base a portion of our message on this 2 Corinthians 3:12—4:2 segment.

Luke 9:28-36 (37-43)

The Lukan writer, like the Matthean redactors, retained a Markan text here and kept it in the same context that it has in Mark. The changes made by the Lukan writer may be noted briefly as follows: Mark's "after six days" became "about eight days after," perhaps to place the Transfiguration on the first day of the week, the "Lord's day." The Lukan writer characteristically inserted "to pray" (v. 28d) and "during the time that he was praying" (v. 29a), drawing lines more closely to the Lukan account of Jesus being baptized. Luke provided substance in 9:31-32 to the conversation between Moses and Elijah in glory and Jesus. The conversation centers around Jesus' departure in Jerusalem. The reference to the sleepiness of Peter, of James, and of John suggests a connection to the text about Jesus in Gethsemane and to the darkness of night. Only the Lukan writer has the disciples and Jesus coming down from the mountain on the next day rather than on the same day. In Luke the voice from the cloud calls Jesus "my Chosen Son" rather than "my Beloved Son." Finally, Luke has Peter speak only as Moses and Elijah were leaving.

As in Mark and in Matthew, the principal purpose of Luke's Transfiguration account appears to be to validate the words of Jesus as the Christ. Like the others, Luke's account shows that Jesus is indeed in the same league as Moses (a symbol of the Torah) and as Elijah (a symbol of the Prophetic traditions). More than that, Jesus is shown to be not equal but greater in importance than the representatives of the Israelite/Jewish Scriptures, for when the cloud and darkness pass away only Jesus is there. At the sound of the voice of God from the cloud proclaiming Jesus to be God's Son, God's Chosen Son, the representatives of the Israelite/Jewish Scriptures have vanished into the darkness. They are presented as having been summoned from the past only that they might disappear in the light of this new Chosen Son of God. Jesus and the Word of God through Jesus replace the chosenness of Israel as God speaks to the three disciples the words about Jesus, "Listen to him!"

The miracle of the Transfiguration of Jesus and of the summoning up of Moses and Elijah all serve the validation theme. The account indicates that Jesus and Jesus' message are valid for us. It makes relatively little difference, therefore, whether we consider this to be a "Resurrection appearance" text or not. It functions here to point ahead to the cross, to the resurrection, and to the ascension glory of Jesus. The use of this text is appropriate here at the end of the Epiphany Season and just prior to Lent.

The "miracle" today lies in our acceptance of Jesus as Christ for us. Jesus, too, comes now out of our past to speak to us and through us in our particular life situations. What does Jesus as the Christ say to us this year where we are, and how shall we respond to what he says? This will be our agenda next Sunday and during the Lenten season.

ASH WEDNESDAY (A, B, C)

As we ponder the meaning of the season of Lent and the significance we would like for it to have this year for us and for the people with whom we live, we begin with these Ash Wednesday texts.

We see that in Joel 2:1-2, 12-17 and in Matthew 6:1-6, 16-21 the emphasis is on appropriate behavior. In Joel 2:1-2, 12-17 the Lord God commands the people to fast, weep, mourn, repent, and return to the Lord. In Matthew 6:1-6, 16-21 the guidelines are to help those who are in need, pray, fast, and to store up your treasures in heaven where they will never be lost. It is obvious that for those who selected these texts for use on Ash Wednesday the behavior commanded in these texts from Joel and from Matthew was very important, especially for the season of Lent. They then selected a portion of one of the best known penitential psalms in the Psalter (Psalm 51) to indicate appropriate prayer to accompany appropriate behavior. Finally, the grace of God was brought into this series of texts with the inclusion of the Apostle Paul's passive imperative verb *katallagete* ("be reconciled" to God) in 2 Corinthians 5:20 and in Paul's entreaty in 2 Corinthians 6:1 not to receive the grace of God in vain. The 2 Corinthians reading provides for us, therefore, a very important addition to the appropriate behavior emphasis of the Joel and Matthew texts. The inclusion of the 2 Corinthians 5:20b—6:10 reading suggests that we emphasize the grace of God along with appropriate behavior during Lent each year and perhaps once each three years make it the primary focus.

During the height of the Civil Rights Movement, many of us found in Isaiah 58 a message that resonated very well with us. It was that unless we are actively involved in social justice, in addressing the conditions in which people suffer economic and political oppression, as well as in being engaged in immediate and continued direct assistance to the oppressed, our fasting is no way acceptable to the Lord God. As a result, Isaiah 58:1-12 is now an alternative reading to Joel 2:1-2, 12-17 on Ash Wednesday. This inclusion of Isaiah 58:1-12 brings a very important dimension to our observance of Lent.

2 Corinthians 5:20b—6:10

Let us look more closely, first of all, at Paul's passive imperative verb *katallagete* in 2 Corinthians 5:20. From a theological perspective, the passive imperative is one of the most significant grammatical constructions in Indo-European languages. Paul exhorts the followers of Jesus in Corinth and, because his exhortation here is sacred Scripture for us, also exhorts us to *be reconciled to God by the grace of God*. We believe that God makes this reconciliation possible by means of the life, death, and resurrection of Jesus the Christ, through the great atonement proclaimed by Paul and elaborated upon by other Christian theologians later.

What, then, is *our* role in this reconciling action? According to the grammatical construction, we are passive. God in Christ is the active one. We are to be passive, to have this done *to* us. "Be reconciled to God!" we are told. We can, of course, choose to reject this reconciliation, but Paul urges his readers and hearers to permit it to be done, to be forgiven, to become a new creation in Christ, as described in the 2 Corinthians 5:20a portion that precedes this text. All are strongly urged to accept this grace of God from God and to live in this grace. In 2 Corinthians 6:3-13 and continuing in 7:2-4 Paul claims that he and his co-proclaimers are trying to put no obstacles in anyone's path. He wants no obstacles of any kind to keep this message of passive reception of the grace of God from anyone who might want to hear it.

Our work, therefore, on Ash Wednesday and throughout the Lenten season, in accordance with this 2 Corinthians 5:20b—6:10 text, is to prevent any and all obstacles from hindering God's action of reconciling us and others to God through Jesus as the Christ.

Let us look now at the other texts appointed for us for this day in the light of Paul's admonition to us that we should "Be reconciled to God by the grace of God through Jesus Christ our Lord." Let us, as Martin Luther insisted, interpret Scripture by the use of Scripture. In this way, we shall be letting the "gospel" — which in the texts chosen for this day is in the "epistle" — shed light on the other texts selected.

Psalm 51:1-17

The portion of Psalm 51 selected here puts emphasis on the penitential prayer. The obstacles to be removed in this instance are the psalmist's sins (and our sins). These sins are great, but the appeal is that God's mercy is greater than our sins. From our Christian standpoint, the forgiveness of our sins is accomplished by God through the life, death, and resurrection of Jesus perceived as the Christ. We recognize, however, that the Israelites and Jewish people prior to, during, and after the pre-Christian era called upon the mercy of God with no reference to Jesus, and we can and should assume that God has been able to forgive them. To assume anything less would be to try to limit God.

In the portion of Psalm 51 that follows verses 1-13, the psalmist shows an awareness that God does not need burnt offerings and other sacrifices in order to be able to forgive sins. God is interested in our broken and contrite heart. When our hearts are contrite, then the offerings and sacrifices will have value.

Has this changed since the time the psalmist wrote or sang this psalm? Which is the more inclusive concept, atonement or forgiveness? Do we today *always* require atonement of each other (of our children for example) before we will forgive them? Within our cultural milieu is it possible that an overemphasis on atonement theology places an unnecessary limitation upon God and upon our perception of God?

Atonement theology is useful and valuable within our understanding of God's grace, but perhaps it should be seen as *only one of the ways* in which we may perceive God's action in Christ and in history. Atonement theology was a way in which some of the followers of Jesus *after* the crucifixion of Jesus saw some very important *good* that God had brought about through that tragic event. Atonement theology is one of the ways in which we continue as Christians to see the crucifixion of Jesus, but it is only one of the ways in which we understand the crucifixion of Jesus. Considered together with the resurrection of Jesus, we see the action of God as a vindication of Jesus and of his life. God did not prevent the Romans from crucifying Jesus, but we believe that God vindicated Jesus and made the Romans powerless via the resurrection of Jesus from the dead. For more about this, see Hans Küng, *On Being a Christian* (Garden City, NY: Doubleday, 1976, pp. 419-436).

Joel 2:1-2, 12-17

This text elaborates on the ideas of Psalm 51 beautifully and even more vividly. Again in relation to this text, let us consider the issues and questions raised above about atonement and forgiveness. Atonement is very important in "classical" Christian theology. There is no subject, however, in which Jews and Muslims are more significantly different from Christians than on the subject of atonement. Jews and Muslims understand and teach that no person, even God, can atone for the sins of someone else. For Jews and for Muslims, each person is totally responsible and accountable for that person's own sins.

Forgiveness, on the other hand, is very important for Jews and for Muslims, as well as for Christians. We agree within these three religions that we should always seek forgiveness from people whom we have harmed and then also from God, asking God to spare God's people, as this Joel 2 text indicates.

For more about the understanding among Jews and among Muslims that no one can atone for the sins of someone else, see Hassan Hathout, *Reading the Muslim Mind* (Plainfield: American Trust, 1995, pp. 33-35), and my *Blessed to be a Blessing to Each Other: Jews, Muslims, and Christians as Children of Abraham in the Middle East* (Second Edition, Lima, Ohio: Fairway Press, 2010, pp. 51-54).

Matthew 6:1-6, 16-21

A glance at the Synoptic parallels shows that except for Matthew 6:19-21 the components of this pericope are peculiar to Matthew. We can say, therefore, that the materials in Matthew 6:1-6 and 16-18 are best understood as teachings of the leaders of the Matthean community in Jesus' name. The positive aspects of these teachings are certainly applicable for us today as Christians. We should help those who are in need, we should pray to God, and we should fast, but we should do none of these in order to be praised. The negative anti-Jewish aspects that condemn the Jews and their leaders in these verses are not applicable for us today.

Isaiah 58:1-12

As indicated above, the inclusion of Isaiah 58:1-12 as a text to be read and reflected upon on Ash Wednesday and throughout the Lenten season brings a very important dimension to our observance of Lent. It reminds us that if we want to do something that is truly important during Lent or at any other time, we should help people who are in need, especially those who are oppressed economically, politically, socially, and in any other way. That is what the inspired speaker and writer in this Isaiah tradition text said and apparently did.

That is what the Jesus of history said and that is what the Jesus of history did. There can be no doubt about that.

Lent is the season of the Church Year in which we focus on our study and reflection upon the Jesus of history. There are a multitude of texts in the Four Gospels that are evidence of words and actions of the Jesus of history in support of those who were oppressed during that time. There is very little evidence in support of Jesus himself fasting, other than at the beginning of his public service in the Synoptic Gospels, and nothing about his giving up for a few weeks a bad habit that was obviously harmful to himself or to others. If we want to be like Jesus during Lent, or better yet throughout the year and during our entire lives, let us do whatever we can to change systems that rob the oppressed and give excess bounty to the rich, within our own nation and throughout the world.

FIRST SUNDAY IN LENT

A unifying factor present in all four of these texts selected for Lent 1 in Series C is the concept of deliverance. According to Psalm 91, the person who trusts in the Lord will be delivered from all danger. In the Deuteronomy 26 confession of faith it is said that the Lord (the God of our Fathers) heard our voice when we were slaves in Egypt and rescued us. The temptation account in Luke 4:1-13 has Jesus demonstrate that if you worship the Lord your God (as perceived by the Israelites, the Jews, and the early followers of Jesus) and serve only the Lord, you will be delivered from the power of the devil. Finally, in Romans 10:8-13 Paul wrote that if you confess with your lips and believe in your heart that Jesus the Risen Christ is Lord, you will be saved.

Psalm 91:1-2, 9-16

This well-known psalm that extols the wisdom of trusting in the Lord God Almighty was obviously chosen for Lent 1, Series C, because Psalm 91:11-12 was quoted by the "devil" in the Luke 4:1-13 temptation of Jesus account, our Gospel reading for next Sunday, illustrating how the Scriptures can be misused when the wrong person quotes them in the wrong way! It is apparent that Psalm 91 in its historical setting in ancient Israel was not referring specifically to Jesus who would be born hundreds of years later, but to anyone who would be wise enough to trust God completely. Certainly the Jesus of history was not to enjoy the "long life" promised in verse 16; neither was the Jesus of history rescued (v. 15) from death on the Roman cross.

Psalm 91 shares the thought in verses 11-12 that was further developed within the Zoroastrian religion of angels guarding faithful people. Although we would certainly support the wisdom of unconditional trust in the Lord God Almighty, there is well-documented evidence that in spite of this trust Jews were tortured and killed by their Seleucid adversaries at the time of the Maccabean revolt, Jesus was tortured and then died on a Roman cross, first-century followers of Jesus were torn to pieces by hungry lions and tigers from Africa for the amusement of decadent Romans, millions of Jews of all age groups were starved, gassed, and slaughtered by the Nazis, and the practice of torture of prisoners continues in the world today. Perhaps we should recognize that ultimately with God there is salvation for the faithful, but that penultimately "the angels" have been known to fail us.

Deuteronomy 26:1-11

Perhaps Gerhard von Rad in his *Old Testament Theology I* (New York: Harper & Row, 1962) overestimated the importance of this great offering response in the formation of Israel's traditions. Nevertheless, we can learn from it not only how Israelites and Jews have perceived the Exodus as a saving act but also how the offering should function liturgically as a central focal point in active worship. Offering, confession of faith, and proclamation through word and sacrament are closely related elements. Nothing is more "dead" liturgically than our "time for the collection." We should return to the earlier Israelite and Christian practice of bringing our own gifts and offerings to the altar with joy, grief, or whatever emotion may be appropriate.

Luke 4:1-13

As we search for new meanings in this temptation of Jesus account, we become aware that there is almost certainly a subtle anti-Roman cryptogram (often now called a "hidden transcript") within the three temptations of Jesus in this account. Only the Roman Emperor was the "devil" who had authority over all of the known kingdoms of the mid-first century world of the followers of Jesus. Only the Roman Emperor at that time, via the powerful Roman Civil

Religion, was demanding that all of the people within that empire bow down in submission to him and to his authority. Faced with this challenge, conscientious followers of Jesus found comfort and gained courage to resist that idolatry from this story about how Jesus had rejected the claims and demands of this Satan, this devil, and they asserted with Jesus that "You shall worship the Lord your God, and God only shall you serve!" With this bold assertion, Jesus and many other first-century Jews and followers of Jesus took the way of the cross. For us also, we shall worship and serve only the Lord our God and no one nor any thing else. That is the way of ultimate deliverance.

Romans 10:8b-13

For Paul, as a Jew, Adonai was Lord and no one who would believe in Adonai as Lord would ever be put to shame. For the Apostle Paul, called to be an apostle of Jesus the Risen Christ, Jesus as the Risen Christ was also Lord and all who would believe that Jesus the Risen Christ is Lord would be delivered, saved from sin, death, and the power of the "devil," whether the devil was perceived as the Roman Emperor or any other personification of evil. With great boldness and excitement Paul proclaimed that now there is no longer any important distinction between Jewish background and non-Jewish background followers of Jesus, because the same Lord (whether Adonai or Jesus the Risen Christ) is Lord of all, of Jewish background and of non-Jewish background followers of Jesus who will believe that God has raised the Jesus of history from the dead as Lord of all. Paul was thrilled by the insight that now Jewish background and non-Jewish background followers of Jesus could be together within the same olive tree (Romans 11:17-24). Paul, and others among early followers of Jesus, with the reluctant consent of Peter and of James, the brother of Jesus, in Jerusalem, brought Adonai and Jesus the Risen Christ together as one Lord and eventually most Christians have followed them. Marcion during the mid-second century CE and other followers of Jesus who have separated Jesus from Adonai as Marcion separated them, have taken a different path. Let us take the path of Paul.

SECOND SUNDAY IN LENT

Jerusalem and the temple in Jerusalem are prominent in many of these texts selected for Lent 2, Series C. It is in Jerusalem and at its temple that the beauty of the Lord is seen (Psalm 27). Jesus' death and his departure from the earth will occur in Jerusalem (Luke 13:31-35), and Jesus expresses his love for the city and for its people.

Transformation is another theme present in several of these texts. In his letter to the Philippians, Paul proclaims that the Lord Jesus Christ will transform our lowly body and make it conform to his glorious body. Within the Genesis 15:1-12, 17-18 promise and covenant text, Abram was said to have been transformed in a sense as the Lord caused the smoking fire pot and flaming torch to pass between the pieces of Abram's offering and made the covenant of land and many descendants with him.

Psalm 27

This psalm of trust in the Lord includes a statement of faith (v. 1), a plea for a response from the Lord (vv. 7-9), and an admonition to the self to wait patiently for the goodness of the Lord during the lifetime of the psalmist (vv. 13-14). The setting, as indicated above, is the temple in Jerusalem. Nothing is asked that is beyond the limits of this life.

Genesis 15:1-12, 17-18

Perhaps the most significant factor for us as Christians in this ancient covenant ratification story is the statement in Genesis 15:6 that Abram believed the Lord that Abram's descendants would be like the stars, too numerous to count, and that the Lord considered Abram's belief in the Lord to be the right relationship for the establishment of a covenant with God. The Apostle Paul drew heavily on Genesis 15:6 in building his argumentation in Galatians 3 and in Romans 4 that our belief in God will be considered the right relationship for us in the sight of God.

Philippians 3:17—4:1

This selection occurs within the sharply polemical portion (vv. 3:1—4:7) of the letter that may have been inserted here by a Pauline editor from another letter of Paul. The polemic in 3:18-19 is directed against "Christians" who claim to follow the cross of Christ, but actually are considered by Paul to be enemies of the cross of Christ. Probably they were Christians who in the opinion of Paul were compromising their Christianity by participating in certain activities of Roman Civil Religion in order to avoid the persecutions that Paul and other followers of Jesus faced and in order to benefit in material ways. In Paul's opinion, the citizenship of such pseudo-Christians was in Rome and they were destined with Rome for destruction. Paul's citizenship, and the citizenship of those who supported Paul against the religion of Roman patriotism and the claims of its adherents, was in heaven, in God's kingdom, not Caesar's, from which Paul waited for Jesus the Risen Christ (not for Caesar) as the Savior who would subject Rome, its Emperor, and everything else to himself.

We are called in our time to proclaim our Lord Jesus Christ rather than the Caesars of today as Savior, and to renounce those who, while claiming to be Christian, follow them.

Luke 13:31-35

This text is one of several in Luke that indicate that many of the Pharisees were friendly and supportive of the Jesus of history, and it is likely that many of them were. His message was also their message. In every instance in the Lukan account, however, the Lukan writer arranged the context and the situation in such a way that the Jesus of this

Third Gospel turns against the Pharisees, denounces them, and embarrasses his Pharisee hosts in front of their friends, even when Jesus is a dinner guest.

With regard to the lament over Jerusalem, it is likely that the speaker here, as in Luke 11:49, was at one time the "Wisdom of God," a supra-historical hypostasis. After the divine Wisdom calls in vain for men to follow her, she departs and will not return until the Messiah comes. Some followers of Jesus, possibly in "Q" material communities, may have seen in the resurrected Jesus the same qualities that had earlier been attributed to the "Wisdom of God." This association was probably particularly appropriate in "Q" communities with their interests in motifs that Richard Edwards in *A Theology of Q* (Philadelphia: Fortress, 1976, p. 84), identified as a) eschatological hope, b) wisdom teaching about the present, and c) either a reference to the prophets as models and examples or the use of the prophetic-messenger forms of speech. In the text represented in Luke 11:49 and 13:34-35 the "Q" communities probably used wisdom and prophetic forms and images in presenting their case against Jews who would not unite with them (Edwards, p. 133). Once the association of the Wisdom of God with Jesus had been made, the Matthean tradition placed the account into a Jerusalem setting *after* the entry of Jesus into the city and made Matthew 23:19 into a prophecy that the inhabitants of Jerusalem would not see Jesus again until they will say, "Blessed is the one who comes in the name of the Lord." The Lukan writer placed the account *prior to* the entry of Jesus into Jerusalem and made it into a prediction that Jesus would not be killed until he would enter the city of Jerusalem, but that once he was there he would surely die at the hands of those whom he would have liked to have gathered together as a hen gathers her chicks under her wings to protect them from danger from predators. The inhabitants of the city would have to wait until Jesus would finally go there and then they would say, "Blessed is the one who comes in the name of the Lord!"

Once the association of the Wisdom hypostasis with Jesus had been made, the lament became virulently anti-Jewish. Jerusalem was then accused of continuously killing the prophets and stoning the ones sent to her. The quotation based on Jeremiah 22:5 and 12:7 became external anti-Jewish condemnation, and Psalm 118:26 was given a variety of new messianic possibilities. For more details about this reconstruction of the development of this tradition, see Barnabas Lindars, *New Testament Apologetic* (London: SCM Press, 1961, pp. 171-173).

Since Luke 13:34-35 and Matthew 23:37-39 as they were developed within the early Church are viciously anti-Jewish with their unfair condemnation of Jerusalem for killing its prophets and in their glorying in the forsaken and desolate condition of the people of Jerusalem after 70 CE, other accounts from the Gospels should be used instead of these in the Church today to demonstrate the love and concern that the Jesus of history had for his fellow oppressed Jews. If these texts *are* used, they should be redacted and addressed to the Christian People of God today self-critically, perhaps in words such as follows: "O my people! O my people! How you have turned from me! How many times have I wanted to gather together your children as a hen gathers her chicks under her wings, but you have not wanted me to do this." A redaction of these verses that would reverse the process of their development within the early Church would put them back once more into a series of sayings of Jesus such as they were when they were circulated in "Q" materials.

If the reader of the lectionary is not willing to redact the texts in this way in order to reverse the process of their development, we may do so in the way in which we use these texts in the sermon or homily for next Sunday, by applying them self-critically to ourselves in the Church. Then they will have a useful impact today.

Luke 9:28-36

See the content of paragraphs 2, 3, and 4 from the consideration of Luke 9:28-36 on Transfiguration Sunday earlier in this Cycle C.

THIRD SUNDAY IN LENT

The profound subject of suffering is a factor in each of the texts selected for next Sunday. Perhaps Siddhartha Gautama (the Buddha) was on target when he reached the conclusion that "to live is to suffer," that suffering is universal — the first of his Four Noble Truths. At any rate, there are few subjects about which we proclaim our message that hold the attention of the members of the assembled congregations as well as the subject of suffering. If we dare to consider seriously the profound subject of suffering that is present in each of these four texts, we can be assured that those who hear us will be involved with us as we proclaim the Word of God next Sunday.

We have an excellent opportunity to show with these texts that on subjects as complex as the subject of suffering, various views are expressed within the biblical accounts, even within the four texts selected for Lent 3, Series C. It should become clear within our study of these texts and in our proclamation based on these texts that the biblical texts do not provide unequivocal answers to all of the questions that we and others may ask about God and the subject of suffering. Nevertheless, the subject of suffering is central in our lives and especially during the season of Lent, reaching a climax in our observance of the suffering of the Jesus of history on what later was to be called "Good" Friday. Therefore, we accept our responsibility of dealing with the subject of suffering here during Lent 3.

Isaiah 55:1-9

The suffering is intense here. There is no food, not even water to drink. With neither food nor water, a person will soon die. When the need is greatest, however, the gift of God and the grace of God are announced. The supply of God's grace is abundant. There is more than enough for all who hunger and thirst. All are invited to come, to buy, to drink, and to eat from the gifts that God provides, gifts of mercy and forgiveness. When those whose lives are polluted with thoughts of evil and wickedness return to the Lord, God will abundantly pardon. By the grace of God, all suffering is overcome.

The thoroughly theocentric view expressed in this joyous announcement of God's grace differs greatly from the thoroughly anthropocentric view of Siddhartha Gautama cited above. Gautama concluded that all suffering is related to and caused by desire and by the desire not to suffer. He taught that the way to reduce suffering is to reduce desire and to live the right way, to follow his Eightfold Path of right thought, right speech, right lifestyle, and so forth. For Gautama, the resources lie within the self. They are not external.

For the inspired poet who wrote the Isaiah 55 text, suffering is overcome when a person returns to the Lord. Only beyond the self, receiving the gifts that God wishes to bestow, can anyone's suffering be overcome. By one's faith in God, a person is given wine, milk, and the food that sustains life, a life that will be lived in accordance with the thoughts and will of God, thoughts that far transcend human thoughts.

Psalm 63:1-8

The situation for the psalmist here is similar to the situation depicted in Isaiah 55:1-9. The psalmist is physically and spiritually dehydrated and famished; with no outside help, the psalmist will soon die. At the last moment the psalmist turns to God, beholds the power and glory of God, receives the steadfast love and mercy of God, and lives! The suffering of the psalmist is overcome externally. Within the shadow of God's protective love, the psalmist sings for joy.

1 Corinthians 10:1-13

The Apostle Paul wrote here, as in the Isaiah 55:1-9 and Psalm 63:1-8 texts, that deliverance from suffering and temptation are gifts that God provides for all who will endure throughout these "last days." Paul urges the Jewish background followers of Jesus in Corinth to remember the history of their people, the spiritual as well as physical food and drink that God provided for them. God especially now by means of the life, death, and resurrection of Jesus, the Son of God, overcomes their suffering. Help comes from God, beyond the self, in mystical union with God in Christ.

Luke 13:1-9

At least initially, in our study of Luke 13:1-9, it is helpful to consider verses 1-5 separately from 6-9. In Luke 13:1-5 the correlation between suffering and specific sins is the issue. Unlike many other biblical texts, it is stated in Luke 13:1-5 that there is no correlation in some instances between suffering and specific sins. We look at our own experiences and at what we observe in other people and we too wonder whether there is always a correlation between suffering and specific sins. We ponder this when we are relatively healthy and when we are ill. According to this Luke 13:1-5 text, we should not always connect suffering with specific sins. Nevertheless, without sincere repentance, all will perish.

We are the fig tree in the Luke 13:6-9 parable. We are expected to be doing more than merely occupying space in the vineyard. If we suffer by being uprooted and destroyed, it is because we have not been fruitful in the vineyard.

As we look back over these four texts, we see that the persons who consider the causes of suffering differ considerably. All are united, however, in their proclamation within these texts that deliverance from suffering is external, a result of actions received from God. We, by our actions cause suffering, directly as well as indirectly. God by God's actions

114

overcomes our suffering. These are gifts from God, received by faith, which itself is a gift from God.

FOURTH SUNDAY IN LENT

The emphasis within most of the texts appointed for next Sunday (Psalm 32; 2 Corinthians 5:16-21; Luke 15:1-3, 11b-32) is on turning to God, acknowledging sin, and receiving forgiveness from God. These are basic motifs within our Christian Lenten season. As we utilize these texts, our proclamation and our parenesis should be focused on these motifs.

Psalm 32

This psalm begins with a beatitude, "Blessed is the person whose sin is forgiven." The wicked are contrasted with the righteous and shown to be foolish for not turning to the Lord. They are like a mule, without understanding. The psalmist demonstrates how reasonable it is to acknowledge sin to the Lord and to receive forgiveness and peace. The individual Hymn of Thanksgiving is most persuasive; those who hear can hardly fail to respond.

Joshua 5:9-12

In this text the Israelites have established a "beachhead" in the land that the Lord has promised to them. They had just circumcised all of the males among them. The manna with which the Lord had sustained them throughout their years of wandering in the wilderness ceased, and they began to eat the produce of the land. They ate the Passover, recalled how the Lord had delivered them from bondage in Egypt, and were prepared for the conquest of Jericho and of the lands beyond Jericho.

Perhaps we should say that thanks to God in Christ we too have a "beachhead" in the promised land. Let us recall the life, death, and resurrection of Jesus as the Christ, remember our baptism, and be prepared to live courageously as People of God here and now and forever as sinners who are forgiven. This is basically the meaning of Lent.

2 Corinthians 5:16-21

Paul announces here that through Jesus as the Christ God has reconciled us and the world to God's self, not counting the sins that have been committed, and has made Paul and those who were with Paul ministers of reconciliation. This is the proclamation in 5:17-20a. The parenesis closely follows in 5:20b in the fascinating form of the Greek 2 Aorist Passive Imperative, "Be reconciled to God!" For a discussion of the significance of this Passive Imperative construction, see the comments on 2 Corinthians 5:20b—6:2 in the Ash Wednesday section a few weeks ago.

Luke 15:1-3, 11b-32

In the Luke 15:1-3 introduction to the three Lukan parables of the lost sheep, the lost coin, and the lost son, the Lukan writer casts the Pharisees and the scribes as objecting to the idea of Jesus having table fellowship with his own followers. Not only the introduction in 15:1-3, but also the three parables in this chapter are exclusively Lukan. We should notice that in every parable of Jesus that is peculiar to Luke the first-mentioned people or things represent religiously observant Jews, while those that are mentioned last represent repentant and grateful followers of Jesus.

Within the context of the other texts selected for next Sunday, our use of this well-known Lukan parable should focus on the graciousness with which the father in the parable invites *both sons* to come to him and be glad, receiving forgiveness for the guilt of their sins. For more elaboration on this, see Helmut Thielicke, *The Waiting Father* (New York: Harper & Row, 1959).

FIFTH SUNDAY IN LENT

The marvelous, amazing grace of God is the most significant unifying factor within this series of texts selected for us for next Sunday.

Psalm 126

In this community lament during a time of depression, suffering, and weeping, there is no reference to the causes of the suffering of the people. All of the emphasis is on release from suffering and on restoration of the harvest by the grace of God. Release from suffering and the restoration of the harvest are attributed to the good favor of the Lord. Since during the distant past and during the recent past the Lord has done great things to relieve suffering, it is the fervent prayer of the community of faith that the Lord will again graciously relieve suffering and provide a bountiful harvest in the near future. An elaborate healing service or at least a specific prayer for healing would be very appropriate for this occasion next Sunday.

Isaiah 43:16-21

The grace of God shown in the parting of the waters to make a path through the sea for the slaves being freed from bondage will be repeated as God does a new thing for the Israelites who have been exiles in Babylon. The Lord, the Creator and Redeemer of Israel, will make a path through the wilderness, will provide rivers of water for the people to drink as they pass through the desert on their way back to Jerusalem. Even the wild beasts will honor the Lord and will not harm the people. In their gratitude, the people will praise the Lord, the king of Israel.

Philippians 3:4b-14

In this very personal section of his letter to the Philippians that is most likely the last letter written by Paul himself that is included within our Newer Testament canon, Paul wrote that he had gladly given up all of his own previously attained egoistic claims in order to receive a mystical relationship with God in Jesus the Risen Christ. Therefore, for Paul the most important prize accessible was the prize of the upward call of God in Christ, the righteousness of God accepted by faith. This righteousness for which Paul was striving through faith in Christ is a gift, given by the amazing grace of God to those whom God in Christ has made God's own.

John 12:1-8

Within the unifying theme of God's grace, John 12:1-8 can be seen to be a testimony that Jesus was with us for a brief time in physical form in order to help, to heal, and to raise Lazarus and us from the dead as an undeserved act of the grace of God. Mary responds to Jesus and to this grace of God as we also should respond to Jesus and to the grace of God, by loving actions of appreciation and devotion. Judas Iscariot, on the other hand, is resentful of Mary and complains that Mary's action is a waste of valuable physical resources. The Johannine tradition interprets Judas Iscariot's action as evidence that Judas was a thief and that he was periodically using the resources of the group around Jesus for his own purposes.

SIXTH SUNDAY IN LENT
(PASSION SUNDAY or PALM SUNDAY)
LITURGY OF THE PALMS

When Lent 6 is designated "Palm Sunday" rather than "Passion Sunday," members of a congregation can more readily identify with the experiences of Jesus during Holy Week as those experiences are depicted within the Four Gospels. Ideally, members of a congregation should come together in a variety of worship and study settings each day from Palm Sunday through Easter Day. Consecutive readings of the passion account in a particular Gospel each day during Holy Week in individual homes and in congregational corporate worship and study sessions help us to "relive" Jesus' passion experiences. In terms of timing, the best time for this is each day or evening during Holy Week rather than at mid-week services throughout the Lenten season or in an extremely long reading on Lent 6.

Most of the texts selected for the Palm Sunday occasion within our Christian tradition emphasize acclamation of the Lord or of Jesus as the Lord. For Israelites and continuing for Jews the Lord (Adonai) is acclaimed through use of Psalm 118 and many other texts and songs. Within our Newer Testament texts there is considerable ambiguity, perhaps deliberate ambiguity, as Jesus as the Risen Christ is called the Lord, and by inference "the King who comes in the name of the Lord" in Luke 19:28-40. In Matthew 26:14-27, 66, as the Lord-who-will-be-crucified, Jesus is betrayed by Judas Iscariot and condemned to death by political and "religious" leaders. Just as it is said in Isaiah 45:23 that to the Lord (Adonai) every knee shall bend and every tongue shall give acclamation, in the "Christ-hymn" in Philippians 2:5-11 Paul wrote that God has exalted Jesus the Risen Christ so that at the name of Jesus every knee will bend and every tongue confess that Jesus Christ is Lord, to the glory of

God the Father. Therefore, in many ways Jesus as the Christ raised from the dead is "the Lord" to us as Christians what Adonai is to Jews, i.e., Lord God, immanent, personal, self-giving, exalted, eminently divine. These similarities as well as differences between Jewish and Christian perceptions of Lord are especially significant during our Palm Sunday worship experiences.

Psalm 118:1-2, 19-29

This beautiful Hallel Psalm was apparently used by many Israelites during entrance processions associated with one or more of the great festivals. Jews continue to read all or portions of Psalms 113-114 prior to their Seder meal and Psalms 115-118 following the meal. Psalm 118 is significant for us as Christians as well, especially on our Palm Sunday.

When we use this Psalm, we should notice the portions of the psalm that are spoken or sung by various individuals and groups. Verse 19 should be spoken, or preferably sung, by someone "outside the gates" (perhaps in the narthex), verse 20 by a choir, another group, or the entire worshiping congregation, verses 21-22 by the person who had read verse 19 as this person now is entering into the sanctuary, verses 23-27 again by a choir or the entire congregation as the person entering the sanctuary approaches the altar, verse 28 by that person at the altar, and verse 29 by everyone.

"The stone that the builders rejected" in verse 22 is widely used in our Newer Testament as a reference to Jesus. Within the context of Psalm 118 it is an expression of the grace of God with many possible applications.

Luke 19:28-40

Comparison of the entry into Jerusalem accounts in the Four Gospels indicates that only in the latter two (Luke and John) is Jesus acclaimed as the King of Israel. Apparently the oppressive Roman military forces who occupied and controlled the region during the first century perceived Jesus to be a political leader who, with the support of crowds of his fellow oppressed Jews, was a serious potential threat to their own security. They did, therefore, what they always did in such situations. They seized the leader of the oppressed, tortured him privately, and then publicly crucified him to show what they would do to anyone who would be acclaimed as "King of the Jews."

Given the political situation in Galilee and Judea at the time of the crucifixion of Jesus, if some of the Pharisees in the crowd urged Jesus to restrain the members of the crowd from shouting political slogans, they were doing so in order to try to protect Jesus himself and the other Jewish people from Roman retaliation. Jesus, however, is depicted as refusing to restrain the crowd.

Among the most significant redactions of the Markan account by the Lukan writer in this instance is the addition of the Lukan motif of "Peace in heaven and glory in the highest places." Also this Lukan motif should ultimately be our focus as we proclaim this text and our faith. The Jesus of history lived this motif. Jesus as the Christ of faith expresses this motif. The Church of Jesus Christ is called to do everything that it can so that there will be peace on earth as there is peace in heaven, to the glory of God. Since only the Lukan entry account expresses this motif, it is especially important for us to focus on this motif during the years that we use Luke's entry into Jerusalem account.

For those who wrote the Four Gospels, Jesus as the Risen Christ was indeed "Lord." In the words of Zechariah 9:9 that they applied to Jesus, he was in every way triumphant and victorious, subduing and riding a young, unbroken colt, and at the same time humble, riding on a lowly beast of burden. He was *their* Lord, coming in the name of the Lord.

From the standpoint of the inspired writers of the Newer Testament documents, what Jesus' followers did proleptically as he entered with other pilgrims into Jerusalem to observe the Passover, God did actually a few days later by raising Jesus from the dead, highly exalting him, and giving him the name that is above every other name. God did this, Paul wrote, so that eventually every knee (including the knee of Caesar) will bend at the name of Jesus, and every tongue (including the tongue of Caesar) will confess that Jesus (not Caesar) is Lord, to the glory of God the Father.

LITURGY OF THE PASSION

Human suffering is obviously the red thread that runs through all of these texts selected for Lent 6 when next Sunday is observed as Passion Sunday. The extensive selections from the Lukan passion account, the influential "Christ-hymn" of Philippians 2:5-11, and the end-of-Lent setting in the Church Year focus attention on the human suffering of Jesus for his people, suffering that he did not avoid. Within a Christian worship service near the end of the season of Lent, the suffering of the Servant of Adonai (Isaiah 50:4-9a), and of the psalmist (Psalm 31:1-5, 9-16) are appropriately placed into juxtaposition with the suffering of Jesus.

Isaiah 50:4-9a

Most people who participate in Christian worship services and hear this text on the Sunday prior to Good Friday probably associate the claims of daily direct inspiration, of suffering at the hands of ruthless tormenters, and of confident trust in the Lord God in this portion of the third Servant Song of the Isaiah tradition with Jesus as they perceive him. As Christians, we can certainly interpret the Older Testament as we choose, and we can certainly picture Jesus as we read and hear about the Suffering Servant of the Lord in this text. Nevertheless, it would be appropriate for us to share in some way with the congregation a recognition that the Suffering Servant Songs have a meaning and a context of their own as a composite expression of the Israelite-Jewish prophetic tradition at its best.

Psalm 31:9-16

Our use of this Israelite individual lament within our Christian worship services indicates that for us also deliverance from human suffering is still futuristic — at the Easter appearance of Jesus and at our own "Easter" appearance.

Together with the psalmist we also cry to the Lord (Adonai for the psalmist, Jesus for us) for deliverance here and now.

Philippians 2:5-11

Perhaps no other text in the entire Bible is used as frequently and in as many different situations of the Church Year as is this text. It can be an Advent text, a Christmas text, an Epiphany text, a Lenten text, and a text for Maundy Thursday, Good Friday, Easter, Ascension Day, and Pentecost. In each different situation we should place the emphasis on the appropriate aspect of the text. For Lent 6 observed as Passion Sunday, we should focus on the suffering of the Jesus of history and on his willingness to go to Jerusalem where it was likely that the oppressive Roman occupation forces would seize, torture, and crucify him because they were afraid that oppressed Jews who were being given hope for freedom and liberation by Jesus would rebel against them.

Luke 22:14—23:56 or Luke 23:1-49

Because of the great length of this reading, comments here will be limited to four segments of the text that depict various aspects of the suffering of the Jesus of history.

Luke 23:1-5, 13-25 (The Trial before Pilate). The specific accusations of the entire multitude of elders of the people, chief priests and scribes added by the Lukan writer to the Markan account of the trial of Jesus before Pilate are strikingly anti-Jewish because they are presented as obviously false and pernicious charges. According to this Lukan account, the purpose of Jesus had always been to bring peace to Jerusalem and to the nations of the world. It had never been to pervert the Jewish nation, as the religious leaders of Jesus' own people are depicted in this trial scene as accusing Jesus of doing. According to the Synoptic tradition accounts, Jesus had advocated the paying of tribute to Caesar and had not called himself a king or a Jewish Messiah. Among the Synoptic accounts, only Luke presents the accusations recorded in Luke 23:2. According to the Luke 23:4, 14-16 account, the Roman official (Pilate) declared Jesus to be innocent of the charges brought against him, but the religious leaders of Jesus' own people charged repeatedly that Jesus had been agitating the people throughout the land. Only Luke specified that the voice of the Jewish religious leaders prevailed and that Pilate delivered Jesus over to their will (vv. 23-25).

The impression is thereby given that not the Romans but the chief priests and the rulers and the Jewish people took Jesus away and crucified him. Since no new subject of the verb is introduced in Luke 23:26, the antecedent of the unexpressed subject of the verb in Luke 23:26 and elsewhere in this section appears to be the Jewish authorities and the Jewish people listed in Luke 23:13. By omitting all of the Markan and Matthean references to Jesus being mocked by the Roman military personnel (Mark 15:16-20a; Matthew 27:27-31a) grammatically the antecedent of the unexpressed subject of the verb in Luke 23:25 and in other verbs that follow is not the Roman soldiers, whom the Lukan writer does not introduce until 23:36, but the Jews. In this manner, the Lukan writer achieved a consistency with the charges made by the same Lukan writer in Acts 2:22-23 and 7:52-58 that the Jews betrayed and murdered Jesus, the Righteous One. The impression is given, therefore, that anti-Jewish invective was more important for the Lukan writer in some instances than was historical clarity.

In the interests of historical accuracy and (belatedly) of justice, we should also specify the subject in Luke 23:26 as "the Roman soldiers" from Mark 15:16 and Matthew 27:27 and from what is known from other sources about execution practices of the Roman occupation forces, so that the subsequent unexpressed subjects of verbs in the crucifixion proceedings in Luke will refer back to Roman military officials rather than to Jews.

Although the Lukan writer's earliest readers were well aware that crucifixion was a Roman prerogative used effectively to discourage opposition and revolt in the various provinces of the Roman Empire, most Christians who read Luke today do not know the extent to which the Roman military used crucifixion in executing leaders of oppressed people whom they perceived to be threats to their security. Most Christians today focus only on the crucifixion of Jesus. They do not realize that the title that the Romans placed over Jesus on the cross, "the King of the Jews," had probably been used many times by the Romans before the day when they used it to apply to Jesus in order to transmit clearly to the Jewish people that "This is what we do to your leaders! This is what we will do to any of you who will try to lead your oppressed people and gain popular support that may be used against us!"

This type of careful attention to context in translation will partially counteract the popular supposition among many Christians even in our time that "the Jews" killed Jesus. Actually, most of the Jews who were aware of Jesus and knew what the Roman occupation forces were doing to Jesus on the day of his crucifixion grieved bitterly that another of their leaders in whom they had hope was being shamefully tortured and executed by the hated Romans and that there was nothing short of suicidal action that they could do about it.

This kind of sensitive translation is essential in our time. Since we have ample evidence of these serious instances of anti-Jewish biases in Luke-Acts, it is our responsibility as spiritual descendants of the Lukan writer to counter these biases by sensitive translation and usage. As Paul M. van Buren put it in his *Discerning the Way: A Theology of the Jewish Christian Reality* (New York: Seabury, 1980, pp. 47-

48), "John Chrysostom in the fourth century, for example, or Martin Luther in the sixteenth, never conceived that their vile words on the subject of the Jews would help significantly to produce a climate which a later pagan ruler would take advantage of in order to destroy six million of God's people," and "If... we leave unchallenged and do not wipe out the tradition of anti-Judaism which we have inherited, we shall have failed those who follow after us. Whatever we may say about the roots and rise of that tradition, we today — after 1945 — can no longer continue it." The extent to which we as Christians today shall be willing to counter the anti-Jewish biases that we see in the Newer Testament within the passion accounts and elsewhere will be determined during the coming decades and centuries in our preaching and teaching as, led by the Spirit of God, we interact with the living, dynamic Word of God and pass it on to our children and to their children.

Luke 23:6-12 (The religious leaders accuse Jesus during his ordeal in Herod's court). Only in Luke's Gospel is there a story about a trial of Jesus in Herod's court. As in every instance of Lukan composition, this account is carefully constructed. At its beginning (v. 6) and at its end (v. 12) Pilate is significant. As we move into the pericope from both its beginning and its ending, we see Jesus presented as in the custody of the soldiers of Pilate and of Herod, subjected to their cruelty. Next the Herod figure is introduced and shown to be curious to see what Jesus would do, and then later depicted as frustrated and treating Jesus with scorn and contempt. At the center of the account (v. 10) the chief priests and the scribes are shown to be accusing Jesus vehemently. Jesus in his innocence will answer to no one.

This literary drama composed by the Lukan writer gives the reader the impression that the attitude and actions of the Jewish religious leaders encouraged Herod and the Roman soldiers to treat Jesus horribly and to mock him. Although it is likely that a very small percentage of the heavily oppressed Jews of Galilee and Judea at the time of Jesus' death cooperated fully with the Roman occupational forces for personal advantage, there can be no doubt that the overwhelming majority of the Jews of that time who knew anything about the Jesus of history were supportive of him, given hope by what Jesus was saying about God and the kingdom of God, and were saddened and grieved when they heard that the Romans with the complicity of the Herodians had seized Jesus and were torturing him. Jesus was one of them, a leader and a hero among his fellow oppressed people. The Jews in Galilee and Judea knew from past experience that once the Romans seized a leader among the oppressed Jews, the people would soon see their leader die on a Roman cross, and as oppressed people they were unable to do anything to prevent this.

Luke 23:27-31 (prophecy against the "daughters of Jerusalem"). The women who were beating their breasts in mourning and lamentation while Jesus was being led to his crucifixion appear to be presented in Luke as sympathizers with Jesus rather than as his mockers. Nevertheless, the Lukan writer has Jesus utter an oracle of prophetic judgment against them in words that are similar to those of the "Q" material saying of Luke 13:34-35 and the weeping over Jerusalem account of Luke 19:41-44. Therefore, the Lukan writer condemned all of the inhabitants of Jerusalem, especially the women who were alive at the time of the crucifixion of Jesus and their children, to a fate worse than death. With devastating effectiveness, the Lukan writer linked the siege and fall of Jerusalem — an event that had occurred after the crucifixion of Jesus but prior to the composition of Luke's Gospel — to the crucifixion of Jesus in skillfully portrayed anti-Jewish polemic. If we are interested in proclaiming what actually happened during the final hours of Jesus' life, we will read only Luke 23:27 and not 28-31.

Luke 23:32-49 (the crucifixion). A comparison of the words of Jesus while on the cross in the Markan, Matthean, and Lukan accounts reveals that the Lukan writer did not use the cry of despair, "My God! My God! Why have you forsaken me?" of Mark and of Matthew and inserted instead, "Father! Forgive them, for they do not know what they are doing," "Truly, I say to you. Today you will be with me in paradise," and "Father! Into your hands I put my spirit." This contrast is clearly indicative of the differences with which the Lukan writer portrays Jesus compared to the Markan and Matthean accounts. In Mark and in Matthew Jesus is a desolate figure as he dies; in Luke Jesus is in control of the situation even while he is dying. The Lukan Jesus forgives those who are crucifying him. He declares that the man on the cross next to him who recognizes the innocence of Jesus will be in paradise with Jesus on that same day, and he puts his spirit into the hands of the Father. (The Johannine writers use neither the Markan and Matthean words of Jesus on the cross nor the Lukan words. Instead, they develop three new sayings for their Johannine Jesus.)

As we speak about the human suffering of Jesus on this Passion Sunday occasion within the context of all human suffering, it will be appropriate for us to relate it in significant ways to the suffering and death of millions of oppressed people during the twentieth century, particularly to leaders of oppressed people such as Dr. Martin Luther King Jr. and Archbishop Romero who spoke out publicly against the oppressors and were killed as Jesus was, each as a leader of the oppressed. As we read the Lukan passion account with its skillfully constructed anti-Jewish polemic, we have a moral obligation to note how the anti-Jewish polemic in it contributed to an environment in which most Christians in Germany raised no effective opposition to what the leaders of their nation did to the Jews of Europe from 1933-45.

HOLY WEEK
MONDAY OF HOLY WEEK
(A, B, C)

John 12:1-11

Monday of Holy Week is introduced with this account that is only in the Fourth Gospel about an anointing of the feet of Jesus by Mary, the sister of Martha and of Lazarus, whom Jesus, according to John 11:1-44, had resurrected from the dead. The account makes a major contribution to the plot of the Fourth Gospel, with Jesus speaking in support of what Mary was doing and in opposition to Judas Iscariot, who was complaining about the pouring of the expensive perfume on the feet of Jesus when the perfume could have been sold and the proceeds given to the poor. The statement of the Johannine Jesus that "you are always going to have poor people with you whom you can help, but you are not always going to have me" presents the greatest challenge for us even today. It raises fundamental questions about how the financial resources of individual Christians and of congregations of Christians should be allocated. Perhaps we should respond to these questions in terms of "both and" rather than in terms of "either or."

Hebrews 9:11-15

The writer of the Epistle to the Hebrews presents Jesus in a way that is very different from the ways in which Jesus is depicted elsewhere in our Newer Testament documents. Within each of the Four Gospels Jesus is opposed by the priests who manage the Temple under contracts purchased from the Romans; he is certainly not presented as the honored priest entering into the Holiest Place in the Temple to offer his own blood to God. This very different way in which Jesus was portrayed by the writer of this document was a major reason that the Epistle to the Hebrews was one of the last documents to be accepted into the Newer Testament canon.

Isaiah 42:1-9

By using this "Servant of the Lord" text, as it is designated by Christians, on the Monday of Holy Week, we are identifying the Servant of the Isaiah traditions with Jesus as we as Christians perceive him. That identification, of course, does not give ownership of the Servant concept to us as Christians. The Servant of the Lord still primarily belongs to the Jews, not to us as Christians. The statements in this text about God putting the Spirit of God upon the Servant in order that the Servant may establish justice on the earth in a sense unites Christians with Jews, since, when we are at our best, we as Christians, together with Jews, long for justice and work together to "repair" the world and to be righteous and just in all that we and Jews do.

Psalm 36:5-11

Here also, when we as Christians use this psalm, or any of the psalms, or any portion of the Older Testament for that matter, ideally we use these materials together with Jews, as devotional guides along with Jews, even during our so-called Holy Week. Although our experiences and our understandings of the intended meanings of the texts in the Older Testament are different from those of Jews, we must remember that these were Israelite and Jewish documents before we began to use them and that they remain basically Jewish documents today.

TUESDAY IN HOLY WEEK
(A, B, C)

John 12:20-36

All except the final verses 34-36 of this text are used also on the Fifth Sunday in Lent and were commented upon above at that place. There we considered the two symbols that are used in this text to signify the death of the Johannine Jesus. His death is compared to the "death" of a kernel of grain, a change and germination that is necessary in order that new life will result. His death is also depicted in this text as a situation in which the Johannine Jesus is lifted up between the earth and the sky on a Roman cross.

On this occasion, let us look more closely at verse 25, a Johannine explication of the "death" and germination of a kernel of grain as a symbol of Jesus' death on the cross. Most translations of verse 25 into English indicate that the Johannine Jesus here said that the person who loves the person's own life loses it, but that the person who *hates* the person's life here in this world will retain it eternally, expressing the form of the Greek verb *miseo* here with the word hates. In most instances of the use of forms of the Greek verb *miseo* in our literature, the English word *hate* is appropriate. Here and in Luke 14:26, however, there are better and more nuanced ways in which this Greek form should be expressed in the English language. It is not a good translation here in John 12:25 to say that a person should *hate* the person's own life here. In the context of this verb in John 12:25, I suggest that the verse should be translated as I express it in my *The New Testament: A New Translation and Redaction* (Lima, OH: Fairway Press, 2001) as follows: "The person who selfishly wants to retain that person's life is going to lose it, and the person who selflessly gives that person's life to others in this world will actually retain it into life eternally."

In the three verses (vv. 34-36) that are used here but not on the Fifth Sunday in Lent the Johannine depiction of Jesus as "the light" is used. The idea that the Johannine Jesus will not be physically present within the Johannine community much longer, as expressed more extensively in the "farewell discourses" in John 14-16, is included.

1 Corinthians 1:18-31

In this text the Apostle Paul proclaims Christ crucified as the one whom God, through the resurrection of Jesus as the Christ, made the primary manifestation of the power of God and of the wisdom of God. The word of the cross (Christ crucified) makes us wise, makes us righteous, makes us holy, and redeems us from the power of sin. This is what God does, not what we do. Therefore, we should not boast about what we have done. If we boast, we should boast about what God in the death and resurrection of Jesus as the Christ has done and continues to do.

Isaiah 49:1-7

In verse 3 of this second of what we as Christians call the Servant Songs of the Isaiah tradition the Servant is identified as "Israel." This identification was probably added to the text at some point after the initial composition and use of this text. It is difficult to see, however, how the Servant could *be* Israel when it is written in verse 5 that the Servant is commissioned by God to bring Jacob back to God, to gather Israel back to God, and in verse 6 to bring back to life the tribes of Jacob, to restore those who will be preserved in Israel. Our Christian identification of the Servant with Jesus as the Christ does not work perfectly either, unless we make the followers of Jesus as the Christ to be the "New Israel." When we do this, we should call ourselves at most "a new People of God," rather than "the New Israel." When we call ourselves "the New Israel," we are being arrogantly supersessionistic.

Within the context of the Isaiah traditions, the Servant, and, farther along in the traditions as we have them, the Suffering Servant, should probably best be understood as a composition of poetic expressions by a variety of inspired Israelites of the ideal prophet, the ideal inspired person in that tradition. In that sense, the Servant or Suffering Servant concept can be used both by Jews and by us as Christians today, with neither group preempting the concept.

Psalm 71:1-14

The psalmist, during the "senior years" of the psalmist's life, calls upon God to rescue the psalmist from those who are cruel and oppressive, from those who are showing no respect. The psalmist affirms that the psalmist has depended upon the Lord God ever since the Lord gave life to the psalmist when the psalmist was born.

WEDNESDAY OF HOLY WEEK
(A, B, C)

John 13:21-32

Not only is the Johannine Jesus in this text depicted as having the foreknowledge of which of the twelve disciples will "betray" him, the Johannine Jesus is portrayed as in a sense mandating that betrayal by saying to Judas Iscariot, "That which you are going to do, do it soon." Various interpretations have been given to this saying within Church history. One is that Judas was predestined by God to betray Jesus so that God's plan of salvation would be accomplished. Personally, I have never felt comfortable theologically with that interpretation. I think that a much better interpretation within the context of the Fourth Gospel is that here as throughout the Fourth Gospel, but not in the Synoptics, especially not in Mark and in Matthew, Jesus is portrayed as being in charge, in command of the entire situation, as the Lamb of God who takes away the sins of the world from the beginning of the Fourth Gospel until he dies on the cross with the words in John 19:30, "All that I have come to do has been done!" The Johannine Jesus directs the orchestra, he is the producer and the director of the play, and he is the coach who calls the plays on the field.

Hebrews 12:1-3

The writer of the Epistle to the Hebrews has a Christology that uses words that differ considerably from the words used by the Johannine writers. Nevertheless, the Christology is similar in many respects to that in John. For the writer of the Epistle to the Hebrews, as in the Fourth Gospel but not in Mark and Matthew, Jesus is completely in charge of God's salvation drama. In the Epistle to the Hebrews, Jesus himself goes into the most holy place in the Temple and offers his own blood as a sacrifice to God for sin, not for his own sin but for the sins of other people. Here in Hebrews 12:1-3 Jesus is presented as the founder, the pioneer, the one who makes our Christian faith perfect, and the one who is now seated at the right hand of the throne of God.

Isaiah 50:4-9a

The ideal prophet to the writers of the Isaiah tradition is given directions each morning by the Lord God. Therefore, the ideal prophet is able to stand up with confidence against those who are evil and to help those who are in need. For those of us who are Christians, Jesus the Risen Christ is like that and even more than that. This does not mean, however, that our interpretation of Isaiah 50:4-9a is the only valid interpretation. Our interpretation was certainly not the original and was not the earliest interpretation, and Jewish interpretations will always remain valid and helpful to us, as well as valid and helpful to Jews.

Psalm 70

For anyone who is suffering distress, whether because of adversaries or because of illness, the cry to God for help at the earliest possible moment expressed by the writer in this psalm is certainly understandable. Since this cry for help contrasts with the situation of the Johannine Jesus more than it complements it, Psalm 70 would be more appropriate in a Christian lectionary when the Gospel reading is from Mark or Matthew rather than from John. Within our message on this Wednesday of Holy Week, we can apply Psalm 70 to us, but hardly to the Johannine Jesus.

HOLY THURSDAY
(A, B, C)

John 13:1-17, 31b-35

For most of us who have been accustomed since our childhood to observe this day as Maundy Thursday and to associate this night with Jesus' words of the institution of the Eucharist on the night when Jesus would within a few hours be seized in the Garden of Gethsemane, it seems somewhat strange that we read Jesus' words of the institution of the Eucharist in the 1 Corinthians 11:23-26 text from the Apostle Paul rather than from one of the Synoptic Gospels. Of course, in the Revised Common Lectionary the Words of Institution (Mark 14:22-25; Matthew 26:26-29; Luke 22:14-20) are read each year, but only in the context of the lengthy Liturgies of the Passion, one of them each year. Unless we are rigidly bound to follow the Revised Common Lectionary with no deviation, we can, of course, supplement the reading from John 13:1-17, 31b-35 of Jesus washing the feet of his disciples on Holy Thursday each year with a reading of the Words of Institution from one of the Synoptic Gospel texts each year. We would then, however, have a nearly duplicated reading of the Words of Institution from Paul in 1 Corinthians 11:23-26 within the same service.

The Johannine reading that has the Johannine Jesus washing the feet of each of his disciples, even of the feet of Judas Iscariot, may appear at first and has often been considered to be an illustration of Jesus' humility. A more detailed study of this text in John 13, however, indicates that what the Johannine Jesus is represented as doing here is not an act of humility, but of control. Simon Peter was not given the option of refusing the washing. Neither was Judas Iscariot nor any of the other disciples. Jesus also, not Peter, had the choice of how much of Peter's body Jesus would wash. In addition in this text, the Johannine Jesus does not merely urge his disciples to love each other; the Johannine Jesus *commands* them to do this. As leaders in worship in the Church we are not, of course, the Johannine Jesus. We should, however, use appropriate care when we talk about humility and when we attempt to be humble, so that our actions will be genuine and not be expressions of a *false* humility.

1 Corinthians 11:23-26

It is essential that we look closely at the context in which Paul presents the Words of Institution of the Eucharist here. We can easily overlook the fact that Paul's primary concern in 1 Corinthians 11:17—14:40 is not the Words of Institution. Instead, Paul's primary concern is to command the followers of Jesus in Corinth to change the ways in which they were eating food when they were gathered together. The ones who were affluent had not been sharing their food with the ones who were poor. Apparently, even when they used the Eucharistic words, they were not participating together, but separately. Some of them were very disrespectful of others in the community of believers. Because they were not resolving these difficulties and problems, Paul sternly chided them for their behavior. He was not scolding them for their lack of intellectual understanding of the mystery of the Eucharist. He was chiding them for their *segregated behavior*, for not eating and drinking in the Eucharist together, for not having love for and respect for one another.

It is tragic and disrespectful to Jesus and to Paul that even into the twenty-first century the "sharing of pulpit and altar fellowship" is still so limited within the Church, even within the same denomination, as it is in my own Lutheran Christian denomination. If Paul, not to mention Jesus, were physically present and evaluating us today, Paul, as Paul indicated in 1 Corinthians 11:17—14:40, would chide *us* sternly, not because we have not achieved a single identical understanding of the mystery of the Eucharist, but because of our *segregated behavior*, because so many of us refuse to receive the Eucharist together with others or to permit others to receive the Eucharist with us. Many of us who are Lutheran Christians refuse to permit even other Lutheran Christians to join with us at our altars and in our pulpits, because we have decided that these other Lutheran Christians are not "Lutheran" enough and that they do not segregate themselves sufficiently from other Christians who are not Lutheran Christians. What would the Apostle Paul, whom especially we who are Lutheran Christians claim to honor so highly, say about us and our failure to honor the Church as the "Body of Christ," comprised as Paul put it in 1 Corinthians 12 of many diverse parts (ears, eyes, feet, and so on.)?

We need much more serious study of Scripture in the Church, especially of Scripture in the context of other Scripture. We need to study and to use the Words of the Institution of the Eucharist in 1 Corinthians 11:23-26 in the context of 1 Corinthians 11:17—14:40, not isolated from their context as we do in the Holy Thursday selections in the Revised Common Lectionary. It would be preferable on Holy Thursday to be using the Words of Institution in the context of their place in Mark 14, Matthew 26, and Luke 22 in successive years, not every year as they are in a secondary position in 1 Corinthians.

Exodus 12:1-4 (5-10) 11-14

This text in the priestly tradition in which the Israelite Passover observance is commanded and which is read when the Seder meal is celebrated in Jewish homes provides a segment, but only a small segment, of the background for the Christian Eucharist. The sacrificial slaughter of an entire yearling sheep or goat to be eaten during the course of one night by an extended family or by several neighboring families has evolved for Jewish families today into the use of only a single bone of a lamb as a symbol of the entire lamb in a Jewish Seder. There is a lamb bone on the table, but meat from a lamb is not necessarily a part of the menu for the Seder meal today.

There is very little direct connection between the Israelite Passover observance as commanded in Exodus 12 and the bread and wine by means of which we as Christians receive the "Body" and the "Blood" of Christ in the Eucharist. There is symbolism, however, in the belief that we have as Christians that because of the death and resurrection of Jesus as the Christ in which we as Christians participate in the Eucharistic action, God "passes over" our sins and we, like the ancient pre-Israelite slaves in Egypt, are spared. It is important that we make this connection on Holy Thursday.

Psalm 116:1-2, 12-19
There are a few connections between these portions of Psalm 116 and the other texts selected for this day in our lectionary. Somewhat like the Israelite slaves in Egypt, the psalmist testifies that the Lord has set the psalmist free from that which had enslaved the psalmist, in this case a very serious illness. We as Christians can link the reference by the psalmist to "the cup of salvation" that the psalmist will raise up as the psalmist will call upon the name of the Lord to the cup within the Eucharist, especially on this Holy Thursday.

GOOD FRIDAY
(A, B, C)

Psalm 22

As early followers of Jesus reminisced about the suffering that Jesus had experienced while he was being tortured and crucified by the Romans and about the significance that they saw in Jesus' suffering for their own lives, no texts within the Hebrew religious traditions were more helpful to them in describing the crucifixion of Jesus than were the Psalm 22 and the Isaiah 52:13—53:12 readings that have been selected in this lectionary for Good Friday each year.

Followers of Jesus used the vivid details of these texts as they told and retold their descriptions of Jesus' crucifixion in order to fill in the gaps within their own knowledge and recollections of that horrible event. Most of the portions of these two texts that could not be used in their recounting of the events during the crucifixion of Jesus because they did not "fit" Jesus' situation were simply not used. Psalm 22, as a detailed individual psalm of lament, and Isaiah 52:13—53:12 served well to depict what his followers concluded must have been Jesus' inner struggles as he was dying and to depict how Jesus had suffered, even though neither of these two portions of the Hebrew religious traditions were originally intended to describe the thoughts of Jesus or of anyone else who was dying on a Roman cross centuries later.

Our Christian hymns written to express Jesus' thoughts as he was dying develop these details even further than the Newer Testament texts develop them, and as we sing these hymns the words that we sing are implanted into our memory. It is important that we read the entire Psalm 22 within its own life situation before we use the Psalm in telling the story of Jesus' passion and death.

Isaiah 52:13—53:12

Most of that which has been written about Psalm 22 above applies also to this climax of what we as Christians call the Suffering Servant Songs of the Isaiah traditions. We can, of course, merely continue to see these texts as amazingly accurate prophecies that describe in vivid detail Jesus' suffering hundreds of years before he was crucified. We can also say that it was necessary for Jesus to suffer and to die in a specific way in order that he might fulfill these Scriptures. It will be in much greater accord with what actually happened, however, and more helpful to the people whom we serve if we suggest within our proclamation that followers of Jesus probably used details from Psalm 22 and from the Isaiah 52:13—53:12 texts as they told and retold what they understood about the death of Jesus during the decades after his crucifixion. Is this not essentially what we ourselves do when we prepare and share sermons and homilies to express our faith and to encourage other people in the development of their faith in God? We too use what we can and what works best within the religious documents that are available to us.

John 18:1—19:42

If these entire two chapters are read, the time that will be used within the service for this reading will mean that if there is a sermon or a homily our proclamations will be very brief and will probably provide very little reflection over most of the details in the reading. If, because of the length of the reading, there will be no sermon or homily of reflection at all, the impression will be given that everything written in the two chapters is simply a compilation of historical facts.

There are three segments in this extensive reading in which the narrative depicts the Jews as extremely cruel and sadistic in their insistence that Pilate order the crucifixion of Jesus. It would be admirable if we would shorten the reading somewhat by not including these three segments (vv. 18:28b-32, 38b-40; 19:4-16a) in our reading. These are the three segments that are the least edifying, the least historically verifiable, and the least appropriate for Christian proclamation. It would be even more desirable to begin our reading with John 19:16b and read until the conclusion of the suggested reading with John 19:42. This is the portion of the two chapters that actually depict actions on Friday rather than on Thursday evening.

It is not surprising that when we compare the passion accounts in all Four Gospels, we see that in the Fourth Gospel Jesus speaks quite extensively, unlike the other three in which Jesus says only a few words. This is consistent with what we have seen throughout the Fourth Gospel in which the Johannine Jesus is basically in charge of the entire situation, even when he dies on the cross with the words, "It is finished," i.e., "I have completed everything that I have come to do."

Also, as we compare the passion accounts in all four of the Gospels, we see that although in the Synoptic accounts there are said to have been various women present at the scene of the crucifixion of Jesus, no mention is made of the mother of Jesus being there. Also, in the accounts of Mark and Matthew it is stated that all of Jesus' male disciples had fled, including Peter who had at least gone along to enter the courtyard of Caiaphas to attempt to see what the bodyguards of Caiaphas would do to Jesus. Apparently the Fourth Gospel presents a different scene in order that its hero, "The Disciple whom Jesus Loved," would be shown as continuing Jesus' responsibilities by taking the mother of Jesus into his own home, or, if the "Beloved Disciple" is a symbol or representative of the Johannine community, into its home. This Johannine story about the mother of Jesus and the "Beloved Disciple" being present during the crucifixion of Jesus is not primarily a contradiction to the Markan and Matthean accounts. It merely presents a different scene for a different purpose.

Hebrews 10:16-25

As an encouragement for those who read or hear this text to enter into the most holy presence of God, made possible because of the blood shed by Jesus on the day that for us has become a Good Friday, this text is appropriate for our use on Good Friday every year. In the words of the writer of the Epistle to the Hebrews, let us rejoice in our new and lifegiving access to God through the "curtain" that Jesus as the Christ has opened for us.

Hebrews 4:14-16; 5:7-9

The prayers and the supplications of Jesus mentioned in Hebrews 5:7 help to bring this document somewhat closer to the depictions of Jesus in the Four Gospels. The designation of Jesus as "a ruler-priest after the order of Melchizedek" in 5:9 takes it farther away from them. We experience an echo of this "great high priest" language applied to Jesus the Christ in the Great Thanksgiving portion of our Holy Communion liturgy. There are those among us, however, who are still somewhat less than comfortable with this "great high priest" terminology in our Communion liturgy, even after many years of usage.

Finally, these texts selected for our use on Good Friday provide the setting for a general appeal for sensitivity during our Good Friday experiences. Our Jewish friends tell us that even now in this country they are at times still somewhat uneasy on this day that we as Christians designate as Good Friday. They remember the instances that their parents and grandparents have told them about verbal and physical abuse suffered by their people in Europe when after "Good Friday" worship services Christians poured out from their church buildings to attack Jews. Some of them remember the abuse that they themselves experienced within this country from Christian children who ridiculed and chased them as "Christ-killers."

There are many Christian people who do not realize that it was a Jew who was crucified by the Romans on that first "Good Friday," and that it was a Jew who became our Lord and Savior within the process of Christian theological development. Rembrandt realized this when he asked a Jew to pose for him while Rembrandt painted his portrait of Jesus, but most other Christian artists have not, and neither have most Christian preachers. Perhaps on Good Friday this year, and every year, we might remember this and in some way share the fact that Jesus lived and died as a Jew. If we do this, we might even be able to invite Jews whom we know to join with us in some way on Good Friday in our remembrance of the crucifixion of Jesus the Jew by the oppressive Roman occupation forces in Jerusalem.

HOLY SATURDAY
(A, B, C)

Matthew 27:57-66

There are two disparate materials in this selection. The first, verses 57-61, is an expression of kindness and love shown to the body of Jesus by Joseph, a relatively rich man from Arimathea. The second, verses 62-66, depicts the chief priests and the Pharisees as gaining permission from Pilate to have guards stationed at the tomb of Jesus to make certain that Jesus' body will remain there. The materials in verses 57-61 are edifying and appropriate for consideration on this Saturday, when we are experiencing with the early disciples of Jesus the sadness of facing the reality of Jesus' death. There is nothing that is edifying or appropriate for our use in the second account. It and its sequel in Matthew 28:4, 11-15 are malicious polemic against the Pharisees, developed and included only by the Matthean redactors. Matthew 27:62-66 and 28:4, 11-15 provide for us in narrative form information about the animosity that developed between some of the Matthean redactors and Pharisees with whom some of the Matthean redactors were having many experiences of frustration over not being able to "convert" Pharisees to the theological position of the Matthean redactors. They provide neither historical information about what happened on the evening of the death of Jesus, nor theological information that we can use as we, together with the early disciples of Jesus, experience the sadness of facing the reality of Jesus' death, a sadness that we should feel on Holy Saturday.

Therefore, it is regrettable that Matthew 27:62-66 and 28:4, 11-15 are included in our Newer Testament documents. It is even more regrettable that they are included in our lectionary. Since they are included in the lectionary, I suggest that we have four viable responses. We can read these verses and use nothing from them in our sermon or homily. We can read them and express in our sermon or homily that we regret that that are in the text and that they are in the lectionary. We can read and use only the edifying and appropriate Matthew 27:57-61 portion. We can attempt to have the hateful verses no longer included in our lectionary.

John 19:38-42

For the reasons discussed above, the use of this text is much more appropriate than would be our use of Matthew 27:57-66. Here we have the Fourth Gospel's version of the burial of Jesus, a version that includes Nicodemus, a figure who is included only in the Fourth Gospel within the Newer Testament, along with the man Joseph of Arimathea from the Synoptic Gospels participating in the kind and loving action of providing an honorable burial of the body of Jesus. Here Nicodemus, described in John 3:1 as a prominent Pharisee and in John 7:5-52 as urging his fellow Pharisees not to judge Jesus unfavorably without listening to Jesus, is presented as bringing a large quantity of spices to place around the body of Jesus. This is the best account within the Four Gospels to read and to use in our worship services on Holy Saturday.

1 Peter 4:1-8

The message of this text, which includes references both to the suffering of Jesus as a human being and the proclamation of the resurrection of Jesus as the Christ, is in every way appropriate for our use on Holy Saturday, the day between the death of Jesus and the proclamation of his reappearing as the Risen Christ. It is also helpful that this text includes both proclamation of the good news of the resurrection of Jesus and parenesis (guidelines for living) that are to be expected of followers of Jesus, since on most occasions our sermons and homilies should include both of these elements and not one without the other.

Psalm 31:1-4, 15-16

The thoughts expressed in these portions of Psalm 31 can be applied to the situation of Jesus on Holy Saturday, as well as to us. The psalmist expresses resolute faith in the Lord God, asks to be rescued from the "hidden net," and commits the psalmist's spirit into the hands of God.

Job 14:1-14

This text is appropriate for this Holy Saturday day of death. It is said, poetically, that the human life and that the human condition is short and fragile, like a flower, like a shadow, like a river that evaporates on the dry sand, unclean. When a tree is cut, there will usually be a new, vibrant, green tree sprouting from its stump. If a man dies, however, it is entirely uncertain, from the perspective of reason, whether the man will ever live again. It may be implied that God has the power to change the human condition, but that hope is not expressed here.

Lamentations 3:1-9, 19-24

In terminology similar to that in Job, the writer of this portion of Lamentations expresses the distress into which God has placed the writer. Although there is no escape from the afflictions that God has brought upon the writer, because the writer believes in the faithfulness of God and in the mercies of God that are new every morning, there is hope. So also it was for Jesus, even as he died on the cross and was dead on Holy Saturday, and so also it is for us.

SEASON OF EASTER
RESURRECTION OF THE LORD
EASTER VIGIL (A, B, C)

OLD TESTAMENT READINGS AND PSALMS (A, B, C)

Genesis 1:1—2:4a

This classic priestly creation account is cosmic in scope. As in other priestly materials in the Torah, the number ten is used, perhaps to teach children with the priestly teacher keeping the gathered children involved by counting off each part on each of the teacher's and the children's ten fingers. Here ten times we read and hear (in vv. 1:3, 6, 9, 11, 14, 20, 24, 26, 28-29) "And God (Elohim) said." At some point in the development of the text, these ten statements were apparently shaped into a seven-day framework of six days of work by God, followed by one day in which it is written that God finished God's work and rested from all of the labor that God had done. We see, therefore, that a primary purpose of the account became that of establishing the concept that God, already in God's wondrous creative activity, instituted the Sabbath. If God rested on the seventh day and made that day holy, so also should the Israelites, as is implied in Genesis 2:2-3. This priestly creation account was then placed at the beginning of the Torah in front of the Genesis 2:4b-25 folktale account in which the primary purpose, as we have it, is to show that God instituted monogamous marriage.

Finally, it should be noted that this creation account is not designed to give detailed scientific or historical information. Instead, it is designed to be a detailed expression of faith. We should recognize this and improve our translations into modern languages by beginning the account and most of the other sentences in it with the words "We believe that," as in "We believe that in the beginning God created (called into existence) everything (the skies/heavens and the earth)." These are all statements of faith, not of scientifically or historically verifiable facts. As statements of faith, they are far more important and substantial than are any so-called facts that can be disproved by new and additional evidence. When we are cognizant of this, we avoid much of the destructive conflict between science and religion that has been detrimental to Christianity during recent centuries.

Psalm 136:1-9, 23-26

Our Easter Vigil in which we recount highlights in our story of salvation (in our *Heilsgeschichte*) continues with this beautiful expression of thanksgiving to the Lord God. Verses 4-9 especially recapitulate portions of the Genesis 1:1—2:4a creation account. Every one of the 26 verses in this psalm includes the worshiping congregation's refrain "for God's steadfast love endures for ever."

Genesis 7:1-5, 11-18; 8:6-18; 9:8-13

The most reassuring segment of this Noah's flood story is the rainbow symbol and the promise that God will never again use a flood that will cover the entire earth.

Psalm 46

The awesome power of God is acclaimed in this well-known psalm. It is a power designed to bring peace upon all of the earth.

Genesis 22:1-18

In this frightful story of the binding of Isaac, God is presented as rewarding the obedience of Abraham. An animal is substituted as the offering. The reader is assured that God will provide, and that Abraham and his descendants will be blessed. From our Christian perspective, God offered no substitute later but freely offered Jesus as the Christ, the Son of God, as a sacrifice for our sins.

151

Psalm 16

The psalmist has faith that God will revive the health of the psalmist and grant to the psalmist an extended period of physical life and pleasure.

Exodus 14:10-31; 15:20-21

In the Revised Common Lectionary it is stated that "A minimum of three Old Testament readings should be chosen" for this Easter Vigil and that "The reading from Exodus 14 should always be used." Why do you think that this directive about Exodus 14 was given?

Exodus 15:1b-13, 17-18

This alternative, which includes the more extensive Song of Moses and of the people of Israel, also expresses rejoicing that God has destroyed the Egyptian soldiers in the waters of the sea. There is the salvation element, of course, in the expectation that the Lord God will establish the Israelite people in their own nation, with a political and religious capital in Jerusalem.

Isaiah 55:1-11

This poetic expression of salvation in restoration Jerusalem is certainly positive and edifying, providing guidance regarding how to live in accordance with the words and thoughts of God. As such, it is in every way appropriate for use in our Christian Easter Vigil.

Isaiah 12:2-6

This too is appropriate for our use here. It is a song of salvation, of faith in God, of praise to God, and of encouragement to live in the peace that God will provide.

Baruch 3:9-15, 32—4:4

As the exile of the former inhabitants of Jerusalem continues, the inspired writer urges Israel to learn wisdom, that is, to walk in the way of God by obeying the commandments and guidelines that God has provided in the Torah.

Proverbs 8:1-8, 19-21; 9:4b-6

Wisdom speaks, calling upon men to seek her, offering to them fruit that is better than the finest gold and silver, the gifts of righteousness and justice, and a place at her table where they may eat of her bread and drink of her wine.

Psalm 19

All of creation proclaims the glory of God. Nevertheless, the Torah that God has given is even more wondrous, more to be desired than that finest gold, sweeter than the most pure honey.

Ezekiel 36:24-28

God will gather the remnants of Israel from among the nations, sprinkle pure water upon them, give them a new heart, and put the spirit of God within them.

Psalm 42 and 43

In both of these psalms the psalmist is oppressed, asking God for help and vindication. Then, when God responds, the psalmist will again be able to return to Jerusalem, to worship the Lord God there.

Ezekiel 37:1-14

When the dry bones in the valley strewn with desolation hear the word of the Lord God, breath will come back into them and they will live again. God will open their graves and raise the entire house of Israel from the dead. Therefore, this text is entirely appropriate for use in our Easter Vigil, especially when we recognize its original situation in life in ancient Israel.

Psalm 143

During the darkness of night the psalmist prays to hear in the morning of the steadfast love that the Lord God has bestowed. The psalmist does not claim to be perfect and righteous. Only God is said to be perfect and righteous.

Zephaniah 3:14-20

This is a joyous expression of faith that the Lord God will return to Jerusalem, whose inhabitants will then no longer fear evil and disaster. Its people will be brought home, and the Lord God will restore their fortunes.

Psalm 98

The people of Israel are commanded to sing to the Lord God a new song, for the Lord has been victorious over all evil. All of nature is commanded to join with Israel in this song, the sea roaring, the floods clapping their hands, and the hills singing for joy.

NEW TESTAMENT READING (A, B, C)

Romans 6:3-11

As proclaimed in this text by the Apostle Paul, by means of our Baptism in the name of Jesus Christ we are united with Christ so completely that our sins actually died with Jesus when Jesus was killed by the Romans. Therefore, when God raises Jesus from death to life, with Jesus Christ we now live in a new relationship with God that is a new life of grace. This means that Easter morning is immeasurably important to us as Christians, by far the most important time in the Church Year.

Psalm 114

The psalmist considers the Lord God who brought the ancient Israelites out of slavery through the sea and across the Jordan to be so powerful that the entire earth trembles in the presence of the Lord. For us as Christians, this is comparable to the power we ascribe to God in bringing Jesus, who had been crucified and buried, out from the earth that can no longer contain him, for Jesus is now the Risen Christ.

Luke 24:1-12

As we read and reflect over the Lukan form of the empty tomb account, our Easter Vigil is complete. Our period of waiting is over. We welcome with grateful appreciation to God the announcement that the crucified Jesus is not in the tomb. "He has been raised from the dead!" Our season of Lent is ended! We again and anew sing the Alleluia! Praise the Lord!

RESURRECTION OF THE LORD
EASTER DAY

The most important sentence of our Easter Day message each year is the statement of faith, "I believe that God raised Jesus from the dead and that God will also raise me and will raise you from the dead." No Easter message is adequate without this statement of faith. It is the Easter message that the people have come to hear. They expect to hear it on Easter. Attendance at worship on other Sundays of the Church Year would be greater also if we would make this statement of faith in various ways in our message on the other, the "Little Easter" Sundays throughout the year.

The statement of faith alone is not, however, sufficient. Our statement of faith must be followed by the invitation, "And I invite you also to believe that God raised Jesus from the dead and that God will also raise you and me from the dead." "We believe. Others have believed. And we invite everyone who hears this proclamation to believe also." The invitation must be explicit. It calls for a commitment of faith.

Subjectivity is far more important than is objectivity in our proclamation, especially on Easter Day, but also on all of the other "Little Easters" of the year. The historians and the news reporters say, "From the data that we have been able to gather, we can say objectively that so-and-so has occurred." We who proclaim the Gospel say, "We believe! We speak from the perspective of faith." The Gospel is a subjective statement of faith, not an objective historical report. For this reason, we begin our consideration of the texts for Easter Day, Series C, with 1 Corinthians 15:19-26, a statement of faith.

1 Corinthians 15:19-26

In this text from the great resurrection chapter of 1 Corinthians Paul extends the effects of Jesus' resurrection to all who will believe that God raised Jesus from the dead and will continue to raise Jesus and all of us from the dead. We should not conclude that when Paul wrote that in Christ all shall be made alive, he was proclaiming an expectation of universalism and that ultimately everyone will be "saved." Paul desired, of course, that ultimately everyone would be saved. All would be saved if all would believe in God. All would be saved is all would believe that God was, is, and always will be active in Jesus as Christ. For this reason, we should translate 1 Corinthians 15:22b as "so also in Christ all who believe shall be made alive."

The emphasis in 1 Corinthians 15:19-26 is on victory over every oppressive ruler and authority and power, even over death itself. Paul was saying the resurrection of Jesus from the dead is an indication that God will nullify and destroy the Roman power that had crucified Jesus, and that, even prior to the nullification of the oppressive Roman power, God will raise from the dead all who "belong to Christ."

Psalm 118:1-2, 14-24

This exhortation to give thanks to the Lord, this proclamation of the mercy of God, this celebration of the action of God in restoring life to the psalmist is appropriate in a Christian Easter Day worship service. It can and should be sung with gladness, for it links us to other People of God in antiquity and to other People of God now in a Christian Easter Day celebration in which we confess our faith in God and rejoice in the redeeming power and love of God.

Isaiah 65:17-25

In this text the inspired writer joyfully proclaimed that soon the Lord God will recreate the sky and the earth for Jerusalem and for the Israelite people. For the People of God, there will be no more weeping and distress; no longer will anyone die short of a long and fruitful life. No one will take from them the products of their labor. God will hear and will respond to help them even while they are still speaking! Wild and rapacious beasts will be gentle and eat grass along with oxen and lambs. The sky and the earth will be resurrected. The People of God will be resurrected. Prophecy will be resurrected. Everything conceivable will be resurrected, except an individual person who has died. What a wondrous setting for the Easter message that God has taken this one giant additional step — to raise from the dead a person, the Jesus of history now perceived as the Christ of faith, and with the Risen Christ also each of us!

Acts 10:34-43

We marvel at the skill of the inspired Lukan playwright. Chapter 10 of Acts is not only an indication of the spread of the early followers of Jesus beyond the Jewish setting of Jesus to Greeks and other non-Jews; it also depicts a *Roman military officer* embracing the new Christian faith, a powerful representative of the oppressors being baptized in the name of the crucified and resurrected Lord Jesus Christ!

In addition, the Lukan writer may have even included a very subtle cryptogram against the Roman Emperor in Peter's speech in Acts 10:38-39 in the home of Cornelius, the Roman military official. The Lukan playwright has Peter describe Jesus as having gone from place to place among his people, healing all who were being oppressed by the devil. The devil here may actually be a coded reference to the Roman Emperor, a code understandable to followers of Jesus during the latter decades of the first century, but so subtle that Roman officials would think that this was only theological jargon!

Luke 24:1-12

The message to the women who had come very early in the morning of the day after the Sabbath to perform the last possible action of love for the crucified Jesus, "Why are you looking here in this place among the dead for someone who is living?" is also our message. "He is not here. He has been raised from the dead! Remember how he explained to you while he was still in Galilee that the Son of Man would be delivered over into the hands of the oppressive Romans and be crucified, and that on the third day after that he would be raised from the dead." Even the powerful Roman oppressors, those skilled specialists in torture and crucifixion, could not keep Jesus dead. They could kill Jesus, but they could not keep Jesus dead! They could not prevent God from raising Jesus back to life in a form in which even the skilled Romans could not kill him again. This text is a biblical condemnation of all who torture and kill other human beings, who torture and kill Jesus and anyone else.

John 20:1-18

It is often noted that Mary Magdalene is a witness to the empty tomb in all Four Gospel accounts. In the Fourth Gospel she also sees and clings to the resurrected Jesus. Our understanding of the nuances of Greek grammar help us to see that it was not the intention of the writer of the John 20:1-18 account to say that Mary Magdalene did not touch the Risen Christ. The negative with the Greek present tense imperative mood in the word of the Risen Christ to her in John 20:17 indicates that the action described should not continue indefinitely, not that it should not begin. Therefore, the words of the Risen Christ to Mary Magdalene should be translated into English as "Do not continue any longer to hold me," not as "Do not touch me!" The latter would have been indicated by using the negative with the Greek aorist tense subjunctive mood. When she could no longer cling to the Risen Christ, she went to his disciples to make her glorious Easter confession of faith, "I have seen the Lord!"

EASTER EVENING
(A, B, C)

Isaiah 25:6-9

The reading of this significant expression of Israelite/Jewish hope has become traditional for us also in Easter Day worship events. We realize, of course, that the expression of hope in Isaiah 25:8 is still not fully realized. It is still futuristic for Jews, for us as Christians also, for Muslims, and for others. They wait. We wait. Must we have animosity against others while we wait? What can we do together as we wait? Dare we include questions such as these within our Easter message this year? Perhaps we can no longer afford not to include them.

Psalm 114

As indicated above in the Easter Vigil listings (Series A, B, and C), the writer of Psalm 114 considered the Lord God who brought the ancient Israelites out of slavery through the sea and across the Jordan to be so powerful that the entire earth trembles in the presence of the Lord. For us as Christians, this is comparable to the power we ascribe to God in bringing Jesus, who had been crucified and buried, out from the earth that can no longer contain him, for Jesus is now the Risen Christ.

1 Corinthians 5:6b-8

When this admonition from the Apostle Paul is utilized in Christian worship on Easter Day, it is a reminder to us that even as we celebrate the appearance to us of the Risen Christ, evil and wickedness among us continues. We are in the words of the Latin expression used by Martin Luther *simul iustus et peccator*, at the same time justified and still sinning.

Luke 24:13-49

There are obviously Eucharistic connotations in this Road to Emmaus and appearance of Jesus to a large group of his followers account. Not only does Jesus break the bread and give it to the two men at Emmaus; Jesus actually is depicted as eating a piece of broiled fish to show a group of his followers that he was indeed physically resurrected from the dead. Easter evening is unquestionably the ideal time for us to read and to consider this text. This text is as "concrete and foundational" as the Mark 16:1-8 text is primordial. Here Jesus is presented as, in terms of the prepositions used by Martin Luther, "in us, with us, and under us" as we receive the body and blood of the Risen Christ in the Eucharistic action.

SECOND SUNDAY OF EASTER

The message that we must proclaim next Sunday in this Series C is expressed succinctly in the words of the Johannine Jesus in John 20:29b. Within the words, "Blessed are the ones who have not seen and have believed nevertheless," we find our identity in this text. Here again the Easter message is a strong invitation to faith. By focusing on this message we shall have a strong sequel to Easter Day. We shall begin our consideration of these texts for Easter 2, therefore, with John 20:19-31.

John 20:19-31

This is one of the three texts (Luke 24:39-43; John 20:19-31; John 21:1-14) that provide for us the most fully developed "proofs" of the resurrection of Jesus within the Newer Testament. The John 20:19-31 account served its purpose well late in the first century. In it Thomas, who as the most important representative of "gnosticizing" Christianity in the Fourth Gospel does not believe that Jesus would appear in a physical form after his resurrection, is forced to confess that the physical form is his Lord and God. For more about this, please see Raymond E. Brown, "Other Sheep Not of This Fold," *Journal of Biblical Literature* 97 (1978, pp. 5-22). This John 20:19-31 text continues to serve us in the Church as a most helpful "proof" text that Jesus was certainly raised in a physical form, similar to his body prior to his crucifixion in recognizable ways, but also different in that he was no longer limited by time and space restraints.

The most important way in which this text continues to serve the Church, however, is that we are in the position, not of Thomas, but of those of whom the Johannine Jesus says, "Blessed are the ones who have not seen and have believed nevertheless." We believe without seeing the resurrected Jesus, and for this we are blessed. We are in the same position in this respect as the members of the Johannine community were late in the first century. To believe without seeing, without proof, is more blessed than to believe because we have irrefutable proof. In this text we have faith, as faith, at its best. We joyfully believe. If we had irrefutable proof, there would be no reason for us to believe.

Revelation 1:4-8

Before this text is read in the congregations in which we serve, there should be some explanation that as we read this we are passing into the language of biblical apocalyptic imagery in which Jesus is portrayed in a way quite different from the ways in which he is depicted in the Four Gospels. Then Revelation 1:4-8 should be read with emphasis and with feeling.

Acts 5:27-32

This is the first in the series of "First Lesson" texts from Acts of Apostles rather than from the Older Testament designated to be read on the Second through the Seventh Sundays of Easter in Series C. It is, unfortunately, a text in which Jewish religious leaders rather than Roman political leaders are condemned as the ones who killed Jesus by hanging him upon a cross.

We as Christian Ministers of Word and Sacrament are called to proclaim a message that is pro-Christ, not one that is anti-Jewish. Some redactional modifications will be suggested here, therefore, as necessary in adapting Acts 5:27-32 for use in Christian worship during our time. These are redactional modifications that should have been made prior to or during the time in which Acts of Apostles was canonized and approved as Scripture for use in the Church. Since the modifications were not made when they should have been made, we must make them now. The Word of God is of tremendous importance to us, but the People of God are of even greater importance. In instances where the Word of God has hurt and continues to hurt the People of God (both Jewish and Christian), it must be modified redactionally. To paraphrase the Markan Jesus in Mark 2:27, "The Word of God was made for the People, not the People of God for the Word of God."

Acts 5:27-32 is a thespian's delight. The inspired Lukan playwright provided for us a historical drama with villains and heroes. The reading and hearing audience is pleased when the villains in the play are made to look ridiculous. The audience, clearly partisan, knows that in spite of great odds and difficulties God is on the side of the heroes and that their success is assured. This text is not unlike a TV drama written for our time.

The following redactional modifications are suggested here as appropriate in adapting this scene for use in our time so that the drama will be effective. Doing this is somewhat analogous to what a director does in adapting a drama script to a specific modern audience for greater effectiveness.

The proclamation of obedience to God and the witness to the belief that God has raised Jesus from the dead come across much more clearly when the vicious anti-Jewish polemic of Acts 5:30b and 31b is relegated to a footnote, or at least is not used. The following is an example of an expression of Acts 5:29b-31 that utilizes this kind of sensitivity.

It begins with what in a drama presentation would be delegated to a chorus, "We must obey God rather than obey people!" From within that chorus Peter would continue alone with the sterling confession, "We believe that the 'God of Our Fathers' raised Jesus from the dead and has exalted him as our Leader and Savior to the 'right hand' of God in order to provide for our repentance and the forgiveness of our sins." In this sensitive expression the onus is taken from "Israel" and from the "villains" of this scene. Instead, the confessional nature of Peter's speech is highlighted. The necessity of "our" repentance and the need for the forgiveness of "our" sins is acknowledged in a manner that theologically is far more attractive than if repentance is demanded of other people while it is assumed that "we" have no need for it.

The apostolic witness that is expressed in Acts 5:32 is enhanced by this biblical expression because it puts the emphasis on *our* confession of faith. When the emphasis remains only on the alleged guilt of other people (the Jews) and on *their* need for repentance, the witness is robbed of much of its power. The zeal of the inspired Lukan writer to incorporate anti-Jewish polemic so frequently in this scene and elsewhere in Acts of Apostles detracts from the witness and from the confession of faith of the writer. It was the purpose of the Lukan playwright to deflect persecution by the Romans of early followers of Jesus from these followers of Jesus to the Jews, to scapegoat the Jews. Other followers of Jesus in their usage of this material and by their incorporation of it into their new canon of sacred Scripture obviously gave their approval. The lives of the followers of Jesus were considered to be precious; the lives of Jews who remained Jews apparently were thought to be of little value. Within a mature Christianity, however, we are no longer bound to the purpose of the Lukan writer, especially when the vicious anti-Jewish polemic that is present in Acts of Apostles and in other Newer Testament documents has been shown to have contributed to the loss of human rights and of human life to Jews for nineteen centuries and when it also detracts from an otherwise clear confession of Christian faith.

Psalm 118:14-29

These verses, similar to the other verses from Psalm 118 used on Easter Day in this Series C, emphasize the victory that God provides for the people who are righteous. They are appropriate, therefore, for Christian worship services also on the Second Sunday of Easter.

Psalm 150

This marvelous hymn of praise in which everything that breathes in every possible way is called upon to praise the Lord God as a brilliant doxology to conclude the Psalter is certainly appropriate for our use next Sunday.

THIRD SUNDAY OF EASTER

A major unifying factor for each of the texts selected for Easter 3 in Series C is the theme, "The Redeemer Revealed." The Lord (Adonai) is, of course, the Redeemer revealed to the distressed psalmist in Psalm 30. The Lord (Jesus) raised from the dead is the Redeemer revealed to Paul in Acts 9:1-6 (7-20), the Redeemer revealed as the Lamb who was slain in Revelation 5:11-14, and as the Host in a shared meal in John 21:1-19.

Psalm 30

Psalm 30 is a good example of an Individual Hymn of Praise. The close escape of the psalmist from death is attributed by faith to the action of Adonai, the Redeemer from death. The grateful psalmist calls upon the members of the community of faith to join in praise and thanks to the Lord.

This is not a resurrection psalm, but it is close to being a resurrection psalm. It is stated that Adonai could have chosen to permit the psalmist to die, to be buried in *Sheol* (the grave, pit, arroyo), and his body to return to the clay from which according to the Genesis 2:4b-25 account Adonai Elohim had made the first man. The psalmist had cried to Adonai for healing, had used the logic that it would be to the advantage of Adonai to restore the psalmist to health, and restoration had been granted. This is an appropriate psalm, therefore, for use by Christians on Easter 3.

Acts 9:1-6 (7-20)

Since the Apostle Paul had written in 1 Corinthians 15:8 that "last of all, Jesus as the resurrected Christ had been revealed" to him and in Galatians 1:13-17 that God, who by God's grace had called him, had been pleased to reveal God's Son to Paul, it is likely that the inspired Lukan playwright used what Paul had written in 1 Corinthians 15:8 and in Galatians 1:13-17 creatively in composing the series of scenes that became Acts 9:1-20. The Lukan playwright was apparently so pleased with these scenes that the playwright used them again with only slight elaborations in Acts 22:4-16 and 26:9-18. For us on Easter 3, the significance of Acts 9:1-20 is that in this text it is said that Jesus the Redeemer was revealed to the Apostle Paul.

Revelation 5:11-14

This segment from the conclusion of the Revelation 4:1—5:14 throne scene is another excellent example of the best of the apocalyptic literature in the book of Revelation. Again, as last Sunday, it is appropriate to comment briefly about the apocalyptic imagery of the account. Then the text should be read with emphasis on Jesus as the Redeemer revealed as the Lamb who was slain to receive power and wealth and wisdom and might and honor and glory and blessing.

John 21:1-19

It may be helpful to provide a few comments selected from Raymond E. Brown's extended discussion of this text in his *The Gospel According to John* (Anchor Bible 29a, pp. 1066-1130). According to Brown, John 21 is best classified as an Epilogue, most likely supplied by a redactor of the work of the Evangelist. It is probable that two separate stories lie behind 21:1-19. In one of them Jesus was recognized through the (Eucharistic?) symbolism of the meal (v. 12). In the other Jesus was recognized by "the disciple whom Jesus loved" (v. 7). The Epilogue was attached to the main body of the Fourth Gospel by use of the typical redactional Greek words *meta tauta* ("After these things"). There are numerous close similarities to the Lukan account of the call of Peter and the miraculous catch of fish (Luke 5:1-11). Brown concluded, therefore, that the Third and Fourth Gospels preserved variant forms of the same miracle story. The primary purpose of this miracle story in each of its accessible forms is to show that Jesus revealed himself, which is emphasized both at the beginning (v. 1) and near the end (v. 14) of the John 21:1-19 account. The catching of fish almost certainly symbolizes the catching of people. According to Brown, the 153 fish signify the all-embracing character of the mission of the followers of Jesus. The unbroken net means that in spite of the inclusion of such a vast diversity of people, the community represented by these disciples is not torn by schism.

It may be added that John 21:1-19 does not indicate that Peter and the others were giving up on Jesus after the crucifixion and after other resurrection appearances and were returning to their earlier occupation of commercial fishing. Peter and the others are fishing here for people. Until Jesus from the shore directed them to cast their net on the *right* side of the boat, they caught nothing. Since in Mark and in Matthew there is considerable evidence that there was during the first century a Jewish west side of the lake and a non-Jewish east side of the lake, it is possible that the Johannine Jesus was said to have been directing his followers to fish for people on the other (east) side of the boat where there were more non-Jewish people rather than on the west side facing Galilee where there were more Jews. At any rate, the account is not merely telling us that if we obey Jesus we shall certainly be successful and prosperous in our business. It is not a "Prosperity Gospel" text.

For our homiletical purposes, the primary consideration here is that Jesus is said to have revealed himself as Risen Lord and Savior in the catching of a multitude of people and in the shared meal of his community of followers just as the Risen Christ continues to be revealed among us in our time. Within that community of "caught people" then and now there is a basic unity in spite of great diversity.

FOURTH SUNDAY OF EASTER

There is a message of confidence and assurance in each of these four texts chosen for Easter 4 in Series C.

Psalm 23

For us as Christians, Jesus as Lord and Savior has become in many ways what Adonai was for Israelites and continues to be for Jews. For us, Jesus raised from the dead is our shepherd who finds green pastures for us and leads us beside still waters, who restores our "soul." For us, Jesus as the Risen Christ is our Lord and God just as for Israelites and for Jews Adonai is, was, and always will be Lord and God.

In English the word "Lord" is used as a title by which both Adonai and Jesus are addressed, signifying in each instance the most significant way in which God is perceived as Active in History. When as Christians we say, "The Lord is my Shepherd!" to some extent we may be thinking about Adonai as Lord as Adonai is perceived as Lord for Jews, but more likely most of us are thinking almost entirely about Jesus the Risen Christ as our Shepherd and Lord, especially on this Easter 4 "Good Shepherd" Sunday. Our use of Psalm 23 together with Revelation 7:9-17 and with John 10:22-30 on Easter 4 encourages us to think about Jesus as the "Lord" who is our shepherd in the symbolic imagery of Psalm 23.

Acts 9:36-43

In this text Peter speaks and acts with the power of God that in the Four Gospels is attributed to Jesus. We note also that in this Acts 9:36-43 text, expressing the prominence of women and the perspective of women in Luke-Acts, it is a very good woman who is brought back to life when Peter addresses her by name, "Tabitha!" and says, "Get up!" The message is expressed with confidence and assurance, just as we are called to express the message of these texts this coming "Good Shepherd" Sunday. Nothing less will be adequate.

Revelation 7:9-17

These words continue to carry for us a beautiful message of confidence and assurance that although we may be weeping in tribulation now, in the future we shall lack nothing when the Lamb of God will wipe away every tear from our eyes, shall guide us as a shepherd guides the shepherd's sheep to springs of flowing water, protects us from the burning sun, and provides for our every need. Our Christian faith and hope are built on words such as this, not on words of accusation and condemnation of people who actually did not do that of which they are accused and for which they have been condemned.

John 10:22-30

Within the message of confidence and assurance recorded in John 10:27-29 the Johannine Jesus speaks as the Good Shepherd whose sheep hear his voice and follow him. The Johannine Jesus says in these verses that he knows his sheep and gives to them eternal life. They shall never perish. No one shall ever snatch them from his hand.

The controversy with "the Jews" in John 10:24-26 distracts and detracts from this otherwise excellent message of confidence and assurance. As in many other instances within the Fourth Gospel, in John 10:24-26 "the Jews" are said to be excluded because they do not believe as the Johannine people believe. We can put the necessary emphasis on the positive on this Good Shepherd Sunday if we do not use this controversy with the Jews portion of this text. As a person who is primarily within the Lutheran Christian tradition, I wonder why the Lutheran and Common Lectionary selections and the Revised Common Lectionary selections were expanded from the earlier (1967) Roman Catholic John 10:27-30 readings to include the anti-Jewish John 10:24-26 verses. Just as we who are non-Roman Catholic Western Church Christians have learned since the Second Vatican Council that we can be for Christ without having to be against the Roman Catholic Church, so also now and during the coming decades all of us who are Christians can and should realize that we can be for Christ without having to be against the Jews and against full participation in the Church by those who are in minority and powerless positions among us.

FIFTH SUNDAY OF EASTER

The texts selected for Easter 5 in the Revised Common Lectionary are indicative of a transition from emphasis on the crucifixion and resurrection of Jesus as a saving action for a limited number of his followers to sharing the message of salvation within a much broader arena. The Johannine Jesus in John 13:31-35 requires that his followers must love one another after he departs from them, just as he has loved them. Within a vivid literary drama in Acts 11:1-18 Peter in ecstasy in a vision is shown and convinced that the saving action of God in Christ must be shared as a gift from God to people beyond the community of initial followers of Jesus. It must be shared not merely with people who have a "clean" Jewish background, but also with non-Jewish background people whom Peter had previously considered to be impure and unclean. In the vision of the new heaven and new earth after the oppressive Roman Empire and all wicked people have been removed, it is acclaimed in Revelation 21:1-6 that God will live among God's people in a situation in which there will no longer be any pain, mourning, weeping, and death. During a much earlier period, this had also been the ideal situation depicted by the writer of Psalm 148, a messianic age in which all the angels of heaven, all of the creatures and elements of God's creation, and all people, men and women, young and old will praise the name of the Lord.

John 13:31-35

Analysis of these five verses indicates that its three units (vv. 31-32, 33, 34-35) are rather disparate elements juxtaposed. Raymond E. Brown, however, in his *The Gospel According to John* (Anchor Bible 29a, p. 609), noted that we can "trace the logic that led to the union of these disparate elements." Brown stated that "Jesus' glorification (vv. 31-32), which is the goal of 'the hour,' is an appropriate opening theme for the great Discourse explaining the hour. This glorification involves his return to his Father and, therefore, his departure from his disciples (v. 33). The command to love (vv. 34-35) is Jesus' way of ensuring the continuance of his spirit among his disciples."

The literary genre here is that of a dying father instructing his children. This text has close parallels in the *Testaments of the Twelve Patriarchs*, which is a Jewish document with Christian interpolations or a Christian work dependent on Jewish sources. For example, in the *Testament of Gad* 4:1-2, we read, "Now, my children, let each one of you love his brother," and in the *Testament of Reuben* 4:5, "My children, observe all that I have commanded you." For other examples, see Brown, *The Gospel According to John* (AB 29a, p. 611).

What we have, specifically, in John 13:31-35 and in many other Newer Testament texts is theological reflection over the tragedy of Jesus' crucifixion, the absence of Jesus from his followers, and Jesus' message and example of love.

Acts 11:1-18

It is interesting to note that Peter, who is described by Paul in Galatians 2:1-10 as reluctant to agree to Paul's request that non-Jewish followers of Jesus should not be required to be circumcised if male and should not have to follow Jewish dietary restrictions, is here depicted as using his own experiences to convince other apostles and believers in Judea that God has given to people of other religious traditions and ethnic backgrounds repentance and access to life.

Revelation 21:1-6

This vision of peace in the presence of God is wondrous for us and for all people. It was especially glorious for the people of the Johannine community who were suffering such intense persecution by zealous advocates of Roman Civil

Religion. Even though most of us are not being subjected to the kind of persecution faced by the Johannine followers of Jesus within the Roman province of Asia during the last seven years of the reign of the Roman Emperor Domitian, many of us are faced with intense pain and anxiety because of terminal illnesses, as well as economic losses and uncertainties.

Psalm 148

All of God's creation, in heaven above, on the earth, and the sun, the moon, and the flickering stars, people of all ages and genders are called upon in this psalm to give praise to the Lord God. As we draw nearer to the conclusion of our Easter Season this year with Psalm 148 and the Newer Testament texts selected for us for our use this coming Sunday, what justification do so many of us have for restricting leadership in the Church to males and to those who have majority power positions and orientations?

SIXTH SUNDAY OF EASTER

The emphasis in these texts selected for the Sixth Sunday of Easter this year is clearly on "good things" and on the belief that all good things come from God, as the Prayer of the Day specifies: "Bountiful God, you gather your people into your realm, and you promise us food from your tree of life. Nourish us with your word that empowered by your Spirit we may love one another and the world you have made, through Jesus Christ, our Savior and Lord, who lives and reigns with you and the Holy Spirit, one God, now and forever. Amen."

These texts in Series C all carry this emphasis without entering seriously into the related question of the origin of "bad things." It is appropriate that our sermons and services next Sunday maintain the emphasis of these texts. There are other opportunities to consider the more difficult issue of the origin of evil.

Psalm 67

The "good things" here are God's gracious interaction with and blessing of the people of the worshiping community. The results of this interaction and blessing are seen most clearly in the good harvest cited in 67:6. This and presumably other blessings will cause people of all nations to fear God and to praise God. God is said to judge and to guide all nations. In this Community Hymn of Praise there is no mention of Adonai. It is entirely Elohim who is acclaimed.

Acts 16:9-15

In this segment of the Acts of Apostles literary drama the "good things" come to the woman named Lydia, a seller of purple cloth who worshiped God and listened to Paul and to the other apostles. The Lord had opened her heart to be receptive to the message of Paul. After she and her entire household had been baptized, she invited Paul and those who were with him to be guests in her home. Together with Lydia, we too are nourished by the Word of God.

Revelation 21:10, 22—22:5
Here in beautiful unrestrained apocalyptic imagery we are given a description of the glorious new city of Jerusalem coming down from heaven from God to become the Bride of Christ, the Lamb of God who takes away the sins of the world. Life is so good in this new city that there is no need of a temple, or of sun or moon, for its temple is the Lord God and the Lamb. The glory of the Lord provides its light and the Lamb of God is its lamp.

John 14:23-29
Three "good things" form the basis of this Fourth Gospel text. They are presented in two promises and in a gift of "my peace" from the Johannine Jesus. The first good that is promised is the Paraclete, the Holy Spirit whom the Father will send in Jesus' name to remind the disciples of all that Jesus had said. The second good that is promised is the assurance that the Johannine Jesus and the Father of Jesus will come to those who keep Jesus' word, and the third is that the Johannine Jesus and his Father will make their home with those who keep the word of the Johannine Jesus.

As the Johannine writers and community, inspired by God, reflected theologically about how Jesus as they perceived him would be and was active among them, they claimed Jesus' peace. Nevertheless, the grammatical condition contrary to fact in 14:28 suggests that they realized their love for Jesus was not adequate. Perhaps this condition contrary to fact construction is the key that provides for us the best entrée into this text and into a homily/sermon based on this text. They perceived Jesus as saying to them, "If you had loved me the way that I wanted you to love me, you would have rejoiced that I am going to my Father, because my Father is greater than I am."

We too look for good things from God as we reflect theologically over the absence of Jesus and claim his presence. Like the members of the Johannine community, we also recognize that we do not love Jesus as the Christ, as the Son of God our Savior, as we should love, and that because of this our joy is not complete. Therefore, the "good things of God" remain for us somewhat elusive, as they were for the community by which and for which this text was composed. They are realized only in part. The full measure of the "good things from God" is still to come.

John 5:1-9

The "good thing" that the man at the pool near the Sheep Gate in Jerusalem who had been ill for 38 years received was to be healed. The question asked by the Johannine Jesus, "Do you want to be healed?" seems at first to be entirely unnecessary. Of course, he wants to be healed! After being helplessly ill for 38 years, would he not want to be healed? On further reflection, however, we see that it is totally essential that he has the will to be healed. Without the will to be healed, he would not have been healed. We too must want the healing and all of the other "good things" that God provides.

ASCENSION OF THE LORD (A, B, C)

The Ascension of the Lord texts in Luke-Acts (Luke 24:44-53 and Acts 1:1-11) accomplish four major objectives. First, they provide an explanation of where the Risen Christ is now. Second, they provide an explanation of why the Risen Christ was seen by many followers of Jesus during the first few weeks after his crucifixion and resurrection but is being seen in the same way no longer. Third, they provide assurance that the Risen Christ is still with us spiritually and that the Risen Christ will return. Finally, they establish more clearly the responsibilities of the followers of Jesus to be witnesses of the Risen Christ throughout the world.

These are very important objectives, and we miss our opportunity to follow through with a dramatic culmination of our forty-day Lenten season and of our forty-day Easter season if we do not have a meaningful and memorable worship service on Ascension Day each year.

Psalm 47

Our use of this psalm on our Christian Ascension Day is an indication that we consider the Risen Christ to be our Lord and God in a way that is quite similar to the way that the ancient Israelites perceived the Lord God for them. They perceived the Lord God to be the one who had won the victory for them over their enemies and over all evil and as the one who was, as it is stated in the picturesque language of this psalm, "sitting on the holy throne of God" the "Most High King over all of the earth." As Christians, we perceive Jesus the Risen Christ in much the same way as the Lord God was and is perceived and acclaimed by Israelites and by Jews in Psalm 47.

Psalm 93

There are numerous similarities between Psalm 47 and Psalm 93. The Lord is acclaimed in Psalm 93 as the king clothed with power and majesty, whose throne is established eternally. The Lord's rule is holy and just and will be for ever.

Acts 1:1-11

Since the principal literary antecedent of Acts 1:1-11 is the Septuagint text of 2 Kings 2:1-18, it is helpful to review the 2 Kings text in preparation for a Christian Ascension Day worship service. Genesis 5:21-24 and Deuteronomy 34:1-7 should also be read to provide the Enoch and Moses analogies.

We note that the inspired Lukan writer linked the Ascension account closely to the Lukan empty tomb account by having "two men clothed in white robes" interpreting the significance of the ascension of the Risen Christ in Acts 1:10-11 just as the Lukan writer had "two men in dazzling apparel" interpret the significance of the resurrection of Jesus in Luke 24:4-7. Perhaps we could benefit from the use of this Acts 1:1-11 drama best if we would begin the Ascension Day service outside the church building with the reading of this Acts 1:1-11 text. It would not be necessary for anyone to play the role of the Risen Christ, but it would help to dramatize the event with two of the men of the congregation dressed in white robes appearing from around a corner somewhere at the point of Acts 1:10 in the reading while the rest of those gathered for the worship service are standing together "gazing up into the heavens." The two men should appear and say to the group, "Why are you all standing here, looking up into the heavens? This Jesus, who has been taken up from you into heaven, will come again as you have seen him going into the heavens!" The worship service can then continue with the people entering into the sanctuary, singing an Ascension Day hymn, and using an Ascension Day liturgy.

Ephesians 1:15-23

At least once during our three-year cycle in the lectionary that we are using, it would be effective to utilize this Ephesians 1:15-23 reading as the primary text for the Ascension Day message. This text articulates what is desired for the People of God in the Church on Ascension Day. It refers specifically to the thought that the Risen Christ is sitting at the right hand of God in "the heavenly places." It uses the analogy of the ancient throne scene to depict how some people in the early Church late in the first century perceived the Risen Christ. What is said here about the power of the Risen Christ over the Roman Emperor and all of the political authorities who are persecuting and threatening the early Christians should be emphasized as we consider this text.

Luke 24:44-53

The Lukan themes of understanding the Scriptures and of claiming that everything about Jesus' life, death, and resurrection written in the Israelite Scriptures has now been fulfilled are prominent in this text. What the Lukan writer did not say in this text about the expected return of Jesus as the Risen Christ is supplied in the Acts 1:1-11 reading. What Luke 24:44-53 does stress is the great joy of the followers of Jesus and their constant worship and blessing of God. Let us continue this joy and this worship and blessing of God for the Risen Christ now and always!

SEVENTH SUNDAY OF EASTER

As is appropriate for this Seventh Sunday of Easter, the Sunday after the Ascension of the Lord, the emphasis within these texts is on the exaltation of the Lord. In Psalm 97 it is the Lord (Adonai) who is exalted. The exalted Lord Jesus and the Most High God are said to have removed the spirit of divination from the slave girl in the Acts 16:16-34 account and opened the gates of the Roman prison. In the Revelation 22:12-14, 16-17, 20-21 text it is said that the exalted Lord Jesus, the Lamb of God, will be coming soon to judge everyone and to give the water of life to those who are thirsty. In the final portion of the prayer of the Johannine Jesus in John 17:20-26 the members of the Johannine community and those who will believe in the exalted Johannine Jesus through their word are said to be one with the Johannine Jesus in the glory that the Father has given to the Johannine Jesus.

Psalm 97

Those who live in accordance with the precepts of the Lord God as perceived by the Israelites will be filled with joy, for the Lord God reigns over all the earth. The Lord God is exalted far above those who are perceived to be God by people among the other nations. Therefore, Zion and the daughters of Jerusalem will be glad; they will be delivered from the hand of the wicked. They shall prepare themselves by hating all that is evil and by giving thanks to the Lord God of Israel.

Acts 16:16-34

With the subtlety that is characteristic of the inspired Lukan writer, the Lukan playwright proclaimed in this account that the power of the Most High God present in the exalted Lord Jesus was infinitely greater than the power of the

Romans and of the Roman Empire. This text is especially meaningful for Christians who practice Believer's Baptism, for in it the jail warden at Philippi who asks what he should do to be saved is told that he should believe in the Lord Jesus and he and his household will be saved. Baptism follows instruction and confession of faith in this account.

Revelation 22:12-14, 16-17, 20-21

This text is a reminder to us that the Seventh Sunday of Easter marks the end of the first half of the Church Year. It is somewhat like a "Christ the King" Sunday. This text in Revelation 22 is particularly comforting to those believers who are heavily oppressed in this world or are otherwise nearing the point of death. The rich symbolism of this final chapter of the Christian Apocalypse should not be unnoticed during our worship services next Sunday.

John 17:20-26

This is the portion of the prayer of the Johannine Jesus that is existentially most significant for us, since we are among those who have believed in Jesus because of the words of the members of the Johannine community. In this text we have the most pronounced ecumenical prayer within the Newer Testament. It is the biblical basis for our most sincere efforts for denominational unity, for Christian unity, and for human unity. Even if the members of the Johannine community wanted unity on *their* own terms (just as most of us do), they did have their Johannine Jesus pray for unity and most likely themselves prayed fervently for unity, particularly for unity with the representatives of the much larger communities of followers of Jesus who produced and used the Synoptic Gospels. Certainly we should reflect theologically over this prayer for unity and make it our prayer next Sunday within the congregations in which we live and serve.

DAY OF PENTECOST

Two lunar months after they reenacted the Passover meal each year, many of the ancient Israelites brought some of the first fruits and vegetables of the spring season as an offering to the Lord and to their priests as they celebrated together their spring religious and social agricultural festival. When the Torah became the unifying factor of those who survived the fall of Jerusalem and the loss of their nation, this agricultural festival, the Feast of Weeks, seven weeks after the Passover, gained additional meaning as a commemoration of the giving of the Torah to Moses by Adonai at Sinai. For Greek-speaking Israelites still later, this festival was called Pentecost because it was celebrated on the fiftieth day after Passover.

The inspired Lukan writer took this process of development one step farther, transforming for followers of Jesus the Israelite agricultural and Torah festival into a Christian celebration of the beginning of Christian prophecy and the "birthday" of the Church. This is one of many instances in which the Lukan writer shaped the emerging Christian traditions by using ideas and materials from the Greek Septuagint translation of the Hebrew Scriptures.

Within our current Christian usage, the significance of our Pentecost observance is much less than is our Christmas and Easter, the other two major Christian festivals. Many congregations have Confirmation ceremonies on Pentecost, but apart from that, relatively little is done to attract interest in the rich traditions of the day. (It is the only one of the three major Christian festivals that has not been commercialized. There are few if any "Pentecost sales" in our department stores and truck and auto sales lots.)

The agricultural significance of this day is not notable for most Christians. Apart from small volume "farmers' markets," within our "supermarket" society we are able to purchase fresh and frozen fruits and vegetables throughout the year. It seems that we have always had the Scriptures and the Church, and because of our multitude of somewhat independent Christian denominations the Church has had many different "birthdays."

There are actions that we can take to educate and sensitize more members of the congregations in which we live and serve regarding the historical and spiritual significance of the Day of Pentecost. We can decorate the chancel areas of our worship centers on Pentecost Day with early produce from our gardens and orchards in the southern areas of our country, or purchase high-quality produce for this purpose in the central and northern regions. We can have someone carry a Bible into the chancel during the opening processional. We could even place a "birthday cake" on the altar to celebrate another year of life for the Church. This will provide numerous opportunities for various members of the congregation to be involved, and everyone should, of course, share in enjoying a small piece of the "birthday cake." Our children (and we as adults also) will learn in this visual, tangible way to have a greater appreciation for our rich Pentecost traditions. With a few variations each year, within a few years we shall have much more interest in the Day of Pentecost and increased attendance on the occasion. If we have a children's sermon, it will be easy to take the children to the produce, to the Bible, and to the birthday cake to teach the traditions represented by each.

Psalm 104:24-34, 35b

This psalm was chosen for the Christian Pentecost observance each year within our three year cycle of texts because of the mention in 104:30 of the *ruach* (Hebrew expressed in English as spirit, wind, or breath) of Adonai giving life to all of the creatures of the earth. The sending of the *ruach* of Adonai, which gives life, is contrasted with Adonai's hiding of Adonai's face (v. 29), which results in the death of all beings as they lose their *ruach*.

It would be helpful to use all of Psalm 104 and not merely the verses suggested in our lectionary. Psalm 104 is a poetic equivalent of Genesis 1:1—2:4a, more beautiful in many ways and perhaps older than the Genesis account. Also, since the Genesis account was at some point redacted into a six days of work and one day of rest liturgical pattern in order to show that God instituted the Sabbath already at the conclusion of God's initial creative activity as the Genesis 1:1—2:4a account has been, unlike with the Genesis account, we do not become embroiled in historicity issues with Psalm 104.

Genesis 11:1-9

Among the many purposes of the Tower of Babel story, three come immediately to mind. First, the account provides an answer in story form for the etiological question, "Why are there so many different and confusing languages among the people of the earth?" Second, the story is a polemical degradation of the "evil" Babylonians and other Mesopotamians who, having no mountains on which to build their altars, built towers (ziggurats) with worship centers at their tops. Third, the account continues the theological theme of Genesis 1-11 that sinful humankind seeks to grasp divinity by force, by eating the forbidden fruit to gain knowledge of everything, by taking human life, mating with Elohim beings, and here trying to reach into the heavens. Genesis 11:1-9 is the Series C selection for the Christian Day of Pentecost because Acts 2:1-21 provides a dramatic indication that through God's sending of the Holy Spirit the Christian gospel will be heard and understood by people of all languages. Even though people are sinful and their languages are confused, the Spirit of God makes it possible for them on the Day of Pentecost to hear about a few of the mighty acts of God.

Acts 2:1-21

This reading in Acts 2 clearly dominates the Day of Pentecost for us. It is a prime example of the Lukan playwright's inspired creativity and literary skill. Therefore, it should be the primary basis for the message on Pentecost each year. We can hardly provide a Christian Pentecost worship service without it, just as we can hardly have a Christmas Eve service without the Lukan writer's Luke 2:1-20 Christmas story.

The "tongues of fire" that are said in Acts 2:3 to have come upon the heads of the followers of Jesus are symbolic of the "tongues" or languages needed to proclaim the Good News about Jesus as the Risen Christ in Jerusalem, Judea, Samaria, and to the ends of the earth, i.e., to Rome and to people throughout the Roman Empire. The inspired Lukan playwright used fire as a visible symbol of the Holy Spirit of God. The fire is a sign that the Spirit of God is resting on the disciples of Jesus. Today we receive the same Spirit of God and are called to proclaim the mighty acts of God to all people in all languages just as the earliest disciples of Jesus were called to do.

Romans 8:14-17

As stated by the Apostle Paul, all who are led by the Spirit of God are children of God, are in a secure relationship with God, and are heirs of the blessings of God, together with Jesus perceived as the Risen Christ, suffering together with Christ and glorified together with Christ. More than that, no one of us can ask, especially on this Day of Pentecost.

John 14:8-17 (25-27)

In John 14:16-17 the Spirit of Truth is called "another Paraclete," who will be like the Johannine Jesus. Unlike the Johannine Jesus, however, the other Paraclete will be able to be with the followers of Jesus until the end of the age. The Spirit of Truth will be requested by the Johannine Jesus and sent by the Father. The Spirit of Truth will live with and within the Johannine followers of Jesus, and the Spirit of Truth will bring peace to them.

We notice that within this chapter 14 of the Fourth Gospel the Trinity perception of God as Father, God in Jesus as Son, and God as the Holy Spirit of Truth are linked together inseparably in order to assure and to comfort the Johannine followers of Jesus. As such this text provides for us a theological introduction to our observance of Trinity Sunday one week later.

SEASON AFTER PENTECOST (ORDINARY TIME) TRINITY SUNDAY (FIRST SUNDAY AFTER PENTECOST)

If we think that we must try to explain God on Trinity Sunday, it is understandable that we face this assignment with apprehension. However, if we see this as an excellent opportunity to praise God by sharing enthusiastically some of the biblical expressions of God, we will be able to enjoy the experience immensely. The texts selected for Trinity Sunday, Series C, provide some beautiful expressions of faith in God with which we can do this.

Psalm 8

One of the advantages of this psalm is that it is understandable and appealing even to the younger children and to the theologically unsophisticated. Because of this, as we use this psalm in the Trinity Sunday worship service we should simplify the vocabulary, using words such as "exalted" with "important," "majesty" with "greatness," and "adversaries" with "enemies." Then the reader should comment that the psalm is easily understood and ask the members of the congregation to close their eyes and to picture the images of the psalm with their imaginations while the psalm is read or sung. The time that it takes to prepare to present our biblical texts in innovative ways during our worship services is well spent. "One size fits all" with no variety in our presentations of biblical texts leads to monotony and boredom, apathy and non-participation. With proper preparation, we can recover much of what was lost when the oral presentation of pre-biblical material was cast into written form.

Proverbs 8:1-4, 22-31

This portion of the personification of wisdom as an attractive female *hypostasis* of God in Proverbs 8 is an excellent text for Trinity Sunday in that it demonstrates that the wisdom *hypostasis*, along with other important *hypostases* of God in Israelite thought such as the *ruach* ("spirit") of God, the *panim* ("faces") of God and the *dabar* ("word") of God were available, along with the *hochmah* ("wisdom") of God and the *shekinah* ("presence") of God in the development of the Christian doctrine of the Trinity. Apparently, elements of the *hochmah, shekinah,* and *dabar* hypostases were applied to the stories about Jesus and the sayings of Jesus by early followers of Jesus, as we see them in what we call the "Q" materials and in the Fourth Gospel particularly. These elements, along with others, were applied to Jesus perceived as the "Son" of God over a period of several centuries in the process by which Jesus after having been depicted as the "Son" of God became within our Christian formulation of the doctrine of the Trinity Jesus as "God the Son." God as the Father of Jesus in a special sense became generally for us as Christians "God the Father." The hypostasis *ruach* ("spirit") became "God the Spirit," and soon more specifically "God the Holy Spirit" to complete the Trinity. While we can know no "facts" about God, we can study, understand, and share information about how our concepts of God have been and continue to be developed.

The potential existed within the Israelite *hypostases* of God for still more complexity in our description of the nature of God. Female figures such as wisdom, or perhaps wisdom incarnate in the Virgin Mary, could have come in but were not adequately developed by the time of the fourth century. It is important for us to note that most of the early Christian Trinitarian discussions were conducted in the Greek language, in which attention was focused on the Son and on the Holy Spirit as *hypostases* of God. When the discussions were expressed in Latin within Western Christianity, the Greek word *hypostases* became *personae*. The Latin *personae* ("faces," "masks") became the English "persons" (one God in three *hypostases*, one God in three *personae*, one God in three "persons").

Especially on Trinity Sunday, we should say with confidence that we believe in *One* God, revealed to us as creative, life-giving Father, as vital, youthful Son and Savior, and as correcting, chiding, comforting, counseling Spirit in God's world for us, in God's Word for us, and in God's life for us.

Romans 5:1-5

In writing this Epistle to the Romans primarily to Gentile background followers of Jesus within their house churches in Rome during the mid-fifties of the first century, urging them to accept Jewish background followers of Jesus back into their house churches as leaders, Paul emphasized that all people sin and fall short of the glory of God. He wrote that it is not on the basis of a person's religious or cultural background or by good works — not even by trying to live in accordance with God's Word — that we have access to the grace of God. It is by faith that God has been active for our salvation now and forever in a very special way through the death of Jesus for our sins and through our belief that God has made Jesus alive again that we shall have peace in the presence of God. After a digression about boasting in the hope of sharing in the glory of God and about boasting in the problems and difficulties that we face for the sake of sharing the gospel, Paul returned to his major point that the love of God has been poured into our hearts through the Holy Spirit given by God to us.

John 16:12-15

The Johannine followers of Jesus, not having the Jesus of history accessible to them, wrote about the Spirit of Truth whom Jesus would send to lead them into all truth. The Johannine followers of Jesus claimed that they had the Spirit of Truth among them and through this Spirit of Truth Jesus continued to speak to them. The Johannine Jesus who speaks in these "farewell discourses" is the Johannine Jesus of many decades after the crucifixion. The Johannine Jesus reveals what the members of the Johannine community believed about Jesus, about the relationship between the Johannine Jesus and the Father, and between the Father and the Son and the Spirit of Truth. What we have, therefore, in the Romans 5:1-5 text and in this John 16:12-15 text are some of the biblical "raw materials" from which the Christian doctrine of the Trinity was formed.

What then shall we proclaim next Sunday? Which texts shall we use as the primary basis for our message? We realize that although we cannot comprehend or understand or explain God, we can and must share these biblical expressions about God and we must apply them to our lives in our own particular situations. We should not try to reduce the Trinity concept to more simple dimensions. We should, instead, expand the concept beyond the ways that it is usually perceived and presented. We should do this by using the rich, biblical images within the texts selected for our use on this coming Trinity Sunday. As always, we should emphasize that our Triune God is one God who is perceived in many ways and in three particular ways by us as Christians.

PROPER 4
(ORDINARY TIME 9)
SECOND SUNDAY AFTER PENTECOST

Sunday between May 29 and June 4 inclusive (if after Trinity Sunday)

In each of the texts selected here for this occasion, there is some indication that the Lord (Adonai in the Older Testament texts and God the Father and Jesus as the Christ in the Newer Testament texts) is God for all people. This will, therefore, be a message that we shall want to share through our use of these texts.

Psalm 96
Psalm 96:1-9
According to this Community Hymn of Praise, the glory of the Lord God of Israel is to be proclaimed among all nations, to all people. Unlike the false gods and idols of other people, the Lord God of Israel is said to be the one who created and sustains the heavens and the earth. All honor and majesty are to be given to the Lord God, and abundant offerings are to be given to the Lord, the King of all.

1 Kings 8:22-23, 41-43
Solomon's prayer of dedication of the temple was probably written or at least augmented considerably during the years between 970 and 540 BCE. We note particularly the theological motif of the Deuteronomic History of Israel in Its Land in 1 Kings 8:23b, "keeping your covenant and showing your steadfast love to your servants who walk before you with all their heart," and in 8:33-34 (not included in this selection), "When your people Israel are defeated by their enemy because they have sinned against you, if they turn again to you and acknowledge your name and pray and make

supplication to you in this house, then hear in heaven and forgive the sin of your people Israel and bring them again to the land that you gave to their fathers."

The writers of these traditions attempted to justify the innovative idea of a national worship center within the recently captured city of Jerusalem, where there had been no consecrating theophany. The place "that Adonai has chosen" was actually in the eyes of most of the rural Israelites not a holy place. It was merely a royal chapel at a site selected by Solomon and built by command of the new king as a focal point for Solomon's empire. There was understandably much opposition to the closing out and abandoning of the traditional local holy places and to the requirement of centralized worship.

1 Kings 18:20-21 (22-29) 30-39

The purpose of this famous story about the contest between Elijah, the only remaining prophet of the Lord God of Israel, and the 450 prophets of Baal is obviously to show that only the Lord God of Israel has awesome, unlimited power to perform a marvelous, amazing act of nature. The 450 prophets of Baal are totally powerless even when the "deck is stacked" in their favor. The story is intended to maintain the faith of those who hear it, even though in their own experience they have seen no phenomenon such as this. The story and our affirmation of faith are intended to have the same result.

Galatians 1:1-12

The Apostle Paul makes the bold claim here that because he has been commissioned by God the Father and by the Lord Jesus Christ the good news that he proclaims must not be altered or changed in any way. He appeals to God to affirm him, to God and God's Son as the only valid authority.

Unless there is an explanation for the people today about the problem between Paul and the Judaizing followers of Jesus, Paul's unwavering condemnation of the teachings of the Judaizing Christians in Galatians 1:6-9 can be misunderstood and misused today by those who wish to reject all innovation in worship and in all other aspects of life and to guarantee the status quo in every situation.

Luke 7:1-10

Apparently a traditional story about a healing by Jesus at a distance from the patient was developed differently in Matthew 8:5-13, Luke 7:1-10, and John 4:46b-54. The Lukan account is the most fully developed. Eric Franklin, *Christ the Lord: A Study in the Purpose and Theology of Luke-Acts* (Philadelphia: Westminster, 1975, pp. 77-79, 178-179), finds in the principal Lukan additions to this account (vv. 3-5), in which the centurion is described as one who loves the Jewish people and built the synagogue in Capernaum, and in the description of Cornelius in Acts 10:2 as "a devout man and one who fears God with all his household, giving alms for all of the people, and prays to God through everything," something that seems to come close to a self-portrait of the Lukan writer. In Franklin's opinion, the Lukan writer was greatly influenced by the Jewish faith (we should more precisely say by the expression of the Jewish faith in the Septuagint) and was led to see in Jesus the fulfillment of the Jewish hopes and the climax of all of God's saving actions.

In 7:3-5 and throughout the entire Luke 7:1-10 account, the emphasis is on the faith of the centurion, a faith that does not request a sign, or even a personal contact, but relies entirely on Jesus' word. The elders of the Jews are merely of tertiary importance in this text. They are made to beseech Jesus in behalf of the Gentile benefactor who according to this account has his request granted, his slave healed, and his faith lavishly praised.

The Greek phrase *en to Israel* should be translated as "among my own people," since this is the sense of the expression within the setting of the Jesus of history, and since this translation has the double advantage of reducing the anti-Jewish polemic and helping the Christian reader or hearer today to employ this text self-critically and become more personally involved.

This text, like many others in Luke, illustrates how the Lukan writer presents Jewish leaders as relatively friendly to Jesus only to find themselves humiliated in the process. For this, see Luke 14:1-24; 17:20-21, and most of all 11:37-54.

Our situation, like that of the Lukan writer, is one in which we relate to Jesus from a distance. The distance is even greater for us, since Jesus the Christ is now for us one with God the Father within the Christian doctrine of the Trinity. We relate to the Son of God by faith and we receive the grace of God, life, new life, and healing by faith. That healing comes to us in many different forms. It does not always come to us in the way that we would like for it to come. Neither did it always come in the manner in which people expected it to come within the biblical accounts. When we receive that healing, we are to thank, praise, and glorify God and Jesus our Savior.

That healing is not limited to Christians. Just as the non-Jewish Roman centurion was a beneficiary of that healing in this Luke 7:1-10 text, non-Christians can also benefit from that healing today. The text does not state that the centurion became a follower of Jesus, although perhaps that may be implied.

PROPER 5
(ORDINARY TIME 10)
THIRD SUNDAY AFTER PENTECOST

Sunday between June 5 and June 11 inclusive (if after Trinity Sunday)

The principal theme in these texts is that the Lord (Adonai in the Israelite Scriptures and Jesus as the Christ in the Newer Testament) renews life. There is a progression in the texts from lifting up those who are bowed down in Psalm 146 to healing those who are at the point of death in Psalm 30 and 1 Kings 17:17-24 to bringing back to life a young man who was being carried out of a city to be buried in Luke 7:11-17. The Galatians 1:11-24 reading may seem to stand outside this theme, unless we articulate "the gospel that Paul proclaimed" (Galatians 1:11) as the good news that God raised Jesus from the dead and will also raise us from the dead.

Psalm 146

It is wise to put one's trust in the Lord God of Jacob, who created and sustains the universe and provides justice for the oppressed and food for those who are hungry, who lifts up those who are bowed down, and opens the eyes of the blind. It is not wise to trust in the political leaders of this world, who are mortal and transient. Not they, but the Lord God maintains and renews life.

Psalm 30

This beautiful Individual Hymn of Praise glorifies the Lord God for bringing the *nephesh* (the life, the animating principle) of the psalmist back from *sheol* (the abode of the dead). In its original setting, this psalm acclaims Adonai for providing a resuscitation, not a resurrection. The restorations to life proclaimed in this psalm and in the Elijah and Elisha stories (1 Kings 17:8-16, [17-24] used here with this text and in 2 Kings 4:8-37) are manifestations of the power and of the love shown by Adonai. They are intended to encourage people to respond to Adonai with praise and thanksgiving.

1 Kings 17:8-16 (17-24)

For the complete picture of this account, the reading should begin with 1 Kings 17:1 and continue to the conclusion of the chapter.

We should note that the power to renew life in the young man in this text comes from the Lord (Adonai). The power is not inherent in Elijah. Also, what Elijah prays for and receives is that the *nephesh* (the life, the animating principle of life) return to the young man. What is said to have left and then to have returned here is the same word (*nephesh*) used in Psalm 30. A person who has lost one's *nephesh* shows no signs of life. A person is still a person without one's *nephesh*, but without one's *nephesh* a person can do nothing.

The primary purpose of 1 Kings 17:8-16 (17-24) apparently is to demonstrate that the power of Adonai was active in Elijah. Elijah was obviously a man of God, divinely inspired and empowered.

Luke 7:11-17

This account is another excellent example of how the inspired Lukan writer used the Septuagint translation of the Hebrew Bible to move beyond Mark's account. In this instance, the event is Jesus' raising the daughter of Jairus who had just died and returning her alive to her grateful parents.

There are differences, of course, between the stories about the power of Elijah and the power of Jesus perceived as the Christ. Within the stories about Jesus as the Christ there is no necessity for Jesus to pray to God for the power to restore life. Jesus as the Christ is represented as inherently having the power and authority of God to be able to restore life. Jesus as the Christ in the Newer Testament is presented as similar to Elijah and to Elisha, but vastly superior to them. For us as Christians, God acts in a unique way in and through Jesus perceived as the Christ.

Galatians 1:11-24

Within the heat of controversy with other early developing Christians over the lifestyle appropriate for non-Jewish background followers of Jesus, the Apostle Paul claimed that the gospel that he was proclaiming came to him through a revelation of Jesus the Christ. Paul's concern was that the gospel from Jesus Christ and about Jesus Christ be accepted by as many people as possible. Paul wanted no lifestyle hindrances to get in the way of people accepting the grace and forgiveness of God, just as for us today no lifestyle hindrances should be permitted to get in the way of people accepting the grace and forgiveness of God. The good news that God has raised Jesus from the dead and will restore and renew life for all who will accept the grace of God through Jesus Christ is the climax of the series of texts selected for our use on this occasion. It should be the climax also of the good news that we proclaim.

PROPER 6
(ORDINARY TIME 11)
FOURTH SUNDAY AFTER PENTECOST

Sunday between June 12 and June 18 inclusive (if after Trinity Sunday)

According to these texts, the greatest need of people and the greatest gift of God are the same — *the grace of God.* The writer of Psalm 5 asks for the help and grace of God and in faith expects to receive it. Psalm 32 emphasizes the importance of confessing to God every type of sin. As each type of sin is acknowledged, God gives God's grace and the sinner is forgiven. The guilt that follows the sin is taken away. In the story about Naboth and his vineyard in 1 Kings 21, even though the grace of God is not expressed, there is great need for the gift of God's grace for all involved: for Naboth who had been murdered, for King Ahab and for his wicked Queen Jezebel who had arranged for the murder of Naboth, and for Elijah the prophet, who had the onerous task of confronting the king. In the 2 Samuel readings for this occasion, through the skillful use of a parable the terrible injustice of David's sin with Bathsheba was expressed to King David and David had declared his own death warrant to Nathan the prophet. King David desperately needed grace and forgiveness from God, and Nathan announced that grace. According to Paul in Galatians 2:15-21, the grace of God is experienced when Christ lives in us and in faith we respond. Finally, in Luke 7:36—8:3 the grace of God is extended to an openly sinful woman who expressed her love and affection for Jesus. All of these people were in need of the grace and forgiveness of God, and whenever they were repentant and receptive, God's grace was extended to them. The guilt of their sins was taken from them, although the destructive results of their sins remained.

Psalm 5:1-8

The psalmist speaks as a person in trouble and distress, yet with the assurance that if the psalmist turns to the Lord God and bows down in humble adoration of God in the temple of God, the psalmist will be delivered from those who want to harm the psalmist. It would be helpful to include the concluding verses 11-12 in the reading so that the call of the psalmist to God in behalf of others who are in need of the grace and protection of God would be included.

Psalm 32

Within the beatitudes of Psalm 32:1-2 and again in verse 5 the three most important words for sin in biblical Hebrew are used. In the sequence of the use of these three words in 32:5 there is an increase in the seriousness of the type of sin from word to word. First, the psalmist acknowledged failure to please God in spite of the psalmist's best efforts. Then the psalmist admitted that the psalmist had broken the rules that God had established. Finally, the psalmist confessed the most serious sin of all, the psalmist's attempted insurrection against God.

As is typical in Israelite Individual Hymns of Praise, Psalm 32 is an attempt to teach all who will hear the wisdom of acknowledging one's sins to the Lord. The greatest need of people and the greatest gift of God are brought together in God's grace here as in many other texts in the Israelite Scriptures. For more about this, see Ronald M. Hals, *Grace and Faith in the Old Testament* (Minneapolis: Augsburg, 1980).

1 Kings 21:1-10 (11-14) 15-21a

As we ponder this text, we may wonder whether perhaps Naboth should have taken the offer of the king to provide a better vineyard in exchange for Naboth's vineyard that was adjacent to the king's palace. We occasionally have somewhat similar issues of the so-called governmental "right of eminent domain." There was no evidence in the story, however, that the property taken would be used for "the public good." There is, of course, also the important factor of Naboth's vineyard being Naboth's ancestral inheritance.

We fully realize as we read this text that King Ahab should not have been so covetous of Naboth's vineyard that he would mope in bed and would not eat. Most of all, we know that Queen Jezebel should not have arranged for the murder of Naboth just so that her husband would be happy and productive again. One could hardly make the case that her action was justified because of her love for her husband and her desire to make him happy. At any rate, the tragedy of the story would not have occurred had any one of the three, Naboth, Ahab, or Jezebel, responded differently. All were in need of God's grace.

2 Samuel 11:26—12:10, 13-15

After the parable used by Nathan the prophet demonstrated to David the enormity of David's sin with Bathsheba, David admitted that he had sinned also against the Lord. Although we might think that Nathan was too quick to announce the grace of God and that the Lord was overly lenient in sparing the life of David, we see that the first child of David and Bathsheba will die and that what David had thought that he was doing privately was to be known throughout Israel.

This story also indicates that the grace of God does not undo the damage that has been done when we have sinned. Uriah the Hittite was not brought back to life, and David's reputation and respect was permanently sullied.

Galatians 2:15-21

The most important portion of this text is obviously 2:16 and 19-21 where the emphasis is on the grace of God experienced when God lives in us and in faith we respond to God.

We see in these texts that faith is best described as our grateful response to the grace of God, both in the Hebrew Bible and in our Newer Testament.

Luke 7:36—8:3

In this text, as in most of the others appointed for this occasion, the emphasis is on the grace of God. In this Lukan composition, the grace of God is extended to a woman who has been openly and blatantly sinful, but expresses her love and affection for Jesus.

This text should be compared carefully with its parallel accounts in Mark 14:3-9, Matthew 26:6-13, and John 12:1-8. Although many commentators think that these accounts record two or three separate incidents (for example, I. Howard Marshall, *The Gospel of Luke* [Grand Rapids: Eerdmans, 1978, pp. 304-314]), it seems much more probable in view of the Lukan writer's stated purpose in Luke 1:1-4 and from a detailed comparison of these four texts that as John Drury in *The Gospel of Luke* (New York: Macmillan, 1973, pp. 87-88), suggests, the Lukan writer took a story from Mark, lifted it from the end of Jesus' ministry to the middle, and changed and amplified the story so brilliantly that Luke's redacted version is the one that most people remember. Comparison of texts such as these indicates how freely the writers of the Four Gospels adapted the stories about Jesus to suit their purposes in their particular situations, not unlike the ways in which we adapt and use biblical texts in our preaching situations today. (It reminds us also of how Richard A. Clarke in *Your Government Failed You: Breaking the Cycle of National Security Disasters* [New York: Harper, 2008] explains that analysts of security data in our governmental agencies often modify their reports in order to be supportive of the policies and wishes of top level policy makers.)

The Lukan writer apparently wished to heighten the act of grace and accomplished this in part by making the woman depicted in Mark 14:3-9 into "a woman who was a sinner" in Luke 7:36-50. Conceivably she may simply have been among the non-religious *am-ha-aretz* (ordinary people of the land), but the Lukan playwright in Luke 7:39 depicted her as a courtesan.

The alternative to the suggestion that the writers of the Four Gospels freely adapted the materials that were available to them in written and oral sources is to conclude that various women, some of whom were engaged in "questionable service" occupations, showered their affection on the Jesus of history. Perhaps most of us would be more comfortable with the idea that the Lukan playwright heightened the act of grace by changing the occupation and identity of the woman of Mark's account.

Only the Lukan writer staged the incident in the house of a Pharisee, setting up the Pharisee in order that the Pharisee might be knocked down and disparaged. This account, therefore, should be compared in this respect to Luke 11:37-41, where Luke even more thoroughly redacted Markan material and produced an account in which Jesus responded to a meal invitation extended by a Pharisee and then engaged his host in direct, abusive condemnation. In our Luke 7:36-50 text the Pharisee is treated less harshly, but nevertheless he is embarrassed in the presence of his friends. More important than anti-Jewish polemic in Luke 7:36-50, however, was the emphasis the Lukan writer placed on the forgiveness of sins, the woman's love, and the role and identity of Jesus as the one who shared and demonstrated the amazing grace of God.

PROPER 7
(ORDINARY TIME 12)
FIFTH SUNDAY AFTER PENTECOST

Sunday between June 19 and 25 inclusive (if after Trinity Sunday)

Perhaps the closest we can come to identifying a unifying theme within this series of texts is to see that in each of them there is either an expectation of a new revelation from God or a declaration of it. In each instance, the new revelation will be redemptive.

Psalm 42 and 43

These two psalms are linked together in this selection because they appear actually to be one psalm. The beautiful poetic expression of desire for a revelation and redemption from God with which Psalm 42 begins endears this psalm to each of us. We long for redemption from God just as a deer searches for flowing streams of fresh water to drink. We too seek to come to God and to be strengthened and refreshed as we as Christian people worship the Lord God.

Psalm 22:19-28

The psalmist expects a revelation of God's saving grace and receives it. With this assurance, the psalmist calls upon the congregation and then all of the families of the nations to worship the Lord God. Even those who are in their graves will bow down to the Lord, and in the future the revelation of deliverance from God shall be proclaimed even to newly born babies.

1 Kings 19:1-4 (5-7) 8-15a

When Elijah flees in despair from the threats of Queen Jezebel and asks God to take his life, God reveals God's self to him at Mount Horeb. The revelation comes not in the mighty gusting wind, nor in the earthquake, nor in the burning fire, but in the awesome silence that follows these powerful displays of force in nature. During the silence nothing will hinder or compete with the revelation of God. The great commission revealed to Elijah surprisingly is not included in this selection. That will be given in the continued reading assigned to the following weekend service.

Isaiah 65:1-9

Here God is said to have revealed God's self even when the People of God had not asked for it. Even though the punishment of God has come upon the rebellious people, a remnant will be saved. How is this applicable also in our lives, especially within the Church?

Galatians 3:23-29

We continue to be amazed Paul wrote that the Torah was our babysitter until the time when faith in Jesus as the Messiah would be possible, particularly when we recognize that what he was referring to as the Torah was the most significant portion of the written Word of God, the Bible as Paul knew it! Although some of the later Pauline editors, redactors, and writers were what we today know as biblical literalists (the writer of 1 Timothy 2:11-15, for example), Paul himself was far from that. Paul went even farther in stating in 2 Corinthians 3:6 that the written Word (the Bible as he knew it) kills, but the Spirit of God gives life. In addition, he wrote in Romans 7:6 that we serve not under the old written Word (the Bible as Paul knew it) but under the new revelation of the Spirit of God.

Apparently Paul was much more radical in his views about Scripture and new revelation than we and most people within the Church today have realized. Paul proclaimed something that he recognized to be new, a revelation of Jesus as the Christ far more powerful than the Bible of that time. In that new revelation there were to be no distinctions between those who were of Jewish background as opposed to those who were not of Jewish background, between slaves and those who were not slaves, and between men and women. Through faith in Jesus Christ his hearers were all to be considered to be People of God, with no one to claim to be or to be acclaimed to be superior to any other person.

What are our responsibilities today in light of this? Certainly we should not claim a revelation of Christ more powerful than that written within the Newer Testament, although perhaps at times we must claim a revelation of Christ that is equal to something that is within the biblical account and stand in judgment over it just as it stands in judgment over us. We do this through interpretation, through sensitive translations, and through selective usage of texts, just as Christians have done throughout the history of the Church. If we think that we and others throughout the history of the Church have not done this and that we should not do this, we are deluding ourselves. Even the most rigid biblical literalists among us do some of this. It is through these means that the Word of God remains living, active, and dynamic, as the Spirit of God guides us and continues to reveal the will of God to us.

Luke 8:26-39

This text and its Synoptic parallels are exceedingly interesting in terms of the developing Christology of the early followers of Jesus and in terms of the theology of the cross. We note that Mark has the great Christological confession of faith occur in the area of the villages of Caesarea Philippi, perhaps one of the areas in which members of the Markan community were awaiting the parousia of Jesus during the first years of the Jewish revolt, in 66-67 CE. The Matthean redactors retained this geographical reference, but the Lukan writer dropped it. In most other respects, the Lukan writer followed the Markan account closely in this text, except for not using Jesus' rebuke of Peter, Jesus' labeling Peter as a representative of Satan.

We can now say that the Jesus of history was probably acclaimed as a *Jewish* Messiah by many of the Jews who followed and identified with him, because he was providing a message and an example of hope to his oppressed fellow Jewish people. It was as a *Jewish* Messiah (Jesus of Nazareth, King of the Jews) that he was crucified by the Romans, not as a *Christian* Messiah. He became *the Christian* Messiah only gradually as a new and separate Christian religion was developed. Perceived as the Risen Christ, he could not be *the Christian* Messiah until there was a Christian community of faith, and he will be *the Christian* Messiah as long as there will be a Christian community of faith.

As Christians, we are called to follow and to worship Jesus as *the Christian* Messiah. That means taking up our cross (giving hope to our fellow oppressed people of our time, just as the Jesus of history did during his time) and, if necessary, losing our life for his sake. Galatians 3:23-29 and Luke 8:26-39 are radical texts. Let us proclaim them as radicals today!

PROPER 8
(ORDINARY TIME 13)
SIXTH SUNDAY AFTER PENTECOST

Sunday between June 26 and July 2 inclusive

The emphasis in these texts on trusting in the Lord (Adonai in Psalm 16 and in Psalm 77 and Jesus as the Christ in Luke 9:51-62) is appropriate for this occasion, near our annual celebration of the anniversary of the Declaration of Independence in the USA. Also useful in this connection is the article by Hans Walter Wolff, "Swords into Plowshares — Misuse of a Word of Prophecy?" (*Currents in Theology and Mission* 12:3, June, 1985, pp. 133-147).

Psalm 16

It is likely that this psalm was selected for this occasion because of its emphasis on trust in Adonai, which may be compared to the emphasis in Luke 9:51-62 on trust in Jesus as the Christ. Just as the psalmist warns against the folly of choosing a god other than Adonai, so also the Lukan writer's Jesus announces that following the Lukan Jesus in the proclamation of the kingdom of God takes precedence over all other responsibilities. The psalmist and the Lukan Jesus differ, however, in that the psalmist enjoys security and happiness within this life but the Lukan Jesus calls people to follow him in a very difficult itinerant ministry of proclamation of the kingdom of God in a very insecure setting of economic and political oppression, a proclamation that is correctly perceived by the Roman oppressors to be a political as well as religious alternative to Roman rule. The psalmist describes a religion that is individual, or at most national, within a henotheistic situation. The Lukan Jesus speaks about a religion that seeks universalistic application, but makes exclusivistic theological claims, and requires priority over all other responsibilities, even within one's own family.

Psalm 77:1-2, 11-20

In deep despair the psalmist cries aloud to the Lord God in the night, to God who seems to have forgotten to be gracious to the suffering psalmist. Then the psalmist recalls the saving acts of God in redeeming the pre-Israelites from slavery in Egypt, leading and guiding them through the waters of the sea. By reflecting over the saving events of the past, the psalmist's trust in the Lord God is restored.

1 Kings 19:15-16, 19-21

First Kings 19:15-16, 19-21 is undoubtedly paired with Luke 9:51-62 in part at least because of the similarity and contrast between Elijah's granting Elisha's request to kiss his mother and his father good-bye and the Lukan Jesus' rejection of the man in Luke 9:51-62 who wanted to say good-bye to his family. Only Luke among the Gospel accounts makes so radical a demand.

This 1 Kings text is a prime example within the Hebrew Bible of the call of the Israelite prophets to speak and act within the political realm, even within the realm of international politics, in the name of the Lord. Elijah is ordered and commissioned by the Lord God to anoint a new king, Hazael, as king in Aram (Syria), a foreign power, and Jehu as king over Israel, his own nation. Jehu will replace the dynasty of Omri and cleanse Israel of the worship of Baal.

2 Kings 2:1-2, 6-14

This dramatic account of the ascension of Elijah into heaven within a whirlwind and in a chariot of fire pulled by horses burning with fire is vivid and spectacular, more impressive than the account in Deuteronomy 34 of the death and burial of Moses and the depiction by the Lukan playwright in Acts 1:6-11 of Jesus being take up into heaven by a cloud. It gave to Elijah an aura of deathlessness, of a person who might somehow return, a person of interest both to Jews and to Christians. Even today during the Seder Jews set a place for Elijah and have a child go to the door to welcome the prophet to a place at their table.

Galatians 5:1, 13-25
Here, as in other Galatians texts and in 2 Corinthians 3:6 and Romans 7:6 (as indicated more fully in the comments on Galatians 3:23-29 for the previous Sunday) Paul contrasts the Torah — the Bible as Paul knew it — with the new life in the Spirit of God and of Jesus perceived as the Christ that Paul claimed and proclaimed. Following the Septuagint, in which the Hebrew word *Torah* was expressed with the Greek word *Nomos*, which in turn has often been translated into English as "Law," many of us have often assumed that Jews have been and are characteristically preoccupied with legalism, while we in the Church stress our freedom through the grace of God. As a result, we neither recognize how radical Paul was in his criticism of the Bible as he knew it, nor do we permit ourselves to be as open to the Spirit of God and of Christ in our times as Paul was in his. If we would dare to do either one or both of these, our homilies and sermons would become much more interesting to us, as well as to the people who are with us. Almost always, however, we prefer to remain "priests" rather than to become "prophets" of the Lord.

Luke 9:51-62
Study of the other Synoptic texts that are closely related to Luke 9:51-62 indicates how freely the inspired Lukan writer composed this account about Jesus heading toward Jerusalem from materials within Mark, "Q" materials and/or

an early draft of Matthew, and the Septuagint. The result is a thoroughly *theological* account. With this text, the Lukan writer has the Lukan Jesus begin his theological journey to Jerusalem. The Lukan writer composed some theological statements about the Samaritans (only in vv. 52-56). Luke expanded upon the "Q" or Matthean Jesus' harsh and un-Jewish demand that a disciple follow him immediately and "leave the dead (here intended to be the Jews who do not accept Jesus as the Christian Messiah) to bury their own dead."

Here, as elsewhere, the Lukan writer was willing to present Jesus as inhumane and un-Jewish in order to express what the Lukan writer wanted to express theologically. Can we communicate the urgency of our task next Sunday and express ourselves theologically through a Jesus who is more historical than the Jesus of this portion of Luke's Gospel, a Jesus who takes his message of hope to the city of Jerusalem, and through us to our own city, town, or rural area? We can if we will be open to the Spirit of God and of Christ as the Apostle Paul was.

PROPER 9
(ORDINARY TIME 14)
SEVENTH SUNDAY AFTER PENTECOST

Sunday between July 3 and July 9 inclusive

Psalm 30

This beautiful Individual Hymn of Praise (considered also in Proper 5 above) glorifies the Lord God for bringing the *nephesh* (the life, the animating principle) of the psalmist back from *sheol* (the abode of the dead). In its original setting, this psalm acclaims Adonai for providing a resuscitation of a life that has lost all of its spirit and all of its power, like a rubber tire that is flat, not a resurrection from death to life in which there was no longer a tire at all. The restoration to life proclaimed in this psalm is a manifestation of the power and of the love shown by Adonai. It is intended to encourage people to respond to Adonai with praise and thanksgiving.

Psalm 66:1-9

As in many other texts within the Hebrew Bible, here also God is praised for delivering the ancient Israelites from their Egyptian oppressors by parting the sea so that the escaping Israelites could pass through it on dry land. The Exodus is remembered as one among many instances in which God is said to have used God's power to keep the enemies of the Israelites away from Israel's borders, to prevent other nations from oppressing them.

2 Kings 5:1-14

The prayer of Naaman to the Lord God of Israel was persistent not in the sense that the one who was asking for help from the Lord asked repeatedly over a long period of time, but in the sense that so many different people persisted in the prayer process in Naaman's behalf. The process was begun by the little Israelite slave girl in this story, and continued with Naaman himself, Naaman's king, Elisha, and Naaman's servants.

For the original intent of the story, we should study the entire chapter (2 Kings 5:1-27). If we read only the first half of the story, we should focus our attention on Naaman's desire to be healed and on the persistence of the various people involved. We see that the chain of action would have been broken if any one of the characters involved had not participated in the prayer sequence. This provides an excellent resource for us to consider in our own prayer activities and in our messages about prayers to God this coming weekend.

Isaiah 66:10-14

Although Jerusalem is not fruitful now, the Lord will cause her again to bring forth children and to provide for them abundantly as a nursing mother, not only for her new babies but for her older children as well. The indignation of the Lord is against the enemies of the people of the Lord. Their enemies shall no longer oppress the servants of the Lord.

Galatians 6:(1-6) 7-16

The guidelines for life that are appropriate for followers of Jesus that were provided earlier in this letter are continued in chapter 6. In order that 6:5 may not seem to contradict 6:2, they should be translated carefully in order to distinguish them and their different situations from each other. We might suggest "Be helpful to one another" in 6:2 and "For each person will be responsible individually" in 6:5.

It is possible that the Judaizing Christians were circumcising male non-Jewish background followers of Jesus and insisting that they be circumcised, in part at least, so that they would be afforded the same limited protection that was available to Jewish males by the Roman oppressors at various times during the first century. This may be what Paul meant when he wrote "in order that they may not be persecuted for the cross of Christ" (v. 12). We have within Paul's letter to the Galatians and elsewhere in Paul's letters only Paul's side of the issue. We have nothing comparable in the Newer Testament texts in which the rationale of the Judaizing Christians is presented. Paul apparently wanted to die as Jesus had died, if necessary, at the hands of the Roman oppressors, to be united with Jesus in his death, in order that Paul might be glorified with Jesus in the cross and in the resurrection from the dead. For Paul, God definitely identified God's self with Jesus and with the followers of Jesus who were oppressed as Jesus had been oppressed.

Luke 10:1-11, 16-20

Comparison of the Synoptic texts indicates that the Lukan writer here as elsewhere used materials from Mark (the Mark 6:7-13 sending of the twelve disciples two-by-two with authority over the unclean spirits), from "Q" material or from an early draft of Matthew (for most of the content of this text) and from the Septuagint translation of the Israelite Scriptures (Numbers 11:16-17 for the number of those who would extend Jesus' work just as the seventy had become assistants to Moses). The number seventy, or 72 as some important early manuscripts of the Greek text of Luke 10 have it, is used here only by Luke. The dependence of the Lukan writer on the Septuagint translation of the Israelite Scriptures for material to be used with inspired creativity throughout this Third Gospel suggests that "seventy" was the number that the Lukan writer used and that some who later made copies of the Luke 10 text modified the number to 72.

As the literary creativity of the inspired Lukan writer becomes more apparent to us, the likelihood increases that the

"Q" materials or Matthean material and the Lukan composition actually depict circumstances not prior to but *after* the death of Jesus. It was after the death of Jesus that followers of Jesus proclaiming their message within the regions of Galilee about Jesus as the *Christian* Messiah who is one with God the Father and the Son of God felt that they were going out "as lambs in the midst of wolves" with little success. Their situation was considerably different from that of the proclamation of the Jesus of history as a *Jewish* Messiah figure talking about God and the coming rule of God, giving hope to the oppressed Jewish people in Galilee *before* Jesus was crucified.

The expressions of power over demons and of the fall of Satan from his position of authority may be subtle cryptograms, hidden transcripts of hope and liberation in Luke 10:17-20. As such, they would be communicating assurance to oppressed followers of Jesus that through Jesus raised from the dead as the Risen Christ they are given power by God over the Satanic Roman state and its representatives whom God through Jesus as the Christ will soon topple from their positions of authority forever.

This Luke 10:1-11, 16-20 text is permeated by a sense of urgency. The message of the coming rule of God must be proclaimed in spite of all dangers. Apparently the Jesus of history had pointed very effectively to the Lord God and to the necessity of acclaiming the Lord God and not Caesar as the one who should be the ruler in the lives of the people around him. Just as followers of Jesus pointed to Jesus the Risen Christ as the one who had himself pointed to the Lord God and to the necessity of acclaiming the Lord God rather than Caesar as the one who should rule in the lives of the people around them, so let us also acclaim Jesus as the Risen Christ and God this coming weekend and every day.

It is a challenge for us to find ways in which we can apply these texts selected for our use on Proper 9/Ordinary Time

14/Seventh Sunday after Pentecost to the concerns of people in the congregations in which we live and serve, many of whom will expect references to the Fourth of July within our Christian worship services this coming weekend. Our biblical texts, including the texts selected for our use this coming weekend, express the mercy of God for the oppressed and the opposition of God to the oppressors, whether they be Canaanite, Egyptian, Assyrian, Babylonian, Persian, Greek, Roman, or within the Israelite or early Christian power structures. If we make applications this coming weekend from these biblical texts to the Fourth of July and to American history and to American Civil Religion, we must be critical of and oppose oppression wherever it occurs, even within our own Church, nation, and culture. We must remember that in the biblical texts it is the Lord God, not any nation or secular power, including our own, who is Supreme.

PROPER 10
(ORDINARY TIME 15)
EIGHTH SUNDAY AFTER PENTECOST

Sunday between July 10 and July 16 inclusive

Within most of the texts selected for us for this occasion there is a stimulating tension between the importance of adequate faith and right living as prerequisites for "salvation." This stimulating tension exists regardless of whether "salvation" is perceived primarily in terms of life as we know it here and now with security, prosperity, and happiness for one's self and for one's family as in Psalm 25 and Deuteronomy 30, or whether "salvation" includes also the dimension of eternal life, as it does in the Newer Testament texts Colossians 1:1-14 and Luke 10:25-37.

Although the concept of salvation took on the added dimension of a future hope beyond this life as we know it during the course of theological development of the People of God, salvation in most of our biblical texts is perceived to be by the grace of God rather than by our own efforts. Our response to the grace of God is depicted as important, however. Adequate faithfulness to God is itself presented as a gift from God, as is our ability to achieve and to maintain right living.

If our proclamation this coming weekend is to be based on these selected texts, we shall want to share with the people in our congregations something about this stimulating tension between the importance of adequate faith and of right living for our salvation as expressed in these texts, without failing to emphasize that salvation, however perceived, is by the grace of God. The emphasis on "faith alone" may have been needed as a corrective in the theology and practice of the Western Church during the sixteenth century, but it should never be proclaimed apart from the related concept of "grace alone." To proclaim faith apart from the related concept of the grace of God is to misuse Scripture by arbitrarily selecting certain portions of the Scriptures and downgrading other portions, losing sight of the stimulating tension between the importance of adequate faith and right living in the process. Neither should we pass too quickly to the concepts of God's love and of our love in response to God and lose sight of this biblical tension.

This biblical tension is essential in our mission among people. Many of the people who will be hearing our proclamation this coming weekend have wondered and are wondering about this tension between adequate faith and right living and perhaps about what and where the grace of God is in all of this. Most people, other than pastors, put a heavy emphasis upon right living to ensure salvation, while many, perhaps most, pastors stress adequate faith, with both frequently tending to forget the overriding importance of the grace of God.

Psalm 25:1-10

Since the Lord (Adonai) is the God of the psalmist's salvation (v. 2), the psalmist asks for guidance from the Lord regarding the lifestyle that will be most pleasing to the Lord (vv. 4-5, 8-9). At the same time, the psalmist declares complete trust in the Lord (vv. 1-2, 5-6, 8), and recognizes that salvation can come only through the mercy, love, and grace of the Lord, not by the efforts of the psalmist (vv. 3, 5b-7). We note that the understanding shared by the Apostle Paul in his letters that are included in our Newer Testament is very similar to what is written in this psalm.

Deuteronomy 30:9-14

This text is near the conclusion of the great, composite "sermon of Moses" building block of the Deuteronomic History that extends from Deuteronomy 4:44—30:20. If we look at the context, we see that the loss of the Israelite nation and the scattering of the Israelite people are known. Hope is expressed that the Lord will restore the people in their land and provide for them even greater prosperity than their ancestors enjoyed. The commandments of the Lord are depicted as a gift of God's grace in an accessible form that will help the restored people to live as their ancestors should have lived. The commandments that the Lord provides have been placed into the hearts of the people, and it is said that the people will enjoy living in accordance with them.

Psalm 82

According to this psalm, the evil that God will soon judge and destroy is the evil of those "gods" whose followers on the earth oppress the weak and the fatherless. Then God (as perceived by the Israelites), who is already far superior to those other "gods," will be supreme and unopposed, and God's oppressed people will be rescued, free to serve God with no impediments.

Amos 7:7-17

Through the words of Amos, a herdsman and worker among sycamore trees, called to be a prophet of the Lord God with a message of condemnation for the king, priests, and others in the Northern Kingdom Israel who were oppressing the poor people of that land economically and politically, God speaks to warn the oppressors about the judgment of the Lord God against them.

This message is consistent with the message of Psalm 82. The oppressive people whose lives were characterized by neither adequate faith in God nor right living are condemned by the prophet of God as directed by God.

Colossians 1:1-14

The Pauline writer puts considerable emphasis in this text on the importance of good deeds to please the Lord (v. 10), without losing sight of adequate faith in God through the Christian Messiah Jesus and the love for all of God's people (v. 4). It is only by the grace of the Father, however, that we are qualified to share in the inheritance of the saints in light, in the kingdom of God's beloved Son (vv. 12-13).

Luke 10:25-37

This Lukan Parable of the Good Samaritan indicates quite clearly that adequate faith alone is not sufficient, since both the priest and the Levite obviously had adequate faith. Where both the priest and the Levite are shown to be lacking in this parable is in the area of right living. It was their responsibility as people who had faith in God to risk their lives, if necessary, to live right by helping the man who had been severely attacked and injured. This they both failed to do, even though they were both people of faith.

The Samaritan is praised in this parable because he demonstrated both faith that God would protect him while he came to the aid of the helpless man and actions that were right for a person who has faith. Therefore, he is praised.

If we limit our proclamation here to a warmed-over rerun of our old, used Good Samaritan sermons, it is likely that we shall provide only a right living emphasis. If we share, however, the stimulating, creative tension between adequate faith and right living that is demonstrated in this and in the other texts selected for us for this occasion, we shall help the people who hear us to grow in their faith as well as in their maturity and ethics, as they reflect theologically over their own lives.

PROPER 11
(ORDINARY TIME 16)
NINTH SUNDAY AFTER PENTECOST

Sunday between July 17 and July 23 inclusive

The stimulating tension between the importance of adequate faith and right living continues from last Sunday. The selections are different, but in these texts also "salvation" is possible only because of the grace of God. Adequate faith and right living are basic essentials expected of the People of God, even though apart from the grace of God these essentials would not produce salvation.

As we move through these texts, we find that in the Lukan characterization of Mary in Luke 10:38-42 the tension between adequate faith and right living is resolved. By sitting near the feet of Jesus and listening to him, she expresses her faith in God, she lives her life right in the sight of God, and she receives the grace of God. She put herself in a position to receive the grace of God. For this she was praised. Because Mary had chosen the good portion that shall not be taken away from her, she is an excellent model for us.

Psalm 52

The person addressed in 52:1-5 has neither adequate faith nor right living and is not receptive to the grace of God. Instead, this person is oppressive to the poor and trusts not in God but in excessive wealth. It is said that God will uproot this person (as a tree is toppled by a storm or a weed is pulled up from among a crop in a garden).

The psalmist, by contrast, in a song of thanksgiving (vv. 6-9), trusts in the unwavering love of God, proclaims the name of God to all who will hear, and gives thanks to God in the house of God. By the grace of God, the psalmist receives the grace of God.

Amos 8:1-12

There is no more incisive prophetic word than this in any of the world's great religious literatures, or one *mutatis mutandis* more applicable to our own or to any other human situation. The specific setting within eighth century BCE Israel and Judah is apparent in this text, but the prophetic word of judgment should be applied boldly to our own situation. The firm demand for justice and God's concern for those who are economically oppressed in this text address our own situation in the United States of greed by many among those who are excessively wealthy and the difficulty of finding the most appropriate ways to make adequate health care available to every person.

Psalm 15

The ancient Israelite cult used this type of Entrance-to-Worship-in-the-Temple psalm to emphasize the importance of right living. Those who would live their lives as depicted in this psalm would have a secure reputation and position in the community. Those who do what is right shall be honored in the temple of the Lord and will be receptive to the grace of God. In this psalm, doing what is right is fully elaborated; having an adequate faith is implied rather than expressed. It is implied that the person who does what is right will also have adequate faith in the Lord.

Genesis 18:1-10a

In this account also, the emphasis is on doing what is right. Abraham does everything in accordance with the best ancient Near Easter hospitality when the Lord appeared to him in the form of the three men. In this account, as in Psalm 15, adequate faith is implied rather than expressed. Abraham is presented as totally receptive to the grace of God. His wife Sarah, however, appears to be skeptical. She had not received evidence of the grace of God during her childbearing years, and as a result she did not anticipate that she could possibly be blessed by a pregnancy now in her old age. The text makes the point, nevertheless, that in spite of her understandably inadequate faith, the grace of God will come to her. The grace of God will be marvelous for her and for Abraham; it will be miraculous. Israel, the People of God, is a marvelous miracle in this text, a special act of God's grace, for through this child to be born, through Isaac, Jacob (Israel) the son of Isaac, will be given life.

Colossians 1:15-28

The grace of God is presented as somewhat provisional in this text, somewhat conditional, contingent on the continuation of an adequate faith, a faith that is firm and unwavering. The writer speaks about Paul's experiences as being in some sense complementary to the sufferings of Jesus as the Christ. Right living, along with an adequate faith, is therefore considered to be of great importance here. This is one of the most significant ways in which the writer of this "Epistle to the Colossians" differed from Paul himself, even though the person wrote in Paul's name. Most of the people who will hear the messages that we shall proclaim next weekend would probably agree with the writer of this Epistle that the grace of God comes to us somewhat provisionally, contingent on our having an adequate faith and on our demonstration of right living. Nevertheless, the gospel of God's unmerited grace is obscured by this kind of thinking.

It would be appropriate to point out in our messages next Sunday that the writer of the Epistle to the Colossians did not maintain Paul's emphasis on salvation by the grace of God alone, what Martin Luther found to be so meaningful and depicted in Latin as *sola gratia*. We have the responsibility to maintain the emphasis of the Apostle Paul on salvation by the grace of God alone, without failing at the same time to emphasize the importance of a lived faith (*gelebte Glaube*).

Luke 10:38-42

In this story, Martha, the good hostess who had invited Jesus to be a very special guest in the house of Martha and Mary, is depicted as doing everything that she can possibly do to make Jesus feel welcome and comfortable. It is not surprising that she is said to have resented her sister Mary's failure to work with her in her tasks as an outstanding hostess for such an important guest. When we look at this text as it is used here in conjunction with Genesis 18:1-10a, we see that, although hospitality extended to the Lord (to Adonai in Genesis and to Jesus in Luke) is good, receptivity of the message of the Lord is far better than such a great concern for hospitality. It is that better activity of receptivity that should receive our greatest attention during our consideration of these texts. To "sit at the feet of Jesus," to "listen to him constantly and with our full attention," is to express our faith, to live right, and to be receptive to the grace of God. In the final analysis, it is not what we do but what God does that is of the most importance. Let us, therefore, be open and receptive to what God does in this world and in all of our lives. This is to be our proper response to the Luke 10:38-42 Jesus with Mary and Martha text.

PROPER 12
(ORDINARY TIME 17)
TENTH SUNDAY AFTER PENTECOST

Sunday between July 24 and July 30 inclusive

The worship services and the messages for next weekend obviously will be focused on prayer. The texts selected for this occasion (especially Psalm 138, Genesis 18:20-32, and Luke 11:1-13) provide models and guidance about how we as People of God should communicate with God. From these texts we see that our prayers to God should be personal and persistent. God is to be perceived as our concerned but transcendent Father and as our generous and always helpful Friend.

Psalm 138

In Psalm 138 prayer is not a peripheral matter, not an action to be performed in a perfunctory, mechanical way. The psalmist is totally involved in the prayer. Although the Lord (Adonai) is perceived to be high above the psalmist in power and in position, the psalmist claims that the Lord is intimately concerned with those who are powerless and in need. The psalmist proclaims the steadfast love and faithfulness of the Lord openly, within the hearing of the kings of the earth. Just as the Lord has responded to the pleas of the psalmist in the past, the psalmist expects the same personal attention in the present and in the future. In a most respectful way the psalmist is persistent, stating that it would not be advantageous for the Lord to neglect the psalmist. The Lord should not neglect the psalmist, for the psalmist is the work of the Lord's own hands!

Genesis 18:20-32

This text is perhaps the supreme example in all of our biblical accounts of personal and persistent prayer. Those who composed this account provided in 18:17-19 an introspective view of the Lord. In those verses the Lord is said to be pondering whether to share with Abraham the plans of the Lord to destroy the cities of Sodom and Gomorrah because of the sins of the people who were living there. (It would be preferable to begin our reading with 18:17 rather than with 18:20 so that this introspective view of the Lord would be included.) The Lord is said in Genesis 18:20-21 to be so concerned about the people of the world that the decision to destroy even the most wicked among them will not be made on the basis of reports provided by subordinates. The Lord will make a personal inspection before the final decision for destruction will be made.

In this story Abraham is said to have approached the Lord closely and to have engaged the Lord in a bold though always most respectful manner in a prayer conversation. In this most interesting and persistent intercessory prayer developed and included within the biblical accounts, Abraham requests that the city of Sodom be spared if fifty, or forty-five, or forty, or thirty, or twenty, or even if only ten righteous people can be found there. Using the same persuasive argumentation that would be used in a human-to-human conversation, Abraham is said to have appealed to the sense of justice inherent with the Lord by making the statement that "It would not be consistent with your character to destroy the righteous with the wicked!" A better model for our own personal persistent intercessory prayers cannot be found.

Psalm 85

The reasoning expressed within this prayer is frequently seen in the psalms of the Israelite canonical hymnal. Just as, the psalmist argues, you, O Lord, have acted favorably toward us in the past, please show your favor to us now. Do not continue to be angry with us. In this psalm the psalmist is confident that the Lord will respond affirmatively.

The psalmist speaks personally to the Lord here, much as a person would speak personally to a dear friend. There is a faith-inducing closeness here, making it easier for us even today to address God in prayer. This is one of the most significant blessings that we receive by using the Israelite/Jewish psalms regularly in our private and in our corporate worship and life.

Hosea 1:2-10

There is nothing specifically about prayer in this puzzling text. Should we understand the text rather literally that God actually commanded Hosea to marry a woman who would have two children during their marriage who would be fathered by other men, in order to illustrate the sinfulness of Israel? Should we consider this to be instead a vivid story to demonstrate dramatically the unfaithfulness to the Lord God of many of the people in the Northern Kingdom Israel? Is the account to be understood as a parable or symbolic action that depicts the message of this prophetic document? Did Hosea actually have an unfortunate marriage situation and used it to speak his words of judgment against Israel? Was there some other purpose for this text? Is this a meaningful and helpful text for us to read in our corporate worship and to reflect upon in our sermons? At any rate, the text is enigmatic, challenging, and illustrative of the tremendous variety of materials in the Older Testament. There can be as many interpretations of the text as there are persons to interpret it.

Luke 11:1-13

In the oldest Greek manuscripts of the Lukan "Lord's Prayer" available to modern text critics, God is simply addressed as "Father." God is not depicted as "in heaven" or anywhere else beyond our hearing. The earliest Lukan "Lord's Prayer" is, therefore, characterized by brevity and simplicity. The context given the Lukan "Lord's Prayer" puts emphasis on Jesus himself praying and, because of the context of the Luke 18:1-5 story about the cold-hearted judge who finally responds to the persistent pleas of the widow who continues to appeal to him, on perseverance in prayer. The Lukan account also uses the technique of comparison between the lesser and the greater in which human-to-human relationships are used as illustrations of the more vital human-to-divine ones. If a friend will eventually relent and meet the needs of an acquaintance who continues to implore him for assistance and if a father will supply good food for his children, how much more will the far-superior heavenly Father give the Holy Spirit to those who persist in their supplications! God, as the greatest Father, will certainly provide the much greater divine gifts to those who persist in their prayers. Therefore, we should continue to pray to God for good things and never become discouraged and discontinue our prayers. We believe that God is a loving Father and not a cold-hearted judge.

Colossians 2:6-15 (16-19)

This text is the third in a series of sequential readings from Colossians over a four week period and has very little connection with the other selections for this occasion, although there is in Colossians 2:7 the mention of thanksgiving and this text does provide some reasons for prayer. The words φιλοσοφίας καὶ κενῆς ἀπάτης in 2:8 should be rendered in our time by something such as "love of human, self-centered wisdom and vain deceitfulness" so that the academic discipline of philosophy is not discredited.

PROPER 13
(ORDINARY TIME 18)
ELEVENTH SUNDAY AFTER PENTECOST

Sunday between July 31 and August 6 inclusive

The central theme of most of these texts is that it is foolish for us to trust in the transitoriness of the things that we can do but wise to place our reliance on God, who gives wisdom and knowledge and joy.

Psalm 49:1-12

In the opinion of the writer(s) of this psalm, there is no reason to be fearful of any human being, no matter how wealthy and powerful that human being may be, because no one can use riches to purchase additional years of life in order to live on forever. In spite of their splendor, all human beings will perish just as the beasts of the field die from old age, illness, or injury. Even though some people may own and control large tracts of land, their graves will be their homes forever.

Although unlike the writer(s) of this psalm, we believe that God will raise us from the dead, that which is written in this psalm is still applicable today. Those who are wealthy may be able to purchase the best possible medical care and prolong their health to some extent by proper diet, exercise, and rest, but eventually all will die. There are limits to the power of all people, even of those who are the most privileged and wealthy, for today as then all of us will die just as the beasts of the field die. Only God does not die. Only God is worthy to be feared.

Ecclesiastes 1:2, 12-14; 2:18-23

According to the writers of this text, everything about this present life is vanity, transitory, lacking in substance.

Nothing is permanent. Apart from God, the writers say, there is every reason to despair; all of the possessions that are gained by the sweat of one's brow must be left to someone else, who probably will not even appreciate them and will probably change everything that you have done back to the way that it was before you came.

Some hope is expressed beyond this text in 2:24-26. There we read that to the person who pleases God, purpose and satisfaction in life are possible. God may give to such a person wisdom and knowledge and joy, even enjoyment in the midst of toil. Those who are wise will recognize their dependence on God and will work to please God.

Psalm 107:1-9, 43

After an introductory section (vv. 1-3) the problems of various types of pilgrims on their way to Jerusalem are described in this psalm. When serious difficulties are encountered, the members of each group cried out to the Lord for help, and the Lord delivered them from danger. This rather lengthy song was probably sung while travelers made their way toward Jerusalem. They sang in order to pass the time, to express their appreciation to the Lord, and because they enjoyed singing.

Psalm 107:4-9 describes the situation of those who wandered through desolate areas, hungry and thirsty, far from food and streams of water to sustain them. Nevertheless, when they cried out to the Lord for help, the Lord delivered them and led them straight to a city where their needs could be met. The Lord is said to provide water for the thirsty and food for those who are hungry.

Some of us may recall singing together as we traveled on our way to youth camps, Bible camps, youth conventions, and on mission service trips. It is important that we continue to provide opportunities for young people to have these "pilgrimage" experiences. In some instances persons who are retired from their work careers have somewhat similar opportunities to travel together.

Hosea 11:1-11

The love and compassion of the Lord God is so great that even though the people of Israel do not deserve such affection from the Lord whom they have rejected, the Lord longs once more to be like parents who lift their infants to their cheeks to cuddle them and to feed them. The Lord will do this to the children of Israel who return from Egypt and from Assyria to their homes in their land.

Colossians 3:1-11

This Colossians text fits well within the theme of most of the other texts selected for next weekend. Addressed to those who "have been raised from the dead together with Christ," it directs them to turn their attention to those things that are above, to the new nature that is to conform to the image of the one who has created it. Those who have been raised from the dead together with Christ are instructed to kill within themselves all inclinations to be involved in things on this earth that are evil and of no value, things such as illicit sexual activity, immoral behavior, disgraceful passion, evil desire, and plotting to obtain more and more material things, which is idolatry. The old labels and descriptions of people are no longer applicable; people are now distinguished by whether or not they have "put on Christ" and are raised from the dead together with Christ.

As is often noted, some of this terminology is similar to what we know about teachings of groups of Gnostic Christians at the beginning of the second century. There are differences also, and to some extent Gnostic Christian terminology that was popular at that time was used here to oppose more fully developed Gnostic Christian groups. Basically, "mainline" Christians proclaimed a physical resurrection of Jesus rather than the spiritual resurrection promoted by Gnostic Christian groups.

Luke 12:13-21

This account about the man who requested that Jesus should put pressure on the man's brother to settle an estate, Jesus' warning against covetousness, and Jesus' parable about the rich fool whose lands were surprisingly productive occurs in our canonical texts only here in Luke's Gospel. The Gospel of Thomas, saying 63, however, should be compared to it. The Gospel of Thomas, saying 63, in *The Nag Hammadi Library in English* (New York: Harper & Row, 1977, p. 125), is as follows:

> *Jesus said, "There was a rich man who had much money. He said, 'I shall put my money to use so that I may sow, reap, plant, and fill my storehouse with produce, with the result that I shall lack nothing.' Such were his intentions, but that same night he died. Let him who has ears hear."*

Comparison of the Lukan and the Gospel of Thomas accounts indicates that Luke's account is considerably more developed, embellished, and interpreted than is the Thomas account. The Lukan account may include traditional materials that originated with the Jesus of history, who would most likely have refused to claim authority to enter into a financial dispute among brothers.

The main point of the Lukan text is not that the rich man was evil because his land was productive. Neither is it that the man was condemned because he planned to build larger storage facilities for his abundant crop. The rich man in the Lukan account is condemned for his unwillingness to share his wealth, for his planning to become lazy and gluttonous, and most of all for his placing his reliance on things

— treasures on this earth — rather than on God. Therefore, the wisdom theme of this account is that the man was foolish rather than wise. The message to us is clear. We too should be wise rather than foolish. We should rely on God, not on things.

PROPER 14
(ORDINARY TIME 19)
TWELFTH SUNDAY AFTER PENTECOST

Sunday between August 7 and August 13 inclusive

Most of the texts selected for this occasion emphasize God's desire to do good things for God's people and for all people who will respond in a positive way to God. This emphasis is also present in the prayer for next Sunday in the words, "Almighty and Everlasting God, you are always more ready to hear than we are to pray, and to give more than we either desire or deserve." Let us, therefore, examine these texts and see how this emphasis is expressed in them. Is this not what we also shall be proclaiming this coming weekend?

Psalm 33:12-22

Not only did the Lord do good things for the People of God by calling into being the heavens and the earth for them even before the Lord brought the people into existence, but also the Lord is said in this psalm to look with grace on all who fear the Lord. The Lord is said to look with kindness at those who put their hope in the steadfast love that the Lord has for them, in order that the Lord may deliver them from death and keep them alive during famine. Therefore, the people of the worshiping community gladly wait for the Lord to act and they trust in the name of the Lord.

Genesis 15:1-6

The Abraham traditions in Genesis indicate that there was nothing Abraham and Sarah wanted more than to have a son, but they were both greatly advanced in years and remained childless. Although the reader is kept in suspense for many chapters in Genesis before the birth of Isaac is announced, there is actually never any doubt that the Lord would bless them with a son because, as this Genesis 15:1-6 text reveals, it was the desire of the Lord to do this good thing for them. The son would be born and in spite of any threats to his existence he would survive. Through him Abraham and Sarah would have many descendants, as many as the stars that can be seen on a clear night in a rural or desolate area.

Even in our human relationships, we have learned from our experiences that if someone who is exceptionally powerful desires to do something good for us, it is almost certain to be done. How much more, therefore, will it be likely to occur when God, who is infinitely good and powerful, wants to do something that will be good for us! According to this text, Abram believed that the Lord would do this great thing that the Lord wanted to do for Abram and Sarah, and Abram's acceptance of this promise of the Lord was considered evidence of Abram's righteousness.

Psalm 50:1-8, 22-23

Although God may want to do good things for God's chosen people, there are times in which it is said that God commands changes to occur among the people before God will share God's gifts of grace. In the situation depicted in this psalm, the people had been offering their animal sacrifices to God regularly, but they had not offered to God a sacrifice of thanksgiving. Instead, they had broken the commandments given by God. Nevertheless, if they will repent, God will save them.

Isaiah 1:1, 10-20

As in Psalm 50, the problem here was not the lack of animal sacrifices and burnt offerings. The problem was that the people were being unjust to the poor and oppressed. They were not caring for the orphans or defending widows. If the people will change, even though their sins are scarlet, they will become as white and clean as freshly fallen snow. God is on their side. God *wants* to help them.

Hebrews 11:1-3, 8-16

Along with the definition in Hebrews 11:1 of the concept of faith expressed in the terminology of Greek philosophy and the many examples of the faith of Abraham, Sarah, and the innumerable Israelites descended from them given in this text, there are statements that God has always wanted to be called their God and to provide for them all of the good things that are implied by God's goodness. It is said that God has prepared for them a heavenly city, the city of God. There can be no doubt in this text of God's desire to provide good things for the people.

Luke 12:32-40

It is in this text that the statement of God's desire to do good things for God's people is most explicit. We see this especially in the words of Luke 12:32, "Do not be afraid any longer, my little flock of people, for God your Father has expressed a strong desire to give to you the kingdom." If God had no desire to provide for the People of God a place within the celestial realm where God's will is gladly done, there would have been no point in urging the readers of the Lukan document to sell their material goods and to provide for the poor, to build up their treasures in the heavens, and to be alert at all times, watching for the coming of the Son of Man. God's desire to do good things for us is the reason that we are urged by faith to accept these good things from God and to be ready when these good things are dispensed so that we will miss no opportunity to receive them. Without a doubt, God's desire to do good things for us is "gospel," good news for all!

PROPER 15
(ORDINARY TIME 20)
THIRTEENTH SUNDAY AFTER PENTECOST

Sunday between August 14 and August 20 inclusive

A unifying motif in most of these texts selected for our use this coming weekend is that in view of the impending word of judgment from God, there is an urgent need for justice and righteousness on the earth. In some of these texts the word of judgment from God is fearful and awesome, a reason for great apprehension. In others the word of judgment from God is needed in order to break the power of the oppressors, both foreign oppressors and domestic oppressors. It is not so much the written, revealed word of God from the past as it is the dynamic, imminent word that is to come that is the concern of the writers of these texts.

Psalm 82

The "divine council" and "the gods" as "sons of the Most High" will probably be problematic this coming weekend for Christians who are not familiar with the theological situation of the ancient Near East during the earlier centuries of Israelite development. At that time, each family, community, tribe, nation, or empire in many instances had its own special name for deity and for its own deity. In this henotheistic (one personal God for each group) system, each group generally thought that its deity was the best for it. The existence of other "gods" for other groups was not denied. Israel as a "nation" claimed that Adonai, its Lord, was God, and that Adonai, its God, was Number One.

Later, after the loss of the Israelite nation, the exile in Babylon, and during two centuries of Persian rule, the Israelites claimed that Adonai was not only the God of the nation Israel, but God over all, the Most High, the King of the Universe, the one who judged the "gods" acclaimed by others. At that point, instead of a henotheistic (one God for us) theology, they had developed a monotheistic (one God, our God, the one God for everyone) theology. They had, in part, learned monotheism from the Persian Zoroastrians, who made that claim for their religion even before it became the state religion of the Persian Empire. (The story of Esther provides for us a reflection of that conflict between competing monotheisms.) After the exilic period, Judaism had become, for the most part, no longer a henotheistic religion but a monotheistic religion. Other monotheistic religions developed after this, including Christianity, Islam, the Sikh religion, and so on. There are residual elements of henotheistic religion in our Older Testament, but the predominant view became monotheistic. Most of our Newer Testament is monotheistic. Judaism continued throughout the centuries, however, to be to some extent still henotheistic as it had been for the ancient Israelites. Much of the religion of the Jews today, especially because of the Holocaust, is basically henotheistic rather than monotheistic. This is also the situation for an increasing number of Christians, almost all Hindus, and a few Muslims today. Henotheists are by nature more likely to be tolerant and respectful of people in other religions than are monotheists.

Israelites understood Adonai as demanding that the Israelites act with justice, and declared that while Adonai is immortal, the Israelites and all other people are mortal. As Word of God for us, Psalm 82 and other biblical texts require justice and righteousness among us and label all of our finite "gods" as less than lasting and less than ultimate.

Jeremiah 23:23-29

This text, in which the transcendence as well as the immanence of Adonai as the God of the Universe is acclaimed, has some similarities to portions of Psalm 82. Here the prophets of Adonai are sharply distinguished from other prophets, and the Word of Adonai is depicted as like fire that consumes everything that will burn and as a hammer that breaks rocks into little pieces. We should note that it is primarily the spoken Word of Adonai rather than the written Word that is described in this manner.

Psalm 80:1-2, 8-19

This psalm is a community plea to the Lord God of Israel who had brought a vine out of Egypt and planted it with loving care in the promised land, where it took root and spread over a vast area from the Mediterranean Sea to the Euphrates River. The community promises that if the Lord God will restore the people in their land, which they have lost, the people will never ever again turn away from the Lord God.

Isaiah 5:1-7

As in Psalm 80, in this Isaiah 5:1-7 "Love Song about the Unfruitful Vineyard" the vineyard and vine analogy is used with reference to the people and nation of Israel. The vineyard is abandoned by the Lord God because the love that the Lord had bestowed on the vineyard has been unrequited. The Lord expected justice and righteousness to be shown in the vineyard. Because there had been neither justice nor righteousness shown in the vineyard, and because the vineyard had produced no good, fruitful grapes, but only putrid, stinking grapes, the fearful judgment and condemnation of the Lord has come upon it.

Hebrews 11:29—12:2

Although it was by faith that the pre-Israelites had been able to cross the Red Sea on dry land, had conquered the promised land, ruled over it, endured defeat and horrible suffering, and although the courageous Israelites were fully commended for their faith and endurance, it is argued by the writer of this document that the Israelites, even the best among them, did not receive what was promised, i.e., Jesus, the pioneer of the more perfect faith, the *Christian* faith.

Luke 12:49-56

This text is a composite of various elements. It most likely is comprised of pronouncements of the Jesus of history given in a variety of settings, along with materials from Mark 10:38, from "Q" materials or from an early draft of Matthew (Matthew 10:34-36 and 16:2-3), and from the life experiences of the inspired Lukan writer. The fire that is to be cast upon the earth (v. 49) is probably a fire of lightning, a symbol of instant judgment, a theme of apocalyptic eschatology. In spite of the Lukan writer's penchant for peace on earth, the "Q" or Matthean call for a sword is included. The Micah 7:6 description of dissension within a household is also used, in which it is in every instance one generation (a father or a mother) against or opposed by the next (a son, a daughter, or a daughter-in-law). The combination of the elements in this text is Lukan, and the text can best be understood in terms of the inspired Lukan writer's personal situation, a situation of a Greek-background Christian who has seen or known about families divided by generation, most likely with the older generation remaining Jewish and the younger becoming Christian.

PROPER 16
(ORDINARY TIME 21)
FOURTEENTH SUNDAY AFTER PENTECOST

Sunday between August 21 and August 27 inclusive

In many of these texts the healing that God graciously offers as a gift from God is featured. It is important that we understand that this healing offered and given by God in these and in many other biblical texts is not limited to physical healing. It includes in most if not all instances mental healing, as well as spiritual healing, and in many instances social, political, and economic healing, the end of oppression for the one who is suffering.

As the Obama administration and the US Congress members struggle to improve the health care system in this nation and attempt to make such care accessible to all people here, we are aware that such care, as in the biblical texts, is not only physical, but is also mental, spiritual, social, political, and economic, designed to reduce and to remove the oppression of the ones who are suffering.

Psalm 103:1-8

In the poetic form in which faith in God and the blessing of God for all of the healing that God provides is expressed in this beautiful psalm, we see that this healing includes the diverse but related aspects of the forgiveness of sins, restoration from the imminence of death, and justice for all who are oppressed. In other words, the healing that God offers and provides encompasses physical, mental, spiritual, social, political, and economic healing.

We note that incorporated into this psalm is the favorite Israelite description of God as merciful and gracious, slow to anger and filled to the brim with steadfast, never-ending love, expressed joyously seven times within the Older

Testament, here in Psalm 103:8, as well as in Exodus 34:6-7, Numbers 14:18, Jeremiah 32:18, Jonah 4:2, Nehemiah 9:17, and Nehemiah 9:31.

Psalm 71:1-6

As in many other poetic expressions of faith and of thankfulness for God's gifts of compassion and healing, the healing and compassion of God is expressed here in Psalm 71 in what we often think to be broad, general, encompassing terminology. The terminology uses words such as deliver me, rescue me from those who are unjust and cruel, listen to my cry, and save me. Not only is the terminology broad in order to include a large number of persons who are afflicted; the broad terminology is used because of a realization that healing encompasses physical, mental, spiritual, social, political, and economic aspects of our lives.

Isaiah 58:9b-14

The text selected for our use here is the concluding portion of this incisive chapter 58 of the Isaiah traditions in which the service that God desires, reducing and removing the physical, mental, spiritual, social, political, and economic oppression of powerless people, is shown to be so much more important and pleasing to God than is religious fasting and other religious rituals. As in the psalms and elsewhere in our biblical canon, healing is understood here in broad, holistic terms.

Jeremiah 1:4-10

While the tasks to which the prophet Jeremiah is called in this text may seem to be primarily destructive, i.e., to pull up the "weeds" and to tear down the structures, to destroy that which is evil and to overthrow power structures, his work is also to be constructive, "to build and to plant." We see in this that the destructive and the constructive elements of his call are actually closely related. The planting and building occurs as the oppressive power structures are torn down.

Hebrews 12:18-29

The series of nearly consecutive readings from the Epistle to the Hebrews continues here. As elsewhere in this document, it is written here that the old, which in this instance is the people who were with Moses at Sinai, has been replaced by the new, which here is Jesus revealed in Zion, the Heavenly Jerusalem, the city of the living God, a symbol of the presence of God in Christ Jesus, the arbitrator of a new covenant, whose sacrificial death accomplished all that is necessary for our salvation.

The anti-Jewish polemic in this and other segments of the Epistle to the Hebrews is not directed against Jews who were contemporary with the writer. Instead, the new salvation offered in Jesus as the great High Priest is contrasted with the older Israelite sacrificial system, the butchering of clean and inspected animals as a religious action, a system of animal sacrifice that was no longer very significant for most Jews in the Temple constructed by Herod and certainly irrelevant after the destruction of that Temple by the Romans in 70 CE. Some explanation of this to the congregation would be helpful.

Luke 13:10-17

The first four verses of this text are an excellent testimony of the broad aspects of the healing that God through Jesus perceived as the Christ provided in this instance for a Jewish woman, one of the fellow oppressed Jews of the Jesus of history. The woman was stooped over and was no longer able to stand erect because of eighteen years of severe physical, mental, spiritual, social, political, and economic oppression by the Roman occupational forces in Galilee and in Judea. In my *The New Testament: A New Translation and Redaction* (Lima, Ohio: Fairway, 2001) I translate these verses as follows:

> And Jesus was teaching in one of the synagogues on a sabbath day. And there was a woman in the synagogue who had been weakened by the burden of severe Roman oppression for eighteen years, and she was stooped over and was not able to stand erect. And when Jesus saw her, he asked her to come to him and he said to her, "You are a beautiful woman! You have been set free from the burden with which they have oppressed you!" And he reached out his hands to strengthen her, and immediately she was able to stand erect again. And she gave praise to God.

This translation is designed to help us to see that the condition of the woman was closely related to the oppressive situation in which she and the other oppressed Jews lived at the time of the Jesus of history. Also, I purposely translated the Greek word γύναι, the vocative singular of the feminine noun for "woman," in this context not as the rather "cold" literal form of "Woman!" but with the affirming words, "You are a beautiful woman." To God (Jesus as the Christ here), this woman was beautiful, even in and especially in spite of her oppressed condition.

I cannot understand the reasoning of those who compiled *The Revised Common Lectionary* (Nashville: Abingdon, 1992) of including verses 14-17 in this reading. "Real" Jews, as opposed to the "literary" Jews portrayed in Luke 13:14-17, interpret the commandment "Remember the Sabbath Day to keep it holy" in terms of "On this day there must be no labor that is intended to make money." "A person should not even think and plan how to make money on this day." For "real" Jews, the Sabbath *is* hallowed by loving acts of mercy and kindness such as the Jewish Jesus of history is portrayed as doing in the Luke 13:10-13 text. Jesus with the divine power of the Risen Christ was not providing comprehensive healing of the woman in order to make money. For whatever reason, the non-Jewish background Lukan writer was polemical rather than pastoral when the writer added verses 14-17. Verses 14-17 are not edifying. Even though the persons from the multitude of denominations of Christians from many nations included these four verses in the Revised Common Lectionary, we should not read these four verses in our worship services. We need additional lectionary revision and selection. The lectionary work has not been completed. We should press for and participate in further lectionary preparations and revisions.

PROPER 17
(ORDINARY TIME 22)
FIFTEENTH SUNDAY AFTER PENTECOST

Sunday between August 28 and September 3 inclusive

Psalm 112

This acrostic psalm, along with Psalm 1, which is similar to it in content, served as patterns for the Beatitudes of Matthew 5:3-12 and Luke 6:20-23. In the Psalm 1 and 112 Beatitudes it is said, "O how happy" is the person who fears the Lord. Such a person will be prosperous, righteous, respected, unafraid, generous, and remembered forever. These Psalm 1 and 112 Beatitudes express the characteristic thought of the Israelites, which continued in the Rabbinic Literature and in most segments of the Jewish religion until the horrors of the Holocaust shattered it for many Jews.

The Matthew 5:3-12 and Luke 6:20-23 Beatitudes carried the thought of "O how happy" into a different area, the area of humbleness and of enduring persecution. An excellent sermon could be developed in which we would ask the members of the congregation at worship together whether in their experience they have found that the Beatitudes of Psalms 1 and 112 or the Beatitudes of Matthew 5:3-12 and Luke 6:20-23 conform more closely to reality as they perceive it. It would be helpful to the members of the worshiping congregations if we would ask them to *think* more than we usually do, rather than simply telling them what they should think. In order to accomplish this, our homilies/sermons should take on more aspects of dialogue rather than merely of monologue.

The Holocaust has caused many Jewish philosophers and theologians to raise questions about the validity for Jews since 1933 of the thoughts expressed in Psalms 1 and 112 and to be attracted to the guidelines for enduring suffering and persecution in the Matthew 5:3-12 and Luke 6:20-23 Beatitudes. These Jewish leaders, because of the Holocaust and because of constructive Jewish-Christian dialogue since 1945, are increasingly interested in the Jesus of history, their brother in the faith who has been largely avoided in Jewish studies for nineteen centuries because of Christian coercive pressures on Jewish people. For an example of this interest, see the article by the Jewish theologian Pinchas Lapide, "Is Jesus a Bond or a Barrier? A Jewish-Christian Dialogue," in the *Journal of Ecumenical Studies* 14 (1977, pp. 466-483).

There are many points of continuity between the thought of Psalms 1 and 112 and the Matthean and Lukan Beatitudes. Each emphasis has been found to be helpful for certain people in particular situations. We should not expect that all of the people in any congregation will find the same emphasis to be helpful for them, to be valid for them, to be "true" for them. We should, therefore, ask the questions, "What do you think?" "What have you found from your experiences?" One way to do this would be to set up a portion of the homily/sermon in the format of a TV talk show in which these theological questions would be discussed.

Sirach 10:12-18

In this wisdom tradition there is a warning against human pride that causes people to turn away from their dependence upon the Lord God. The results are disastrous, the opposite of what is acclaimed in the Beatitudes.

Jeremiah 2:4-13

The people who have so richly been blessed by God are condemned here for their forsaking the fountain of living water provided for them by the Lord and instead digging their own cisterns for themselves, cisterns that are cracked and hold no water during dry times.

Psalm 81:1, 10-16

Here also the people are condemned by the Lord for turning away from the Lord God who loves them. Even after this, the Lord greatly desires to feed the people again with the finest harvests and with wheat and honey in the land.

Proverbs 25:6-7

Humbleness and modesty in the presence of those who are in high positions of authority (kings and rulers, and by implication the Lord God) are emphasized here. Luke 14:7-11 is an application of this in the context of a marriage feast, continuing the idea of this Proverbs 25:6-7 text that it is wise to humble one's self rather than to be humbled and humiliated by other people.

Hebrews 13:1-8, 15-16

Among the many parenetic admonitions in this text are the requirements of providing hospitality for strangers and care for those who are afflicted. Each of these admonitions is said to be especially important because of our faith in Jesus perceived as the Christ, who is the same person yesterday, today, and forever. It is through Jesus perceived as the Christ that we offer up our sacrifice of praise to God and share our resources with those who are in need.

Luke 14:1, 7-14

Many of us as Christians seem to be so willing to obey the admonition in Luke 14:7-11 to sit in the lowest place at a marriage feast by sitting as far back in church as we can and so reluctant to obey or even to notice the admonition in Luke 14:12-14 to invite people who are poor, physically and mentally challenged, blind, and in other ways different from the majority of people to be guests in our homes and to full participation in our worship services. Nevertheless, it is in Luke 14:12-14 rather than in Luke 14:7-11 that the related themes of many of the texts selected for this occasion are brought together. Let us together experience the joy of sharing and of providing in personal, meaningful ways for those who have the greatest needs and who have the greatest appreciation for the care that we provide.

PROPER 18
(ORDINARY TIME 23)
SIXTEENTH SUNDAY AFTER PENTECOST

Sunday between September 4 and September 10 inclusive

Human reasoning and human relationships are ephemeral and transitory. Only through the wisdom given by God and through our relationships with God can we survive and live joyously, blessed by God.

Psalm 1

The lives of those who are wicked are worthless. Their lives are like the chaff that the wind blows away. Happy, meaningful, and blessed are the lives of those who delight in the Torah, the way of the Lord. The Lord watches over them and they are like trees planted along streams of water. Their leaves never wither and die.

Deuteronomy 30:15-20

These words in the final six verses of the "Sermon of Moses" in Deuteronomy 4:44—30:20 express the admonition of Psalm 1 and of many other texts in our Older Testament, as well as of the Apostle Paul in Galatians 5:13—6:10 and elsewhere, and in the first portion of the Didache in the Apostolic Fathers. In the words of the "Sermon of Moses" here, we, as well as the Israelites and Jews, are given by God the choice between life and death. It should seem to be such an easy choice to make! Why do we and others so often choose the path of death?

Psalm 139:1-6, 13-18

In this text the psalmist marvels at the infinite wisdom of the Lord God, who brought the life of the psalmist into being and knows every thought, word, and deed of the psalmist.

The Lord God is everywhere, in the heavens, everywhere on the land and sea, and even in the graves of those who have died (vv. 7-12, which should be included in this selection). It is only because of the love and wisdom of God that the psalmist has life.

Jeremiah 18:1-11
The same basic message of the other texts chosen for our worship services this coming weekend is expressed in this account of the symbolic act of Jeremiah and his visit to the potter's house. God is the potter; we are the clay. God can and will smash and destroy any person, nation, or religious community that does evil, but will shape into a beautiful container all who choose to establish and retain a faith relationship with the Lord God.

Philemon 1-21
The relationships that exist between Paul, Philemon, and Onesimus are all bonded together by the relationship that they share "in Christ." It is because of that relationship they share "in Christ" that Paul asks his friend Philemon to accept Onesimus, the runaway slave, back as a brother "in the Lord." Paul makes his request so forcefully that we may assume that Philemon could not refuse Paul's request without jeopardizing Philemon's own relationship with the Lord. This short letter, therefore, provides for us a paradigm to follow in our relationships with each other as Christians.

Luke 14:25-33
The overall theme of the texts selected for us for use next weekend that human reasoning and human relationships are ephemeral and transitory unless they are linked into our relationship with God continues here in Luke 14:25-33. It is probable that on many occasions the Jesus of history said in one way or another, "Whoever is not willing to give up

all other relationships and to put God first is not ready to let God rule."

For Jesus and for most of the top leaders of the early Church, the cost of discipleship was very high. To let God rule meant that they would no longer let Caesar rule over them. If as a leader among Jews in Galilee and Judea or as a leader in the early Church you publicly rejected the authority of Caesar in favor of the authority of God, you would soon be carrying your cross to your own crucifixion event. You would have to give up all human relationships and give up your life at that point. The cost was very high for this level of commitment! Before you would make this level of commitment, you would do well to determine whether you possessed enough strength to make this commitment. Jesus obviously had this level of strength and commitment.

Unless we have some understanding of the oppressive political situation in which Jesus and his earliest followers lived, we cannot understand Luke 14:25-33 and many other similar Newer Testament texts. As we are able to understand more about what it is like to live in some of the totalitarian states that exist in our time, we gain an increased understanding of many of the Newer Testament texts. Jesus believed, the leaders of the early Church believed, and we believe that by the grace of God our relationship with God, and in some sense on a different level our relationships with each other, will continue even after we die.

PROPER 19
(ORDINARY TIME 24)
SEVENTEENTH SUNDAY AFTER PENTECOST

Sunday between September 11 and September 17 inclusive

The most important theme for the texts selected for next weekend is God's gracious rescue from sin and death of those who are lost. It is shown in these texts that as sinners we do not deserve God's mercy and forgiveness. Nevertheless, God forgives us because God wants to forgive us. It is always appropriate for us to respond to God with joyful gratitude.

Psalm 51:1-10

This well-known psalm is especially significant to us because of the intense sense of sin expressed in it and because of its emphasis on repentance and contrition rather than on animal sacrifices. The psalmist is fully aware that God would be totally justified in destroying the psalmist. In spite of this, the psalmist asks God to be cleansed from sin and to be filled with God's joy and gladness.

The feelings expressed in this psalm are our feelings also as individuals and as members of congregations in worship. When God creates a new heart in us and gives to us a spirit that connects with the Spirit of God, our worship experience is complete.

Psalm 14

According to this psalm, in the eyes of God all people are sinful; there is no one who does good things. God, however, delivers those who are poor and oppressed. When God rescues God's people, they rejoice. They are glad. So, also, do we rejoice. So also are we glad.

Exodus 32:7-14

We may wonder how the early pre-Israelites could so quickly have turned away from the Lord (Adonai) who had brought them out of slavery in Egypt and, instead, gathered in worship around a golden idol in accordance with Egyptian practices. Actually, this text, together with others such as Joshua 24:14, is an indication that while they were slaves in Egypt the people who participated in the Exodus had worshiped other gods according to the custom of the Egyptians. As slaves they had participated in the civil religion of the Egyptian people. When Moses was not among them as their leader, they quickly reverted to the religion that they had known.

In Exodus 32:13, portions of the theological motif of the J source, that God had promised many descendants and the land of Canaan to the patriarchs of Israel, are reiterated by Moses. In this story about a divine-human encounter between Adonai and Moses, it is surprisingly said that Moses had functioned the more nobly! The selfless logic of Moses results in the preservation of the people who would inhabit the land promised by God to the Israelites.

Jeremiah 4:11-12, 22-28

Judah and Jerusalem are depicted as barren and desolate here as a result of the destruction brought upon the land by the Babylonians, in accordance with the will of the Lord. There is, nevertheless, in verse 27 a glimmer of hope that there will be a remnant that will remain. God will forgive and restore a few of the people. As in the flood stories of Genesis 6-9, God will save a few and make a fresh start in the land.

1 Timothy 1:12-17

In this text the Apostle Paul is portrayed as an example of how the worst sinner can accept Jesus as "Christ our

Lord" and receive eternal life. All of this came as a free gift from God. Jesus the Christ is proclaimed as the means of the grace of God. There is only one God, and that one God is praised in the 1 Timothy 1:17 doxology that concludes this selection.

Luke 15:1-10

The inspired Lukan writer suggests in these two parables that the sheep that was lost and found and the coin that was lost and recovered are representations of tax collectors and sinners, people who were surely lost in the opinion of most "religious" people such as we are. In order to pursue the intention of the Lukan writer, we probably should present this text for our time next weekend in a way in which most of those who hear us will be offended by it and, as a result, recognize their own sins and selfishness, repent, and bring joy to God and to themselves.

The recovery of every person — regardless of how odious that person may appear to us — is said in this text to bring great joy to God. Therefore, we should try to motivate those who hear us to participate in the recovery of those who are lost. This "lostness" and this "recovery" can take many forms. For example, we could ask those who hear us to think about what we would describe as "lost" people and about how we can be involved in the "recovery of those whom we consider to be lost." Perhaps some of us may consider ourselves to be lost. Emphasis should be placed on recovery actions and on recovery attitudes in which the grace and forgiveness of God will be felt and all will have joy, the joy offered by God even to the least of us who are lost.

PROPER 20
(ORDINARY TIME 25)
EIGHTEENTH SUNDAY AFTER PENTECOST

Sunday between September 18 and September 24 inclusive

Most of the texts selected from the Israelite Scriptures for this occasion praise the Lord for raising the poor, the needy, and the barren from the dust, and condemn those who oppress the poor. The Newer Testament texts urge the followers of Jesus as the Christ to express themselves to God with all types of prayers (1 Timothy 2:1-7) and to use material things prudently (Luke 16:1-13).

Psalm 113

This beautiful Israelite Hallelujah psalm is sung or said together with Psalm 114 at the beginning of the Seder by many Jews as a reminder that the name of the Lord is always to be praised and blessed. In this psalm the Lord is acclaimed for divine majesty and for divine concern for the poor and for the woman who is childless. From our Christian perspective, we attribute these qualities also to Jesus, who is Lord for us, our Risen Lord and Savior, the Christ.

Amos 8:4-7

There is no more incisive prophetic word of judgment than this in any of the world's great religious literatures, or any *mutatis mutandis* more applicable to our own or to any other human situation. The specific setting within eighth-century Israelite religion is apparent in this text, but the prophetic word of judgment should be applied boldly to our own situation. This firm demand for justice and for concern for the poor among the people of the Lord is closely linked to the acclamation of the Lord as the God of justice and of concern in Psalm 113.

Psalm 79:1-9

In this first portion of this psalm the Lord is implored to remove God's anger and wrath from the desolate people of Jerusalem and to punish instead those who have devoured the people of Jerusalem and destroyed the city and its temple.

Jeremiah 8:18—9:1

Jeremiah is represented here as in deep anguish over the pain and illness of the people of Jerusalem when the Lord is no longer in Zion. The Lord is presented in 8:19c as explaining that the Lord God is not with the people of Jerusalem because the people of Jerusalem have provoked the anger of the Lord with their worship of the images of other lords and gods. Jeremiah wishes that he would have enough tears to weep day and night for the slain people of Jerusalem.

1 Timothy 2:1-7

Within the liturgical prayers of the Church we try to comply with the urgings of this fine Pauline admonition and of its standard, orthodox Christian theology. On the other hand, we should not be bound by the directions of the verses that follow in 1 Timothy 2:9-15 regarding the clothing, hairstyles, jewelry, and the subordinate position of women. We must reject the theological demands of the writer of 1 Timothy 2:15 — so different from the theological position of Paul himself — that women will be saved not by the grace of God but by bearing children. It is tragic that the leaders of the developing Church during the second century did not delete 1 Timothy 2:11-15 when they through usage canonized this document along with others written by or attributed to the Apostle Paul. They could have spared most women and most men since that time and especially during recent decades and today many problems and anguish about the authority of our Scriptures. We can only conclude that leaders in the developing Church during the second century were in agreement with the sentiments expressed in 1 Timothy 2:11-15 and that they with their majority power overrode the objections of the minorities of men and of women who opposed them.

The inclusion of 1 Timothy 2:11-15 into the canon is a strong indication that God permitted majority powers in the developing Church to put into canonical status whatever they wished. This leaves us with the sober responsibility of repudiating the directives and theology of 1 Timothy 2:11-15 today. Our concern for people and for the authority of other far more important portions of Scripture demands that we repudiate elements from the texts that should have been repudiated and deleted by our spiritual fathers. If God permitted them to put 1 Timothy 2:11-15 into this document and to leave it in this document, then God will certainly permit us to repudiate it by printing it in small print status or eventually even into footnote status as a testimony to future generations that we care about our sacred Scriptures and about them.

Luke 16:1-13

This is perhaps the most problematic of all of the parables in our Four Gospels. The last four verses of the text selected here (vv. 10-13) provide a secondary application of the parable that is different from what we have in 16:1-9. For this reason, many pericopes do not include 16:10-13 with the reading of the parable itself in 16:1-9.

We may find helpful the conjecture of J.D.M. Derrett in "The Parable of the Unjust Steward," *New Testament Studies* 7 (1961, pp. 198-219), and in " 'Take thy Bond… and write Fifty' (Luke xvi.6) The Nature of the Bond," *New Testament Studies* new series 23 (1972, pp. 438-440), summarized in I. Howard Marshall, *The Gospel of Luke* (Grand Rapids: Eerdmans, 1978, pp. 614-617), that the steward had previously included the accumulated interest due, but now, facing the termination of his employment, reduced the debtors' account balances to the amount of the principal of the loans, thereby pleasing the debtors and making many new friends while obeying the requirement within Israelite religion that the rich should charge no interest on loans to the poor. The problem with this conjecture is that we still have the judgment in 16:8 that the steward was dishonest. Perhaps he was dishonest in the parable in terms of his agreement to handle his employer's business matters in accordance with the wishes of his employer, but faithful to the requirements of his religion. Possibly the "sons of this age" was used by the Lukan writer to refer to the Jews, while the "sons of light" was intended to be a reference to the followers of Jesus. That would be consistent with the techniques of the Lukan writer within Lukan parables elsewhere in the Third Gospel.

Because of our uncertainty regarding the interpretation intended for this parable, this may be one of those occasions in which the readings from the Israelite Scriptures are more usable for us than are the selections from the Newer Testament. Therefore, we may be wise to use the Older Testament readings, especially Psalm 113 and Amos 8:4-7, as our basic texts for our message this coming weekend.

PROPER 21
(ORDINARY TIME 26)
NINETEENTH SUNDAY AFTER PENTECOST

Sunday between September 25 and October 1 inclusive

It is made abundantly clear in most of the texts selected for next Sunday that rich people who indulge themselves in luxury with no regard for the poor and needy will suffer in the future. The Lord will provide wonderful things for the poor and needy who turn to the Lord for help. Those who are rich and selfish can avoid future suffering if they will be generous to the poor now in the name of the Lord.

Amos 6:1a, 4-7

The rich are warned in these Amos tradition "Woe" sayings that those who selfishly and idly indulge themselves with unneeded luxury with no concern for the poor will be the first to go into exile where they will have none of these things.

What is the Word of the Lord for *us* in this text? What shall we do with this text in *our* situation? What is God saying to *us* through it? What implications does this text have for us in the USA on issues such as health care, adequate wages, educational opportunities, and so on? What actions does this text suggest that we should be taking as individuals, as the Church, and as citizens in the United States?

Jeremiah 32:1-3a, 6-15

In the face of the impending surrender of the Israelites in Jerusalem to the attacking Babylonian army, Jeremiah purchases a field in Anathoth from his cousin Hanamel. A secure record of the transaction is made, so that during the restoration Jeremiah or his heirs will be able to claim the property. This action suggests in vivid detail the belief that at some time in the future the people of the land will again be able to own property and live in freedom in Judea. It is implied that the people who will be able to return in peace to the area will have learned that only within their relationship with the Lord God will they be sustained.

Psalm 91:1-6, 14-16

Assurance is given by the Lord God that those who trust in the Lord will be protected by the Lord from all harm and danger. The Lord God is portrayed as an eagle sheltering its offspring. Our beautiful hymn "On Eagle's Wings" depicts this message dramatically and should be used along with this text.

Psalm 146

In so many ways the Lord God provides love and care for those who are suffering and oppressed. The assurance given and expressed here is similar to what is written in Psalm 91. Even if the benefits promised in these psalms are not received immediately or even over long periods of time, we must maintain our faith in God and in the unmerited grace of God. That is expected of us.

1 Timothy 6:6-19

It is in verses 17-19 that we have the closest connection to the other texts selected for this occasion. Instead of merely condemning the rich and providing no guidance for them, these verses spell out quite clearly the course that should be taken by "the rich of this world." They should set their hopes on God. They should be rich in doing good things. They should be liberal and generous, for they have the means to do this. In this way they will lay up for themselves a good foundation for the future, for life that is life indeed.

Since we have relatively few texts in our Newer Testament that express positive and constructive guidance for people who are rich, it is especially important that we use 1 Timothy 6:6-19 in a significant way next Sunday. People who are wealthy receive considerable positive guidance and reinforcement in Islam and in Hindu religions and to some extent in the Jewish tradition. Rarely do they receive positive consideration and guidance within the Newer Testament of Christianity. How are wealthy people in the congregations guided and assisted in our congregations? What is their role in the "Body of Christ"? How can we from our Newer Testament texts guide them without departing from the texts into the fallacy of a "Prosperity Gospel"? For useful suggestions here, see Karl N. Jacobson, "Unhappy business: Why the prosperity gospel doesn't add up — in good times or bad," *The Lutheran* (August 2009, pp. 34-35), or www.theluther-an.org.

Luke 16:19-31

This graphic Lukan parable, which probably draws upon the Egyptian folk tale of the journey of Si-Osiris to the underworld and upon the Jewish story about the condition after death of the poor scholar and of the rich publican Bar Ma'jan, has anti-Jewish overtones, even though anti-Jewish polemic may not be its only or its most important function. The rich man in it — mentioned first, along with his five brothers who remain in his father's house — seems to represent the Jewish religious establishment. As such, he is buried, and in the Lukan viewpoint consigned to Hades, where he will soon be joined by his five brothers. He calls across the chasm to Abraham, whom he claims as his father. Abraham answers, but will offer no special favors at this point. The brothers are to be referred to their own Scriptures, but there is little likelihood that they will repent either on the basis of their own Scriptures or if someone raised from the dead (Jesus!) would come to them. Lazarus, mentioned second (generally the "Christian" position in Lukan pairing of contrasts in Lukan parables) had been poor and oppressed, but now enjoys the favored position in Abraham's bosom.

In all of this, we see how creatively the Lukan writer developed the Lazarus figure as a Christian symbol of the resurrection, a symbol developed also in a somewhat different way in the Fourth Gospel in which it is denied that the Jews are any longer sons of Abraham. We are increasingly cognizant of the creativity of the Lukan writer and of the Johannine traditions. Furthermore, the Lukan context for this parable suggests that the parable was directed against the Pharisees. There are other indications as well that among the parables of Jesus peculiar to the Third Gospel this is one of the most likely to have been largely a Lukan composition, a skillful expression of the Lukan writer's evaluation of the Jews who would not "repent" and join the associates of Lazarus who, although they may be poor in this life, will be secure with Abraham after their death. Because this parable is so well-known to us, we can easily fail to notice how uncharacteristic it is of the parables of the Jesus of history. Most of the action in it is not drawn from everyday life in Galilee, but from the life to come.

Having emphasized the importance of faith, of hearing the Scriptures, and of how one's position in this present life determines one's eternal destiny, the parable ends on a note that is almost completely pessimistic regarding the fate of the Jews who do not associate with Lazarus-type people during this life. How, therefore, shall we today respond to this text? What is the basic theological message of this text, and how shall we state that message in terms that will be relevant at our particular time and place?

The text is a beautiful example of religious language, the language of faith, in which words that are symbols of faith are combined into stories that describe divine-human encounters, as Paul Tillich described it. In the telling of this story there is much use of descriptive detail, which many generations of Christians have used in their efforts to picture as well as they can what it shall be like after their own death. We can, along with millions of our fellow Christians, merely live in that seemingly secure world of unbroken mythological consciousness (again Paul Tillich's terminology) and do no more than repeat the vivid descriptive detail and even elaborate on it from our own rich imaginations. Should we not, however, undertake the alternative to this of seeking to determine the theological message of the text and then of stating that message in terms that will be meaningful to our own situation this coming Sunday? In this instance, the task is arduous because this parable is designed to fit a particular situation of Christian animosity against Jews in the first century.

It appears that there are two messages in the parable. One is that we may anticipate a reversal of roles and of positions in the life that is to come. The other is that most people will continue to live a life of wantonness and ease in spite of repeated warnings within their religious traditions. Here again, therefore, the "gospel" for this occasion is heard more clearly in the other texts selected than it is in Luke. It is heard in the 1 Timothy call for conduct that will result in our access to eternal life and in the psalm readings in which there is a great joy for those whose hope is in the Lord God who is Creator, Savior, and Eternal King.

PROPER 22
(ORDINARY TIME 27)
TWENTIETH SUNDAY AFTER PENTECOST

Sunday between October 2 and October 8 inclusive

The unifying factor in most of the texts selected for us for next Sunday appears to be the call to "patient faithfulness." It is a message first of all for those of us who are ministers of the Word and Sacraments. If we are willing to accept this message and to apply it in our lives, we may then with integrity and enthusiasm share it with other people.

Psalm 37:1-9

Those who are wicked and oppressive may gain a temporary economic advantage, but their advantage will soon be lost. Soon the wicked will be cut off and destroyed. It would be foolish to be envious of them. The Lord will show mercy to those who are righteous; they will dwell securely in the land long after the wicked are gone. Those who are wise will trust in the Lord and wait patiently.

Habakkuk 1:1-4; 2:1-4

After the introduction provided in Habakkuk 1:1, verses 2-3 are a lament by the prophet. Habakkuk 2:1 is an indication of the prophet's readiness to hear and of the expectation that the Lord God will no longer be silent. The response from the Lord begins in 2:2. The response marks a transition to apocalyptic, for the message is to be written. It calls for patient faithfulness until the time when the Lord will act decisively, another important characteristic of apocalyptic.

The good news in the latter portion of 2:4, that "the *tsaddik* (righteous person) who remains consistently in *emunah* (faithfulness to the Lord) shall live," was a favorite for the Apostle Paul in his letter to the Romans, was very important for Martin Luther during his theological crisis, is significant for all of us as Christians, and certainly has been a basic guide for Israelites and Jews down through the centuries. The *tsaddik*, who within the outer limits set by the commandments in the Torah makes the necessary decisions in life, assigning priorities among the many demanding relationships of the righteous person, shall live in security, in firmness, in a covenant relationship with the Lord, with all responsible people, and with the material things of this world. It is the same for us.

Lamentations 1:1-6
Lamentations 3:19-26
Psalm 137

Among these three texts, only Lamentations 3:19-26 offers hope that because of the steadfast, enduring love of the Lord the desolation of Jerusalem will some day end. Only Lamentations 3:19-26 suggests that the Lord will not reject forever and that it is good for a person to wait patiently for the salvation that the Lord will provide.

Although it is understandable that there are biblical texts depicting conditions and people to whom all hope seems to be in vain, we may wonder why texts such as Lamentations 1:1-6 and Psalm 137 should be included in our Lectionary and read during our worship services. We want to encourage people to have hope in the Lord God and to wait patiently for the Lord to help them. Why should we offer to them biblical texts depicting situations of total despair, in which there are no vestiges of hope?

2 Timothy 1:1-14

This portion of the most personal of the Pauline Pastoral Epistles is perhaps based on correspondence of Paul to Timothy, but reworked and rewritten by a later writer-redactor during what that writer considered to be "the last days." This admonition to remain faithful until the "Day of the Lord" is closely linked to the Habakkuk 2:4 text, though modified by the thought and practices that developed within later Pauline Christianity.

Luke 17:5-10

A variety of teachings are juxtaposed in these verses, including a redaction by the Lukan writer of a warning in Mark 9:42 about putting any *skandala* in front of these "little ones," a call for repeated forgiveness included in various ways in Matthew and in Luke, a saying regarding the potential power available in faith, and a parable peculiar to Luke about a slave who was expected to labor unflinchingly for his master.

Comments here will be limited to the Luke 17:7-10 parable, because it is the most interesting portion of the text and because it includes the unifying theme for this occasion of "patient faithfulness." The situation described in the parable is that of a farmer who has one slave to do his plowing, tend his cattle, and prepare his meals. The message of the parable appears to be that even with all of the diligent service that we might muster we cannot obligate God to do anything for us. Any attitude that causes us to seek rewards from God, to think that because we have done so much God must certainly respond with the things that will please us, is misguided. We are slaves to God. God does not owe us anything. Whatever God may give to us is given because of God's grace; our only proper response is thanksgiving to God. We see this also in the parable about the ten lepers, which is placed immediately after this text.

Therefore, we are not to seek thanks *from* God, but are always to give thanks *to* God. Some of the most respected Jewish fathers wrote basically the same thing as this, as is indicated in Pirke Aboth 1:3 in the Rabbinic Literature, "Do not be like slaves who serve their master in order to try to receive a reward," and Pirke Aboth 2:8, "No matter how diligently you have studied the Torah, do not claim merit for yourself, for that is simply what you were created to do." We are to serve God with patient faithfulness, "in sickness and in health," much as we indicate that we will do for our partner in marriage when we express our marriage vows.

PROPER 23
(ORDINARY TIME 28)
TWENTY-FIRST SUNDAY AFTER PENTECOST

Sunday between October 9 and October 15 inclusive

The emphasis in most of the texts selected for us for next Sunday is on obedient, faithful response to God for all that God has done. Therefore, the service and the message for the service should also be a faithful, thankful response to God by all who participate in the worship events.

Psalm 111

This important Individual Hymn of Praise includes in brief form the traditional Israelite description of the Lord God as gracious and merciful, the faithful provider, the God of power and of justice, the one who gave the heritage of the Canaanite "nations" to Israel. The psalm reiterates the hope that the covenant of the Lord with David will continue forever and includes the wisdom theme that the fear of the Lord is the beginning or heart of wisdom.

Psalm 66:1-12

As in many other texts within the Israelite Scriptures, here also God is praised for delivering the Israelites from the Egyptian oppressors by parting the sea so that the Israelites could pass over on dry land. The Exodus is remembered as one among many instances in which God used God's power to keep the enemies of the Israelites away from Israel's borders and to prevent other nations from oppressing them.

2 Kings 5:1-3, 7-15c

Naaman, the Syrian general who has just been cured of his leprosy, stands in front of Elisha and expresses his belief that there is no God in all of the earth except the God of Israel who rules in Israel. Therefore, in the verses that follow this text Naaman requests permission from Elisha to take back with him to Syria two mule loads of Israelite soil on which Naaman will construct an altar to worship the Lord God of Israel, for now Naaman will worship no other God.

Israelites in exile in Babylon where this story was told and perhaps originated faced the same situation as that of Naaman. How could they worship the Lord, God as perceived in Israel, in a foreign land? Would the Lord forgive them if they, like Naaman in the portion of 2 Kings 5 that follows our text, ask that the Lord pardon them if they would be compelled to worship a different god (Marduk) in a different land (Babylon)? The answer that this Naaman story provides is simply "Go in peace." They would have to answer those questions themselves. However, they could perhaps worship the Lord (Adonai), God as perceived in Israel, in a foreign land, and the Lord perhaps would forgive them if they asked the Lord to pardon them.

Jeremiah 29:1, 4-7

In the letter that Jeremiah is said to have sent to the leaders among the Israelite exiles in Babylon, Jeremiah, in the name of the Lord, told them to settle down, marry, and have children. They should even pray to the Lord God of Israel for the welfare of the Babylonian cities in which they would live. It is implied that they should be faithful in response to their Lord God while they were to do whatever was necessary in order for them to survive. How shall *we* express this idea next Sunday?

2 Timothy 2:8-15

Regardless of whether these words were composed by the Apostle Paul or by an admirer of Paul later to express what was thought that Paul would have said under these circumstances, this text is an eloquent call for faithfulness to Jesus as the Christ. The hymn (vv. 11-13) defines the mainline Christian position over against Gnosticizing Christians by maintaining against them in 2:11 that we should live with Christ and that our resurrection has not yet occurred. It provides encouragement to followers of Jesus to endure. It affirms that even if we do not believe in what Jesus is acclaimed to be, Jesus as the Christ remains faithful (as God remains faithful), for he cannot deny what he is. We, therefore, also are to be obedient, faithful, and thankful in our response to God.

Luke 17:11-19

Here again the inspired Lukan writer provided a story that is so vividly told that we can practically "see" every detail in it. The Lukan Jesus is near the end of his theological journey toward Jerusalem. He is passing theologically between the Galilean Jews and the Samaritans. All of them (perhaps symbolically represented by the number 10) are unclean. They stand at a distance, acclaim Jesus as their Master, and ask for his mercy. When they are obedient to Jesus, they are cleansed. Only one of them, however, when he sees that he has been cleansed, abandons the traditional way of going to show himself to the priests for certification of his cleanliness, and returns to Jesus, giving glory to God and falling at the feet of Jesus in thankfulness. The nine who go the Jewish way, even though they have been cleansed by Jesus, are compared unfavorably with the single Samaritan who returned immediately to thank Jesus and to praise God.

The extent to which this account can be traced back to the Jesus of history is uncertain. It is probable, as Hans-Dieter Betz suggests in "The Cleansing of the Ten Lepers" (Luke 17:11-19), *Journal of Biblical Literature* 90 (1971, pp. 314-328), that the identity as a Samaritan of the one who returned to Jesus to praise God was given at the point in the transmission of the account when the mission of the followers of Jesus to the Samaritans became prominent, and that the resulting anti-Jewish polemic is an additive that stems from the period of 80-90 CE when the breach between the developing Church and the Synagogue became irreparable. As G.B. Caird notes in *The Gospel of St. Luke* (Baltimore: Penguin, 1963, p. 195), for the Lukan writer the most attractive portion of the story was that the appreciative Samaritan showed up his Jewish fellow sufferers. As also typically in the parables peculiar to Luke, the characters mentioned first are observant Jews who are discredited, while the ones mentioned last (the tenth here) are types of those who follow Jesus and are acclaimed. We see that both Luke and the Fourth Gospel praise the Samaritans and renounce the Jews, but in different ways. The *positive* emphasis in this Lukan text and in all of the texts selected for this occasion is the obedient, faithful, thankful response to God for forgiveness, life, healing, and salvation. That is what we are called to proclaim.

PROPER 24
(ORDINARY TIME 29)
TWENTY-SECOND SUNDAY AFTER PENTECOST

Sunday between October 16 and October 22 inclusive

Perseverance by people and by God is the unifying theme in the texts selected for next weekend. The writer of Psalm 119:97-104 claims to continue in meditation over the Torah all day long. It is proclaimed in Psalm 121 that the Lord who keeps watch over Israel neither slumbers nor sleeps. Both the Lord and Jacob persevere in the hero of faith saga about Jacob wrestling with the divine figure in Genesis 32:22-30. According to Jeremiah 31:27-34, in the new covenant that the Lord God will make with the house of Israel and with the house of Judah, the Lord will watch over the people constantly, writing the commandments of the Lord on their hearts. Finally, we have the admonition to Timothy in 2 Timothy 3:14—4:5 to continue steadily on the course that he has taken, and the Gospel account is the parable in Luke 18:1-8 about the widow who persevered so persistently that the judge ruled in her favor even though her cause may or may not have been just.

An emphasis on perseverance, therefore, can hardly be avoided within expository preaching based on these texts. This makes these texts excellent selections for use during Confirmation services in the growing number of congregations in which the Confirmation ceremony is scheduled for late October rather than late May in the calendar year. They are also excellent texts for services of Baptism.

Where, however, is the "gospel" in this emphasis on perseverance? Is the "gospel" adequately expressed in the Lukan parable in which the message seems to be that if a thoroughly secular and selfish civil judge will finally rule in favor of a widow who pesters the judge constantly with her entreaty, how much more will God who is holy and self-giving respond affirmatively to our prayers if we bring them persistently to God? Is the "gospel" for Christians adequately expressed in the hero of faith saga about the struggle between Jacob and the divine man in Genesis 32? Perhaps the "gospel" is most clearly proclaimed within these texts in the assurance in Psalm 121 that the Lord keeps watch over the psalmist every day and every night. The psalmist reacts positively to the Lord, Timothy is urged to react to God through faith in Jesus as the Christ, and God is said to react positively to us if we pray persistently following the example of the widow in the parable in Luke 18:1-8.

Possibly an alternate theme that could be as good or even better than the theme of perseverance — at least in terms of the "gospel" — would be the theme that the good news in these texts is that God interacts positively with us.

Psalm 121

This psalm is almost entirely an expression of faith in the unmerited grace of God. As a psalm of trust, it is excellent for use in the evening, before we enter into rest and sleep. It is also appropriate for the morning hour, or for the beginning of corporate worship experience. The theme of divine-human interaction as "gospel" is more pronounced in this psalm than is the theme of perseverance.

Psalm 119:97-104

The interaction between the psalmist and God in this portion of this extensive psalm is the interaction between the psalmist and the Torah (the instruction, guidance, word of God), as it is in every section of this psalm. The psalmist begins with an acclamation of love for the Torah, on which the psalmist meditates at all times. Because of meditation on the Torah, the psalmist becomes more wise, more understanding, more perceptive, and more satisfied and fulfilled than anyone else can be. Through the Torah, God sustains and guides every aspect of the life of the psalmist.

Genesis 32:22-31

The interaction of God with Jacob (Israel) causes the "wrestling" to occur, continues throughout the "wrestling" experience, and remains relevant after the "wrestling" ceases in the morning. The "wrestling" interaction is itself good news, especially when we realize that the opposite of this interaction of "wrestling" would be the silence and inaccessibility of God. For those who trust in the grace of God, interaction with God is always good. It culminates in a mutual blessing, as it does in this text.

Jeremiah 31:27-34

For Jeremiah and for those who were inspired to develop the written Jeremiah traditions, in this account there is a message of the judgment of the Lord on their own religious heritage and an optimistic expression of hope for a more intimate interaction and experience with the Lord, an individual experience written in the hearts of the people wherever they might go.

Jews have interpreted this text as an expression of their dynamic covenant relationship with the Lord and have recognized that their covenant has innumerable ever-unfolding manifestations, rich in meaning for them and for all people. Jews have seen in this text one of many blueprints in their tradition for life as it should be, for life as it will be "when the Messiah comes," or more likely during the anticipated Messianic Age when everyone — whether Jewish or not — will be forgiven and will "know the Lord."

Christians usually interpret this text as a prophetic prediction of the "new covenant" that God established through Jesus as the Christ, and perceive each Christian Baptism and

Eucharist as a sacramental action of the "new covenant," a divine-human interaction instituted by Jesus himself.

Luke 18:1-8

This text includes the rather unusual feature of providing a brief description of the purpose of the parable before the parable is given. This description of purpose in 18:1 suggests that the life setting of the parable is most likely that of the early Church during the period of 70-85 CE when many followers of Jesus were "losing heart" (v. 1b) because of the long, unexpected delay during which God had not vindicated the elect (v. 7) and when there was a question in the mind of the inspired writer over whether when the Son of Man comes he would find faith on the earth (v. 8b). Interaction between God and the followers of Jesus during this period seems to be lacking. The message of the parable in the face of this problem is that the believers of Jesus should persevere in prayer and that God eventually would provide a positive response. If the secular, unjust judge, who neither feared God nor had any compassion for the poor, finally vindicated the widow who persevered in her pleas to him, certainly God, who is God and cares greatly for God's elect people, will respond favorably to them. The followers of Jesus, therefore, should persevere in their prayers; God will certainly then interact favorably with them. This text and this parable provide the same message for us today.

2 Timothy 3:14—4:5

Problems similar to those addressed in the Lukan parable of the Unjust Judge appear to be factors in this text. *Vaticinia ex eventu* seem to be operative here. The situation of what is the present time of the inspired writer is described from the vantage point of the past by means of the literary medium of a letter sent by Paul to Timothy at a much earlier date. At any rate, there was (or was to be) a situation in which many who had been participants in the community of faith composed of followers of Jesus were no longer with them but were involved in Gnostic Christian speculation (vv. 4:3-5). Interaction with God is said to be readily available through use of the "sacred Scriptures," which in this context were probably the Torah and the Prophetic traditions of the Jews. It is claimed here that God also interacts with God's people through Jesus Christ, as indicated in 2 Timothy 3:15 and 4:1. How do we believe that God interacts with us today?

PROPER 25
(ORDINARY TIME 30)
TWENTY-THIRD SUNDAY AFTER PENTECOST

Sunday between October 23 and October 30 inclusive

The primary theme of the texts designated for next Sunday is expressed most elegantly in a verse just beyond the end of the Sirach 35:12-17 selected reading, in Sirach 35:21ab, "The prayer of the humble pierces the clouds, and it will not rest until it reaches its goal" (NRSV).

Psalm 84:1-7

This psalm is a beautiful expression of appreciation to the Lord for the dwelling place of the Lord in the temple in Jerusalem. The pilgrim who is able to be in the temple for only brief periods of time considers those who can be there at all times to pray and meditate to be especially blessed. Even the sparrow (the most common and ordinary of all of the birds) finds a home there, and the swallow builds a nest high above the altar, where it is safe from cats and people and other predators.

Psalm 65

The Lord is praised in this psalm in Zion as "O God of our salvation!" Salvation here is defined as forgiveness of sins, control of nature, a bountiful harvest, and the opportunity to worship God in prayer and meditation in the temple in Jerusalem. Therefore, the People of God and all of the earth shall shout for joy.

Joel 2:23-32

The land, which had usually been productive, had been thoroughly devastated by drought and by hordes of locusts, grasshoppers that jump from place to place in every direction, devouring all vegetation, so that nothing can survive. These invaders may refer to a multitude of insects that sweep down from the north that often arrive during a drought. More likely, the "northerner" whom the Lord will remove from the land (v. 20) is a cryptic reference to the successive waves of Assyrian, Babylonian, and Persian invaders who came from the north and ravished the land, like grasshoppers do in nature.

The Joel traditions proclaim that the Lord who has punished the people of Israel will now heal the land and its people. The Lord who sent the army of ravishers will now provide bountifully food and the spirit of revelation to the sons and daughters of the people. Everyone who calls upon the name of the Lord will be saved (v. 32).

Jeremiah 14:7-10, 19-22

In spite of the horrendous sins of the people and the punishments that they deserve, the prophet and people call unceasingly to the Lord for help, for they believe that only the Lord can bring relief from the prolonged drought that threatens the survival of the people.

Sirach 35:12-17

It is possible that the inspired Lukan writer was familiar with the wisdom material in this text from Ecclesiasticus, the Wisdom of Jesus Son of Sirach. There are no direct quotations of this text in the Third Gospel, but the text may have been a resource in the development of some of the material in Luke, including the Luke 18:9-14 parable about the Pharisee and the tax collector praying in the temple, especially what is written in Sirach 35:21ab about the prayer of the one who is humble. It is a valuable text also for us.

2 Timothy 4:6-8, 16-18

The Apostle Paul is presented, or presents himself, in this text as about to be sacrificed. This and the reference to his having been rescued from the mouth of the lion at the time of his first defense are indications that the life of Paul was threatened and eventually taken by the oppressive advocates of Roman Civil Religion whom Paul publicly and repeatedly opposed by proclaiming that Jesus the Risen Christ, not Caesar, is "Lord."

It is said here that Paul humbly credited the Lord with providing the strength to proclaim the message that Jesus is Lord, not only with Paul's words but also with Paul's actions.

Luke 18:9-14

It is important for us to recognize that the tax collector in this parable was praised not because he was a tax collector but because he was humble as he prayed and admitted that as a horrible sinner he needed the grace of God. The Pharisee was said not to have been fully justified, not because he was a Pharisee but because in the parable he exalted himself. Fasting, tithing, and good ethical behavior are not rejected in this parable; neither is sinful behavior condoned.

PROPER 26
(ORDINARY TIME 31)
TWENTY-FOURTH SUNDAY AFTER PENTECOST

Sunday between October 30 and November 5 inclusive

The theme of "salvation" in many of these texts relates our worship services for the coming weekend to our need for the ongoing Reformation of the Church in our time on October 31 and to All Saints' Day on November 1, as well as being a reminder to us that we are nearing the end of our annual Church Year cycle.

Psalm 32:1-7

Within the beatitudes of 32:1 and again in 32:5 the three most important words for sin in the Hebrew Bible are used. In the sequence of the use of these three words in 32:5 we see the increase in the seriousness of the type of sin from one word for sin to another. First the psalmist acknowledged the lowest level of sin: the failure to please God even when we try. Then the psalmist admitted that the psalmist had moved to the second level of sin: breaking the rules that God had established to be helpful to God's people. Finally, the psalmist confessed the most serious sin of all: attempted violent insurrection against God.

As is typical in Israelite Individual Hymns of Praise, Psalm 32 tries to teach to all who will hear the wisdom of acknowledging one's sins to the Lord. The greatest need of people and the greatest gift of God are brought together here, as in so many other places in both our Older Testament and in our Newer Testament, in God's gracious gift of salvation.

Psalm 119:137-144

The interaction between the psalmist and the Lord is expressed here in terms of the righteousness and covenant-faithfulness of the Lord God. The Israelite and Jewish perception of righteousness and covenant-faithfulness is that it is a condition in which God and the People of God are just and fair in all of their interpersonal relationships. Faithfulness to the covenant requires ongoing and enduring interaction between God and the People of God. In this covenant God provides security and salvation to the people and the people receive their security and their salvation from God.

Isaiah 1:10-18

Even though the people of Jerusalem are addressed as Sodom and as Gomorrah and are said to be as evil as Sodom and Gomorrah, offering animal sacrifices while making no effort to rescue the orphans, widows, and other weak and heavily oppressed persons among them, if they wash themselves and learn to do good, God will provide salvation for them. Although their sins are like scarlet, crimson red, their sins will be like clean wool, as white as the falling snow.

Habakkuk 1:1-4; 2:1-4

Since this text is one of the options for use in Proper 22 earlier this year, a modified portion of the notes given for Proper 22 are offered again here.

The good news in the latter portion of 2:4, that "the *tsaddik* (righteous person) who remains consistently in *emunah* (faithfulness to the Lord) shall live" was a favorite for the Apostle Paul in his letter to the Romans, was very important for Martin Luther during his theological crisis, is significant for all of us as Christians, and certainly has been a basic guide for Israelites and Jews down through the centuries. The *tsaddik*, who within the outer limits set by the commandments in the Torah makes the necessary decisions in life, assigning priorities among the many demanding relationships of the righteous person, shall live in security, in firmness, shall have salvation within a covenant relationship with the Lord, with all responsible people, and with the material things of this world. It is the same for us.

2 Thessalonians 1:1-4, 11-12

The Thessalonians are praised in this text for their fortitude, for their faith, and for their love for one another, even while they are enduring manifold struggles and tribulations. The writers testify that they are praying that God will make the followers of Jesus in Thessalonica worthy of their calling and will fulfill for them every desire that they have for that which is good. All of this is said to be done in order that the name of our Lord Jesus may be glorified among the Thessalonians.

The people to whom this is written are said within 2 Thessalonians 1:5-10, the portion of chapter 1 that is not included within the text selected for us for this occasion, to be worthy of rest and salvation *because of their suffering, not by the unmerited grace of God that the Apostle Paul himself emphasized so strongly within the seven basic letters written by Paul and included in the Christian Scriptures.*

Luke 19:1-10

This story about Zacchaeus is familiar to us, especially because it has been a favorite in our children's education curricula and because of the action song for children, "Zacchaeus was a wee little man, and a wee little man was he...." The story is in Luke only.

Because Zacchaeus in this story welcomed Jesus joyfully and because he made ample restoration to his associates and to the poor, he has salvation. It would be interesting to share within our message this coming Sunday the various ways in which salvation is said to be received within each of the texts selected for this occasion.

PROPER 27
(ORDINARY TIME 32)
TWENTY-FIFTH SUNDAY AFTER PENTECOST

Sunday between November 6 and November 12 inclusive

Perhaps the theological motif that best unites most of the texts selected for this occasion is the statement in Luke 20:38 that God is not God of the dead, but God of the living, and that all who are alive live because of their relationship with God. Some of the texts also proclaim that all life, therefore, should praise and glorify God.

Psalm 17:1-9

The psalmist claims a close relationship with the Lord, using vivid, personal imagery. Throughout the night and as the psalmist wakens in the morning, the psalmist draws near to the Lord, the God of the living. Although there is no expectation of the resurrection of the individual from the dead here, the concept of awakening to new life was incorporated into the resurrection faith of later Israelites, Jews, and Christians.

Psalm 145:1-5, 17-21

For many Jews, Psalm 145 is the most important psalm in the Psalter. It is used daily by many observant Jews in their private devotions to praise and bless the Lord God. It declares the Lord to be the Savior and Preserver of all who call upon the Lord and love the Lord. Millions of Jews were driven into the gas chambers of the Nazi Holocaust or earlier to their death during the pogroms in Easter Europe with the words of this psalm on their lips. The use of this psalm by Christians is much less, but is significant nevertheless. We can add to its use among us as we worship God this weekend.

Haggai 1:15b—2:9

In this text, salvation is proclaimed in the form of an action by the Lord in which the heavens, the earth, the sea and land, and all nations will be shaken so that the treasures of all nations will be brought to Jerusalem. The hope is expressed that then the temple will be furnished with even more splendor than it had at the time of Solomon. Then the people of Jerusalem will prosper because the Spirit of the Lord will be among them.

Job 19:23-27a

The meanings originally intended by numerous words in this text are not clear and unambiguous. For example, the word that within translations into English by many Christian translators is expressed as "Redeemer" in verse 25 is basically an Avenger or Vindicator. It may be "apart from" my flesh rather than "in" my flesh that the character Job in this drama expects to be in verse 26. Although we as Christians would like to see in this text evidence of an early expectation of the resurrection of the body, this is accomplished for us in part only through interpretative translations from the Hebrew words. Nevertheless, especially within this series of texts selected for us for use this coming weekend, we can see in this text support for the concept that God is the God of the living and that all life should praise and glorify God.

2 Thessalonians 2:1-5, 13-17

References to "the glory of our Lord Jesus Christ" and to "eternal comfort and good hope" in these verses connect us to the "being raised from the dead" and to the "God of the living" emphases of Luke 20:27-38, to which we now turn.

Luke 20:27-38

Among the Synoptic texts of this dialogue between Jesus and the Sadducees, this Lukan reading is to be preferred. It would be even better if we were to include Luke 20:39: "After that, even some of the scribes said, 'Teacher, you have spoken well.'" Luke 20:27-38 does not use the provocative retort of Jesus present in Mark 12:24 and Matthew 22:29. Therefore, Luke 20:27-38 probably takes us back closest to the Jesus of history of any of the canonical texts of this conversation.

The references in Luke 20:27-38 and its parallels in Mark and Matthew to "the God of Abraham and the God of Isaac and the God of Jacob" from the burning bush accounts of Exodus 3:6, 15; 4:5; and 6:2 are used to indicate that God is God of the living and that those who are alive live because of their relationship to God. When we concentrate on the sayings of Jesus in this text rather than on the controversy with the Sadducees, we can focus on the resurrection proclamation, especially Luke 20:36 and 38, providing, therefore, an "Easter in November" message.

PROPER 28
(ORDINARY TIME 33)
TWENTY-SIXTH SUNDAY AFTER PENTECOST

Sunday between November 13 and November 19 inclusive

The proclamation in most of the texts selected for next weekend is that God will soon act decisively to destroy rampant evil and those who remain faithful to God will survive because God will strengthen them. The parenesis is that the faithful must believe in God and that they must not be afraid. Until all of this occurs, the faithful must continue to be actively praising God and living in accordance with God's good will for them.

Isaiah 12

The concept of the corporate personality of Israel is apparent in the two psalms (vv. 1-3, 4-6) that comprise this concluding portion of the Isaiah chapters 1-12 traditions. The nation, or remnants of the nation, will give thanks to the Lord as if they were one person on the day when the Lord forgives and restores them, as the context from 11:10 onward indicates. The hope expressed in 11:10—12:6 has been only partially realized even to this day for Israel.

Because of the nature of the reading, two persons should be involved in leadership roles. One person should provide a brief setting from Isaiah 11:10-16 and speak the liturgical rubrics 12:1a and 4a and the liturgical comment 12:3. The other person should speak or chant the psalm portions, turning toward a symbol of the presence of God for 12:1b-2 and stepping toward the congregation for 12:4b-6.

Isaiah 65:17-25
(as used also on Easter Day of this Series C)

In this text, the inspired writer joyfully proclaimed that soon the Lord God will recreate the sky and the earth for Jerusalem and for the Israelite people. For the People of God, there will be no more weeping and distress, and no longer will anyone die short of a long and fruitful life. No one will take from them the products of their labor. God will hear and will respond to help them even while they are still speaking! Wild and rapacious beasts will be gentle and eat grass along with oxen and lambs. The sky and the earth will be resurrected. The People of God will be resurrected. Prophecy will be resurrected. Everything conceivable will be resurrected, except an individual person who has died.

Psalm 98

In this psalm it is proclaimed that the Lord God has come to gain the victory over all evil forces on the earth. Not only the people of Israel, but also all of the other oppressed people of the earth and even nature itself are urged to join together in singing to the Lord a new, joyful song of praise and thankfulness, for they are all free. Evil no longer has any power over them.

Malachi 4:1-2a

All who are arrogant and all evildoers will be consumed as in an oven when the great and terrible day of the Lord comes. Elijah will return on that day in order to gather the faithful together to protect them. After that day of judgment and destruction has passed, those who fear the name of the Lord will spring forth, like young calves released from their stalls, to skip and jump over the ashes of the wicked. The parenesis here is that those who fear the Lord should live in accordance with the instructions provided in the Torah.

2 Thessalonians 3:6-13

This text is almost entirely parenesis. While followers of Jesus wait for the expected future coming of the Lord Jesus Christ in glory, they are to follow the example set by Paul, Silvanus, and Timothy, working quietly to support themselves and gladly serving others without weariness or complaint. This example and admonition holds also, of course, for us today as we experience the conclusion of another Church Year cycle.

Luke 21:5-19

The catastrophic events that occurred during the unsuccessful attempts by Jews in Galilee and Judea to free themselves from the oppressive Roman occupation forces during the Jewish War of 66-72 CE fulfilled some, but not all, of the predictions recorded in this Luke 21:5-19 text. Followers of Jesus also suffered during this period, and were supported by the assurance provided by the words of Mark 13, Matthew 24:1-36, and Luke 21:5-36 that Jesus understood their situation and would give them courage and the ability to endure. Only Luke, however, has the strangely contradictory statement that "some of you will be put to death" in 21:16b, followed almost immediately in 21:18 by "But not a hair of your head will perish." Perhaps the writer intended this to mean that even those who are put to death because of their faith will not perish.

The proclamation here is that Jesus will lead and guide his followers through very difficult times, and that most of them will endure and survive. The parenesis is that Jesus' followers must believe and trust in Jesus regardless of how terrible their conditions may become. That same proclamation and that same parenesis are applicable for us today.

PROPER 29
(ORDINARY TIME 34)
LAST SUNDAY AFTER PENTECOST
(REIGN OF CHRIST or CHRIST THE KING)

Sunday between November 20 and November 26 inclusive

With the texts chosen for this occasion, the Church Year ends in a note of triumph. The Lord is King! The Lord rules in these texts in a great variety of ways, but in each in some way the Lord is King. This is the message that we shall proclaim next Sunday. It shall be our task to proclaim with all of the skill given to us by God the many ways in which the Lord is King in these texts and in our lives.

Jeremiah 23:1-6

In its specific context within the Jeremiah traditions, this selection is a word of the Lord for a specific situation before and after the fall of Jerusalem to the Babylonians in 586 BCE. The word from Adonai is addressed to an Israelite audience that has Israelite expectations of a dynamic political leader, someone who would be like David at his best, or better than David had been.

Although the Jesus of history did not fulfill the messianic expectations of Jewish partisans that included military action for the restoration of Israelite/Jewish national independence and political power, some aspects of those expectations were utilized by followers of Jesus. These aspects helped to inform and to add detail to the portrait of the Christ painted by the early Christians who claimed to be the "New Israel" and who proclaimed the Christ of faith as their King, the fulfillment of texts such as Jeremiah 23:1-6.

In our time, it is essential that the descendants of the original Israel and the descendants of the claimant "Israel" together also with contemporary Muslims share in dialogue their futuristic messianic expectations. This dialogue is urgently needed when distrust and animosity against people who are in the other religious communities are increasing for many Jews, Christians, and Muslims.

Psalm 46

This familiar psalm of trust in the Lord is one of the relatively few eschatological psalms in the Psalter. It is particularly appropriate in times of war and of great stress such as Martin Luther faced during his struggles as a major reformer within the Western Church during the sixteenth century.

Even though the earth may be returned to its primal chaos, Jerusalem, the city of God, is said to be secure because God is in its midst. As perceived by the psalmist, the Lord God brings desolations upon all of the earth, but also brings the peace that shall follow them. The people of the city are merely to be still and to recognize that the Lord is God. Luther gave this psalm of trust a sixteenth-century application. It is our responsibility to give it an application in our time and place. That is our call.

Luke 1:68-79

In this eloquent "Benedictus," the Lukan writer provided as words of the now-believing and jubilant Zechariah a blessing of the Lord God that will be actualized in the work of Zechariah's son, John the Baptist, who shall go before the Lord Jesus to prepare his way. In this "Benedictus" the dawning of a new day is anticipated in which Jesus of Nazareth, as the one proclaimed by John the Baptist, will become the King forever.

Colossians 1:11-20

This great confessional hymn to Christ in Colossians 1:15-20 is perhaps the most significant of the texts selected for this occasion. We sense that the inspired writer had access in some form to Philippians 2:5-11, to Paul's expressions of the followers of Jesus as "the body" of Christ, to Matthew's description of the community of faith as the "Church," and perhaps also to John 1:1-18. The result is a masterpiece composed in opposition to persons in Hellenistic syncretism — incipient, or developed Gnostics — who mythologized the elemental spirits such as earth, fire, water, and air, and the stars whose constellations were thought to control the order of the entire universe and with it the fate of each person. Even though our situation differs considerably from the setting of this Christ-hymn, the impact of this hymn is not lost to us. It is an expression of our theology.

There may be concern for some about what the writer of Colossians 1:24 (beyond our text) meant by "I complete the things that are still needed of the afflictions of Christ in my flesh in behalf of Christ's body (the Church)." The reference is most likely to the suffering that Paul endured at the hands of oppressive Roman political and military authorities who were similar to those who in Jerusalem had crucified Jesus. Paul is represented as accepting such suffering as somehow necessary in obedience to the will of God. It was not a way in which Paul added to the atonement as accomplished in Christ, but was a way in which Paul identified with that atonement and with that Christ. We might add that the Jesus of history was crucified by the Romans because large numbers of his own Jewish people were being filled with hope by Jesus' message that God, not Caesar, is Lord. The Paul of history was killed by the Romans because many followers of Jesus were being filled with hope by Paul's message that Jesus as raised from the dead, not Caesar, is King and Lord.

Luke 23:33-43

Comparison of the Synoptic parallels here indicates that the Lukan writer did much editorial rearranging and new composition in preparing this text. Primarily from the materials available in the Markan Gospel, the inspired Lukan writer was able to compose this impressive, memorable scene. Within a composition designed to be superior to its antecedents (Luke 1:1-4), the Lukan writer did not hesitate to change the Mark 15:32b text, "Also the ones who had been and were being crucified along with Jesus reviled him," into a scene in which one of the two sided with Jesus and the other against him, and did this so skillfully that the impression of continuity is given, that at first both reviled him but that then one sided with him. This little theological drama scene also provided an opportunity for the Lukan writer to demonstrate that Jesus and his friend will be together yet that same day in Paradise, an idea not present in Mark or in Matthew.

ALL SAINTS

November 1 or the First Sunday in November

As we pause to remember those loved by us who have died during the past twelve months or within the scope of our memories, we turn to the inspired writers of each of the texts selected for this occasion. Shall we not also on this All Saints' Day worship God with these writers, along with all whom we remember who have lived among us? Let us boldly worship God as God is perceived within Christianity, as Creator Father of Jesus and of all of us throughout the expanse of time and space, as Redeeming Son, the Risen Christ our Savior, and as Loving, Active, Sustaining Spirit, continuously involved in our lives. Let us *acclaim the saints* of all times and places, and let us *worship God* as God is revealed to us, with no limitations or reservations.

Psalm 149

The reason for the selection of this psalm for this occasion was probably the reference to the assembly of the faithful in 149:1 and the cry "Let those who are faithful rejoice triumphantly in glory" in 149:5. The reading should be limited, however, to 149:1-5 to avoid the use of the holy war command for violence and vengeance that is in 149:6-9a.

Daniel 7:1-3, 15-18

Together with the oppressed of ancient Israel and with all others oppressed up to the present time, we share in joyful anticipation the hope expressed in this apocalyptic text that soon the oppressed saints of the Most High will receive and possess the kingdom. The text reminds us that apocalyptic literature is not merely other-worldly and theological; it is also this-worldly and political. This text reminds us also that our emphasis on this All Saints' Day occasion must be both a joyful anticipation of release from suffering and a powerful protest against economic, political, social, and spiritual oppression in *our* time and place.

Ephesians 1:11-23

In this portion of the blessing section of this epistle the Pauline writer was assuring those who would read the document that both Jewish-background followers of Jesus and non-Jewish-background followers of Jesus would share in the glorious inheritance of the saints. The amazing power and grace of God are said to have been shown both in the raising of Jesus from the dead as Lord and Christ and in the sealing of both Jewish and non-Jewish background followers of Jesus with the promised Holy Spirit of God.

Luke 6:20-31

With the insights that have come from oppressed Christians in Latin America, Africa, Asia, and elsewhere during recent decades, we recognize that the sense of Luke 6:20 is probably "Blessed are you who are *oppressed* (rather than merely poor), for the kingdom of God belongs to you!" "Poor" is the more general sense of the Greek word πτωχοί used here; "oppressed" is the more specific. Those who are oppressed are also always poor, since the oppressors take everything from them. People who are oppressed economically, politically, socially, and spiritually are always hungry and lacking of adequate shelter, clothing, and medical care, and they often weep bitter tears of helplessness.

THANKSGIVING DAY

Fourth Thursday in November (United States)
Second Monday in October (Canada)

National days of thanksgiving within the United States and Canada are by nature primarily expressions of civil religion, not of the ecclesial, individual, family, community, or universal levels of religion, even though every level in which we express our religion may be involved. Because civil religion at its best is *inclusive* of the religions of all of the people living within a nation, in nations such as the United States and Canada in which there are Native Americans, Jews, Christians, Muslims, Hindus, Buddhists, Atheists, and many other groups, observance of National Days of Thanksgiving should include participation by all of the groups represented and use resources drawn from the oral and written traditions of every group represented. Civil religion at its worst, however, *excludes* minority groups and uses the power of the state to promote the religion of the powerful majority within the nation. Therefore, worship experiences at the national level should be inclusive of all of the people, and the celebration of national days of thanksgiving in local areas should also be inclusive of all of the people in the local area.

Leaders in worship at the national level of religion ideally should not be pastors, rabbis, imams, and so on, but should be public, national, state, and local officials, and the most appropriate texts should be selected from national documents such as the United States Constitution and Bill of Rights, and comparable documents in Canada. There have been few instances in which such inclusive expressions of religion on national days of thanksgiving have been attempted and have been successful. It would be meaningful to participate in more of these, if they are planned and implemented appropriately, expressing repentance for national acts of oppression, and inclusive of all persons.

National level of religion within our biblical texts is for the most part centered on the political manifestations of the religion of ancient Israel and of Israel as a nation. That nation provided a positive example in some instances and a negative one of exploitation of the poor by the rich and powerful in many others. Deuteronomy 26:1-11 is one of the best of the positive models available to us. The other texts selected for our use on this occasion: Psalm 100, Philippians 4:4-9, and John 6:25-35 are basically expressions of ecclesial rather than national and civil religion. They are expressions of thanksgiving but not at the level of national, civil religion. They can be used in ecclesial religion on many occasions, but are not designed specifically for civil religion observances.

In summary, since there were no constitutional democracies comparable to the United States and Canada during the lifetimes of the writers of our Scriptures, there are no biblical texts that are ideal for our use on National Days of Thanksgiving in the United States and Canada, even within ecclesial worship services.

Deuteronomy 26:1-11

As indicated above, among the four texts selected for our use on the occasion of a national day of thanksgiving, this text is the most useful and relevant. The use of first fruits of the season in this text provides the emphasis on offering food and dedicating it to the Lord, as well as on sharing food with others. Our practice of sharing baskets of food during the Thanksgiving and Christmas seasons with people who cannot afford good food is at most a token effort if those who receive it lack adequate nutrition during the rest of the year.

Psalm 100
This is a beautiful psalm of praise and thanksgiving for any occasion, even though it is not set in the context of a national, civil religion.

Philippians 4:4-9
This also is a very meaningful expression of faith that with considerable adaptation can be used within an ecclesial level of worship on a national day of thanksgiving.

John 6:25-35
The Johannine Jesus is depicted in this text as the "true bread from heaven" giving life to the world. This text can, of course, be used within a totally Christian setting on any day of thanksgiving. It would not be helpful in a civil religion setting that includes Jews, Muslims, and other groups.

www.ingramcontent.com/pod-product-compliance
Lightning Source LLC
Chambersburg PA
CBHW070724160426
43192CB00009B/1303